SAN BERNARDINO

FOR

N

FAWNS

FAWNSKIN

Little Bear Pk

Delamar Mtn

Holcomb Valley

Upper Holcomb Valley

Moon

Camp Marrone's Lost Frontier

38

Air Strip

B

Grout Bay Public Camp

Windy Pt.

Grout Bay

BIG BEAR LAKE

Stanfield Cutoff

North Shore Landing

Gray's Camp

Gilliner Pt.

Metcalf Bay

18

Lake Shore Landing

18

Butler Peak

Craft's Peak

Holloway's Landing

Pleasure Point Landing

Treasure Island

Boulder Bay Landing

BEAR

Cedar Lake

Big Bear Lake Village

Ski Area

Moonridge

Ski Area

Ski Area

Castle Rock

Bluff Lake

YMCA Camp

Grand View Point

Ski Area

Green Valley

Lookout Point

Clarks Summit

Camp Radford

Slide Peak

Keller Peak

Converse

SBNF

Slide Lake

Seven Oaks

S

N

BERNAR

Seven Oaks Resort

Wesha Club

Jenks Meadows

Cienaga Grande

CAMP AREA

38

Pinanita

Jenks Lake

Horse Meadows

38

Poopout Hill

Glen Martin

Angelus Oaks

SBNF

Constance Peak

Mountain Springs

Thomas Hunting Grounds

San Bernardino East Peak

SAN GORGO

Shields Peak

High Meadow Springs

San Bernardino Peak

Anderson Peak

33

San Bernardino Mountain

Dollar

WILD

A

Chanton Peak

NATIONAL

FOREST

38

Mill Creek Campground

MILL

Those Magnificent Mountain Movies

(The Golden Years)

1911 - 1939

by
W. Lee Cozad

A Rim of the World Historical Society Publication

This book is dedicated to my friend, my lover, and my editor — all of whom happen to be my wife, Mary.

Acknowledgements

I would like to thank the following organizations, individuals and friends who made this book possible:

The Academy of Motion Picture Arts and Sciences and their staff of researchers and librarians and especially Matt Severson and Sue Guldin; the research staff at the American Film Institute; the staff at the Arts Library Special Collections at UCLA and Lauren Buissom, Head of Operations; the staff at the UCLA Film Archives; the Library of Congress research staff and Rosemary C. Hanes, Film and Television Research Librarian; the librarians at Redland's Smiley Library and the staff in the California Room at the Norman Feldheym Central Library in the City of San Bernardino; the County of San Bernardino Library in Blue Jay and their entire staff; the research staff at the Internet Movie Data Base; the San Bernardino County Archives staff; the Rim of the World Historical Society; the Mountain News and Crestline Courier-News.

A special thanks goes to: the late Audrey Mac Kay for getting me started; Tom Core for all his wonderful photos; Pauliena LaFuze for pictures and her marvelous stories and history; Russ Keller and Roger Hatheway for their priceless collection; Les Adams for his great western collection; Larry Don Vito for his photo collection and many favors; Rhea-Frances Tetley for many historical photos; Marc Wanamaker for his valuable advice; June Lockhart for her fabulous stories and history; Wilmer and Helen Jaun for their remembrances; Art Arciniega for his background material; Joseph Putnam "Putty" Henck for all the great historical stories; Jim Price for his knowledge of the star's homes; Jim Grant for all the lake history; Steve Watt for his remembrances; Jerry and Kay Fulton for pictures and historical data; Stoney DeMent, Jr. for his background information; Alan Mac Kay for his terrific stories; Stan Bellamy for keeping my history straight; James Cozart and Kim Tomadjoglou with the AFI for all their research efforts; Jerry Schneider at Occidental University for his invaluable research and history; and Marko Perko for pushing me onward.

Finally, I would like to gratefully acknowledge Jackie Manning, my editor, for making sure I was in the right tense and not making a fool of myself.

If I have inadvertently missed anyone, please forgive me as no slight is intended.

Selected Bibliography

Adams, Les and Buck Rainey. *Shoot-Em-Ups: The Complete Reference Guide to Westerns of the Sound Era.* Arlington House Publishers, 1978.

Ankerich, Michael G. *The Sound of Silence: Conversations With 16 Film and Stage Personalities Who Bridged the Gap Between Silents and Talkies.* McFarland & Co., 1998.

Barbour, Alan G. *The Thrill of It All: A Pictorial History of the B-Western.* Macmillan Co., 1971.

Bellamy, Ralph. *When the Smoke Hit the Fan.* Doubleday & Co., 1979.

Bellamy, Stan. *My Mountain, My People, Volume 1: Arrowhead!* Second Edition. Little Bear Historical Conservative, 1999.

Black, Shirley Temple. *Child Star: An Autobiography.* McGraw-Hill Publishing Co., 1988.

Blum, Daniel. *A Pictorial History of the Silent Screen.* G.P. Putnam's Sons, 1953.

Braff, Richard E. *The Universal Silents: A Filmography of the Universal Motion Picture Manufacturing Company, 1912 - 1929.* McFarland & Co., 1999.

Brownlow, Kevin. *The Parade's Gone By.* Alfred A. Knopf, 1968.

_____ *Hollywood: The Pioneers.* William Collins Sons and Co., 1979.

Carpozi, Jr., George. *The Gary Cooper Story.* Arlington House Publishers, 1970.

Champlin, Charles. *The Flicks or Whatever Became of Andy Hardy?* Ward Richie Press, 1977.

Chaplin, Charles. *My Autobiography.* Simon and Schuster, 1964.

D'Agostino, Annette M. *Filmmakers in the Moving Picture World: An Index of Articles 1907 - 1927.* McFarland & Co., 1997.

Dickens, Homer. *The Films of Ginger Rogers.* Citadel Press, 1975.

Dooley, Roger. *From Scarface To Scarlett: American Films in the 1930s.* Harcourt Brace Jovanovich Publishers, 1979.

Edwards, Anne. *The DeMilles: An American Family.* Harry N. Abrams, Inc., 1988.

Essoe, Gabe and Raymond Lee. *DeMille: The Man and His Pictures.* Castle Books, 1970.

Everson, William K. *A Pictorial History of the Western Film.* Citadel Press, 1969.

_____ *American Silent Film.* Oxford University Press, 1978.

Fairbanks, Jr., Douglas. *The Salad Days.* Doubleday, 1988.

Fenin, George N. and William K. Everson. *The Western from Silents to Cinerama.* Bonanza Books, 1962.

Ford, Dan. *Pappy: The Life of John Ford.* Prentice-Hall, Inc., 1979.

Fowler, Gene. *Good Night Sweet Prince: The Life and Times of John Barrymore.* Viking Press, 1944.

Fox, Charles Donald and Milton Silver. *Who's Who on the Screen.* Ross Publishing, 1920.

Fussell, Betty Harper. *Mabel: Hollywood's First I -Don't -Care Girl.* Ticknor & Fields, 1982.

Gish, Lillian with Ann Pinchot. *Lillian Gish: The Movies, Mr. Griffith and Me.* Prentice-Hall, 1969.

Gordon, William. *Shot On This Site.* Citadel Press, 1995.

Griffith, D. W. *The Man Who Invented Hollywood: The Autobiography of D. W. Griffith.* Edited by James Hart. Touchstone Publishing, 1972.

Griffith, Mrs. D.W. *When the Movies Were Young.* E.P. Dutton & Company, 1925.

Hancock, Ralph and Letitia Fairbanks. *Douglas Fairbanks: The Fourth Musketeer.* Henry Holt and Company, 1953.

Hanson, Patricia King (Editor). *The American Film Institute Catalog of Motion Pictures Produced in the United States: Feature Films, 1911 - 1920.* University of California Press, 1993.

Hanson, Patricia King (Editor). *The American Film Institute Catalog of Motion Pictures Produced in the United States: Feature Films, 1931 - 1940.* University of California Press, 1993.

Harris, Warren G. *Gable & Lombard.* Simon & Schuster, 1974.

Hart, William S. *My Life East and West.* Benjamin Blom, 1929.

Herman, Jan. *A Talent for Trouble: The Life of William Wyler.* G. P. Putnam's Sons, 1995.

Higashi, Sumiko. *Cecil B. DeMille and American Culture: The Silent Era.* University of California Press, 1994.

Holland, Dave. *On Location.* The Holland House, 1990.

Holmes, Bernese Gay. *Tales of the Pioneers of Big Bear Lake.* West Valley Letters, 1956.

Jacobs, Jack & Myron Braun. *The Films of Norma Shearer.* Oak Tree Publications, 1976.

Karney, Robin, (Editor). *Chronicle of the Cinema.* DK Publishing, 1995.

Koszarski, Diane Kaiser. *The Complete Films of William S. Hart.* Dover Publications, 1980.

La Fuze, Pauliena B. *Saga of the San Bernardinos.* San Bernardino County Museum Association, 1971.

Lahue, Kalton C. *Winners of the West: The Sagebrush Heroes of the Silent Screen.* A.S. Barnes and Co., 1970.

Lamparski, Richard. *Whatever Became of . . .?* Crown Publishing, 1973.

Lee, Raymond. *The Films of Mary Pickford.* A.S. Barnes & Co., 1970.

Madsen, Axel. *William Wyler.* Thomas Y. Crowell, 1973.

Milland, Ray. *Wide-Eyed in Babylon.* William Morrow & Co., 1974.

Moore, Colleen. *Silent Star.* Doubleday & Co., 1968.

Moore, William G. with John H. "Fritz" Fisher. *Fun With Fritz: Adventures in Early Redlands, Big Bear and Hollywood.* Compiled by William G. Moore. Redlands: Moore Historical Foundation, 1986.

Munden, Kenneth W. (Editor). *The American Film Institute Catalog of Motion Pictures Produced in the United States: Feature Films, 1921 - 1930.* University of California Press, 1997.

Moving Picture World. January, 1911 to December, 1919.

Niven, David. *Bring On the Empty Horses.* G. P. Putnam's Sons, 1975.

Niver, Kemp R. *Early Motion Pictures.* Library of Congress, 1985.

Ott, Frederick W. *The Films of Carole Lombard.* Citadel Press, 1972.

Parish, James Robert with Steven Whitney. *George Raft File.* Drake Publishers Inc., 1973.

Phillips, Baxter. *Cut - The Unseen Cinema.* Lorrimer Publishing Ltd., 1975.

Pickford, Mary. *Sunshine and Shadow: An Autobiography.* Doubleday & Co., 1955.

Preminger, Erik Lee. *Gypsy & Me.* Little, Brown and Co., 1984.

Quirk, Lawrence J. *Films of Gloria Swanson.* Citadel Press, 1984.

_____ *Films of William Holden.* Citadel Press, 1973.

_____ *Norma: The Story of Norma Shearer.* St. Martin's Press, 1988.

Rainsberger, Todd. *James Wong Howe: Cinematographer.* A.S. Barnes & Co. Inc., 1981.

Redlands Daily Facts. January, 1911 to December, 1914.

Redlands Daily Review. January, 1913 to December, 1918.

Ringgold, Gene and DeWitt Bodeen. *The Films of Cecil B. DeMille.* Cadillac Publishing Co., 1969.

Robinson, John W. *The San Bernardinos.* Big Santa Anita Historical Society, 1989.

Rogers, Ginger. *Ginger, My Story.* Harper Collins Publishers, 1991.

San Bernardino Daily Sun. January, 1911 to December, 1918.

Schutz, Wayne. *The Motion Picture Serial: An Annotated Bibliography.* Scarecrow Press, 1992.

Scott, Evelyn F. *Hollywood When Silents Were Golden.* McGraw-Hill Book Co., 1972.

Sklar, Robert. *A World History of Film.* Harry N. Abrams, Inc., 2002.

Smith, Albert with Phil A. Koury. *Two Reels and A Crank.* Doubleday & Co., 1952.

Steen, David. *Clara Bow Runnin' Wild.* Penguin Books, 1988.

Swanson, Gloria. *Swanson On Swanson: An Autobiography.* Random House, 1980.

Teichmann, Howard. *Fonda: My Life.* New American Library, 1981.

Thomas, Bob. *Golden Boy: The Untold Story of William Holden.* Berkley Books, 1984.

Wallis, Hal and Charles Higham. *Starmaker: The Autobiography of Hal Wallis.* Macmillan Co., 1980.

Wray, Fay. *On the Other Hand: A Life Story.* George Weidenfield & Nicolson, 1990.

PREFACE

It would be impossible to chronicle all the moving pictures that have been made in the San Bernardino Mountains. I began with those that had been reported in various publications, including newspapers, books, and magazines, no matter how wrong I felt they were. I started out with a short list of about fifty films, but gradually this list was pared down because of mistakes and errors, but then started growing once my real research began.

After the project was started, people would come up to me and say that such and such movie had been made up in the mountains. Unfortunately, I had to view a lot of bad movies, and a few good ones, to get to my present list of over 260 films that have been made in the San Bernardinos. As I said, not all of the movies can ever be known because many have been lost to time and the elements. The old nitrate film that was used up until the 1950s deteriorated at an alarming rate. Some studios deliberately destroyed their old films in order to recycle their silver content. Then too, many films were short one or two-reelers that were not thought important enough to even leave production notes about. The fact is though, the San Bernardino Mountains, from the Cajon Pass east to Big Bear Lake, were and still are a rich terrain needed by the film makers for their magnificent mountain movies.

Lee Cozad

THE EARLY YEARS

The fledgling moving picture business came early to the San Bernardino Mountains. Mr. Edison's moving pictures had caught the fancy of just about everyone. Well not exactly everyone, as this medium was still thought of as vulgar by many of the upper classes, but a godsend to the masses of immigrants who could barely speak or understand the difficult English language. The silent movie became a learning tool and introduction into their adopted country and an escape from the drudgeries of everyday life. Their nickels turned into dollars and eventually into thousands for the early producers and distributors.

During the early 1910s, there were three movie theaters in Redlands and five theaters in San Bernardino showing the latest films from moving picture companies such as Selig, Bison, Kalem, Pathé, Universal, Lasky, Edison, Lubin, Keystone, Biograph, Essanay and Vidagraph. In the East, the moving picture industry, tired of cold winters and unpredictable weather, began to trek west to the milder climate of Southern California.

The public's thirst for adventure films was appeased by tales of the great Southwest in the form of the Western. Los Angeles had become a mecca for the budding industry by 1909. The San Bernardino Mountains beckoned the early film makers with the promises of tall timber, grassy meadows and crystal clear lakes. Location shooting was easy because hunting and fishing lodges were already available to house the film crews.

Although films were probably made earlier in the mountains, the first documentation was an item in the Redlands Daily

Early Essanay Poster

G. M. Anderson—Broncho Billy
Essanay Pictures
circa 1913

Facts, February 6, 1911. Essanay Film Company of Chicago set up shop along with six other unnamed moving picture companies. They anticipated making as many as twenty-one films per week! The building was located on Lugonia Avenue, two blocks west of Orange Avenue in Redlands. Production must have gone well, because by the 20th of the month they needed additional cowboys, who were brought in from Wyoming, Arizona and New Mexico. Exactly one week later, those same actors went on strike for higher wages because of the dangers they encountered while filming. The cowboys soon learned that falling off horses on purpose exacted a heavy price on their own hides. At this time, Essanay also began hiring local Indians from the Banning and San Manuel reservations to perform in their pictures.

On March 9, 1911, Essanay announced their first picture made in the San Bernardino Mountains, *The Romance of the Bar O,* filmed on the Smith Ranch in eastern Highlands near the Pacific Light and Power powerhouse. The plot revolved around the rancher's daughter who asked her father to give a saddle tramp a job. Later, of course, this same saddle tramp saved the daughter and her horse as they tried to cross the swollen Santa Ana River. The picture was shown later that month to overflowing crowds at a local Redlands theatre. It is no wonder because the star of the film was none other than Gilbert "Broncho Billy" Anderson, probably the most famous movie and cowboy star at that time. Unfortunately, like so many other early films, this film is lost to us.

Anderson, born Maxwell Aronson, led

the posse in what is credited with being the first featured Western. It was *The Great Train Robbery* made by Edison's Movie Picture Company in 1903. It was all of ten minutes long and made in New Jersey, not the wild and woolly West. Later, Anderson created the rugged persona of "Broncho Billy" and went on to make hundreds of one and two reelers starring his character.

The motion picture company Essanay was, in fact, the formation of the letters S and A. The S stood for George Spoor, Anderson's wealthy Chicago partner and the A was for Anderson. The company made hundreds of Westerns and was a huge success, but dissolved later because of differences between the partners. Many of their films were destroyed at that time.

Most of these early films were one or two-reelers* meant to fill out the program for an evening's entertainment. The majority of what were considered feature films were still being made back East.

In April, 1911, Essanay filmed *Across the Plains* which was called the "Greatest Western Picture ever made" — to that date. It starred Anderson and Arthur Mackley. This was followed with the release of *The Faithful Indian* in May, which was filmed in Santa Ana Canyon and Arrowhead. (The area around Arrowhead Springs Hotel was called Arrowhead at that time.) There is an earlier mention of the film being made near "the" Arrowhead, a large natural rock and vegetation formation on the side of the mountain. Essanay then released a slew of pictures: *Thwarted Vengeance; Widow of Mill Creek; Bad Man's Downfall; The Cattleman's Daughter; Badman's First Prayer; Indian Maiden's Lesson; Circle C Wedding Present; What a Woman Can Do; The Puncher's New*

Ray Meyers and Ethel Grandin in
Across the Plains (1911)
Essanay-Ince

Thomas Ince and Chief Eagleshirt
circa 1912

*One reel was usually 10 to 15 minutes long and depended upon a person turning the crank at the same speed at which the orginal film was shot.

Augustus Carney
(Alkali Ike)

Photo courtesy of Andrew Dzamba

Love; Hidden Mine; The Count and the Cowboys; and *Alkali Ike's Auto.* This was the first mention of "Alkali Ike," a very famous series that Essanay created.

On July 7, 1911, The Bison Company arrived in Redlands on their way to Big Bear Valley where they set up a studio. They had fifty people, ninety horses, six canoes and several carloads of equipment. Included in the cast were Del Blanchart, Milton Brown and Art Acord, a twenty-one year old Oklahoma cowboy, who had been playing the part of Indians for Selig Polyscope in Los Angeles. Glass's Pine Lake Hotel was used for housing the stars and crew. Spectators to some of the filming going on in Big Bear, reported back to the newspaper that they were entertained by the realistic attack on the settlers camp by a group of Indians just above the dam. Actually, they had at first been frightened by the gunfire because they were unfamiliar with blanks.

On August 8, 1911, a bad accident occured while filming an Essanay stage coach robbery. Four actors who were riding in the coach were hurt: Gladys Field, Louis Morrisette, Charles Guerro and Augustus Carney, who played Alkali Ike. Specifically mentioned as not hurt were Mackley and Anderson, their main stars, who were evidently chasing after the stagecoach when it overturned.

The Bison Movie crew was also churning out a number of Westerns, but the

Early Movie Crew at Pine Knot Resort
in Big Bear
Photo courtesy of Tom Core

management back in New York was not happy with the results and so they sent a new man out to manage the cast. Unfortunately he alienated enough of the crew, that they refused to work until he was replaced. Bison management finally resolved matters because by late August and September, *Cowboy's Vacation*, a Bison western comedy, *Brave Swift Eagle's Peril* and *Saved From the Redman* arrived in Redland's theaters. Bison was again noted by locals for its realism during a hanging scene, which they duly reported back to the *Redlands Daily Facts*. By this time Bison was filming an entire movie every day.

William S. Hart and Lillian Red Wing St. Cyr
in an unknown movie

Later in August, a U.S. Calvary Troop from Los Angeles made its annual trek up Waterman Canyon to Grout Bay on Big Bear Lake. The Bison crew took advantage of the fully dressed troop and filmed them galloping across a meadow with bugles blowing "Charge."

By September, Essanay had moved on to San Rafael and later to Niles, California, to set up shop. They were so successful by this time, that they were able to lure Charlie Chaplin away from Mack Sennett's Keystone Studios. But before they left Redlands, they completed *Buncho Game at Lizardville* in May, *The Infant at Snakeville* in June, and *Mustang Pete's Love Affair* in July in the San Bernardino Mountains.

In September of 1911, one of the first Bison pictures made its way to the public, *Little Dove's Romance*, starring Red Wing, Charles Inslee, and Red Wing's husband, James Young Deer. Young Deer, like his wife, was a Native American, and he starred and directed in hundreds of films during this early era of film making. *Little Dove's*

Mona Darkfeather
Courtesy of The Academy of Motion
Picture Arts and Sciences

Romance may be the film that onlookers again reported to the Redlands newspaper, because the story revolved around a young Indian maiden thrown from her horse by the sound of gunfire. She was rescued by the white hunter and taken back to his camp next to a lake. At least one reel of the film still exists at the Library of Congress and at the George Eastman House Archives in Rochester, New York.

In the East, there was a great hunger for more stories about the Indians. In 1912, the Bison company, under the direction of Thomas Ince, began a series of two reelers starring a thirty year old actress using the name of Princess Mona Darkfeather. She was neither a Princess nor a Native American Indian. She was, in fact, from a prominent pioneer family and had been born Josephine M. Workman in Boyle Heights near Los Angeles. She did have Spanish ancestry and with makeup and costume, she was able to pass for a local Indian.

The year 1912 brought a flurry of activity to the mountains. With the huge success of the one and two reel Westerns back East, Ince and Bison continued to turn out movies as well as other producers like Kalem and Kinemacolor. These.companies used the Squirrel Inn and Pine Crest Resort, near present day Twin Peaks, as headquarters while shooting forest and snow scenes. The titles, for the most part, had an Indian theme: *Star Eye's Stratagem; Tattoo; A Red Man's Love; An Indian Ishmael; The Half Breed Scout; A White Indian;* and *Darkfeather's Strategy.*

By 1913, filming in the San Bernardino Mountains was commonplace. The Redlands Daily Review, January 19, 1913, indicated that the Selig Bear Valley Company was in the mountains filming *The Cattle Rustlers.*

Late in February of 1913, the auto stage from San Bernardino transported twenty-four players from the Kinemacolor Company up to the Squirrel Inn, near Twin Peaks, to make a picture in the snow. At the time, it was reported that there was four feet of snow and drifts of ten feet. The action took place in an Indian village set up nearby and later the players were actually marooned when new snow fell. Local residents dug them out and transported them back down the hill, utilizing horse-drawn bobsleds, to a series of switchbacks where they then could be motored out. Another group of actors from the Nestor Films, was waiting at the switchbacks to be transported back through the snow to the Skyland Inn, in Skyland. Neither of these films were named, unfortunately.

During the Spring of 1913, a company of actors came up to Pine Crest Resort* to film another picture. For years the photograph of this group was thought to have been from the cast of the *Squaw Man*, and was labeled "The Squaw Man—1913." The picture came from the Kate Cooley estate and somehow was mislabeled over the years. George M. Cooley had a hardware store in San Bernardino in 1913 and a summer cabin at Pine Crest Resort where these photos were taken.

However, on closer examination by movie historian, Marc Wanamaker, who worked for the DeMille estate, it was determined that none of these actors was in the *Squaw Man* which was actually filmed in January, 1914, at Mount Palomar, California.

Unknown movie cast at
Pine Crest Resort circa 1913
Photo courtesy of Pauliena B. LaFuze

* Pine Crest Resort was the original name for the retreat founded by Dr. John N. Baylis located near present day Twin Peaks. The name was later changed to Pinecrest Resort.

Wallace Reid and Dorothy Davenport

Mona Darkfeather
circa 1914

There is one actor, Chief William Eagleshirt, a member of the Sioux nation, in one of the photos and it is known that he worked a great deal with Thomas Ince, the director. Native Americans, like Eagleshirt, were integral to the authenticity and success of the Ince-Bison 101 Company's Westerns.

Although DeMille did not choose the San Bernardino Mountains for the *Squaw Man*, he did travel to the area several times in the ensuing years with many famous silent stars, including Gloria Swanson, Elliot Dexter and Wallace Reid.

It was reported that Wallace Reid arrived with a group of actors around Thanksgiving time, 1913, and asked for the honeymoon cottage at the Squirrel Inn. He had just married his leading lady, Dorothy Davenport, a month earlier. The rest of the cast was housed at Pine Crest Resort. John Dexter, a young local man, was the new caretaker at the Squirrel Inn. He reported that Reid and another star, Florence Vidor, filmed the *Moonshiner's Daughter* in the rocks between the two resorts. Majestic Motion Picture Co. did release a film by that name on March 9, 1914, but little is known about the film. Another Majestic film also released in 1914, *Moonshine Molly*, starred Mae Marsh, but again little is known of the film other than it was a backwoods romance. Reid was a star at Majestic and made seventy plus films for them and other companies in 1914.

It is interesting to note that in 1913, *Moving Picture World*, the leading industry magazine, reported that: "Indian dramas . . . are played out" and that film companies were hanging out "No Indians Wanted" signs. Little did they know that the Western was far from dead.

In early June, 1913, about forty members of the New York Motion Picture Co. came up to Pine Crest Resort to make a series of movies. Fred J. Balshofer was in charge, but little else is known of the films they made. However, an interesting side note is that on the 6th of June, Kitty Howe, described as a chorus girl, was killed returning from Pine Crest when she leaped from the car on Waterman Canyon Road. Could this have been the first reported incidence of Hollywood immorality?

In July, 1914, the Kalem Company headed by Frank E. Montgomery, Production Manager and D.F. Whitcomb, Scenario Writer, motored up to Pine Crest Resort with a group of twenty actors and several car loads of equipment to begin filming a series of Indian dramas. Mona Darkfeather was the featured actress, but little else is known of the films. Mona is credited with twenty-five films in 1914, twenty-three of which were filmed with Kalem. At this time it was not unusual for a company to make a complete film story in a day. Titles like *The Vanishing Tribe, Squaw's Revenge* and *Kidnapped by Indians* could easily have been made at that time.

The San Bernardino Mountains have always lent themselves to the Western genre of film, as well as many a "Mountie" picture. The golden age for film making in the mountains was during the Twenties and Thirties. One old timer recalled that "there were so many companies up here shooting pictures . . . that they were practically tripping over one another."

Actress White Dove and unknown male actor on top of Castle Rock in an unnamed film overlooking Big Bear Lake
Photo courtesy of Tom Core

THE CALL OF THE NORTH
(1914)

CAST:
Robert Edeson.................Ned Stewart
Theodore Roberts...........Galen Albert
Winifred Kingston..................Virginia
Directed by.................Cecil B. DeMille
Produced by...............Jesse L. Lasky
                        Feature Play Co.

With the tremendous success of *The Squaw Man* just completed, Jesse Lasky and Cecil B. DeMille immediately decided to duplicate their effort with another book/play/movie combination. This time they took Stewart Edward White's book, *The Conjuror's House*, which was adapted to a play named *The Call of the North* by George Broadhurst. They needed a mountain and lake locale for the French trapper story which revolved around the monopolistic Hudson Bay Company in Canada.

DeMille, with a group of actors including Dustin Farnum and Winifred Kingston, along with the author White and his wife, motored up to Pine Knot Lodge in Big Bear. White was brought to work on the script and for authenticity. Farnum's role is still unclear because he was not chosen as the lead nor any other character in the movie. Robert Edeson, a well known forty-six year old theater actor was selected to recreate the dual father/son role of Graehme and Ned Stewart which he had played in the theater. Anxious to have Edeson starring, Lasky and DeMille gave him a contract that allowed him great latitude with choosing cast and locations. He insisted on authentic Canadian Indians and locations, but was finally talked out of it due to budget restrictions.

Teaching little Ned to snow shoe. *Robert Edeson in* "CALL OF THE NORTH"

Robert Edeson and Winifred Kingston teaching little Ned how to snow shoe. Salt was used as substitute for the real thing.

Actual filming began in mid-June. Big Bear sometimes will have snow last into June, but mother nature was not on the side of the crew that summer. The snow scenes had to be shot in salt, a common substitute in those days. The arctic-clad actors suffered terribly in temperatures that soared to over 100 degrees. The altitude of 6,000 feet didn't help either as the actors complained of headaches and slight hemorrhages.

The story revolves around the efforts of the son to clear and avenge the death of his father, who had been unjustly accused of adultery with the wife of the factor, the powerful boss of the trading post and the only law in this vast northern wilderness. The father was sent on "la longue traverse," which is a polite way they had of saying a journey of death. The accused is given a canoe, but no weapons nor food and told to leave the settlement. He was followed by an Indian loyal to the company who is aptly called "The Shadow of Death." Twenty years later, the son is also caught trading in defiance of the company and he too is sentenced to the long journey of death. However, he is rescued by the daughter of the factor, played by twenty year old Winifred Kingston, who had just finished the role as the heroine in *The Squaw Man* that same year. The villain Rand, who sets everything into motion, is played by character actor Horace B. Carpenter. His death bed confession makes all things right in the end which was to become a Hollywood tradition.

The reviews of the movie, which was

Cecil B. DeMille (in puttees behind camera) and Alvin Wyckoff watching Winifred Kingston and Robert Edeson go through a scene at Big Bear Lake.

first shown in August, 1914, were ecstatic and glowing. One reviewer declared, "Such pictures as these amply confirm my faith in the approaching kingdom of quality." DeMille's second attempt in films established him as a director of compelling influence in the years to follow. His choice of Alvin Wyckoff as cinematographer was one of the best decisions he ever made and they would collaborate on forty-four films over the next decade.

This series of three prints from *Call of the North* (1914) is from the San Bernardino County Archives and the Bill Threatt Collection. Scans courtesy of Roger Hatheway

AFTER FIVE (1915)

Long before he played Colonel Saito in *Bridge on the River Kwai,* Japanese born Sessue Hayakawa had been a silent film star. He appeared in more than seventy films over a span of forty years. In *After Five,* Hayakawa played the valet to Edward Abeles, the lead in William and Cecil B. DeMille's successful adaptation of their stage comedy about the foibles of unwise investing in the stock market.

Ted Ewing (Edward Abeles) believes that his broker, Sam Parker (Monroe Salisbury) has led him astray and that he has lost his entire fortune as well as that of his ward, Nora Hildreth, in Potash Preferred. When the broker disappears, Ted, thinking that he has squandered his fiancee's money, purchases an insurance policy on himself for $50,000 with Nora named as beneficiary. But the policy has a clause invalidating it in case of suicide, so he arranges an "accidental death."

Naturally, everything he tries goes astray. The train he falls in front of suddenly switches tracks and the fall out of a window is broken by an awning. Frustrated, he hires the S.S.S., a local Black Hand organization to "do him in" and gives the money to Oki (Hayakawa), his valet, as payment if they will kill him after five that afternoon. Waiting in panic for the fateful moment, Ted receives word from his broker that Potash Preferred has doubled in value. Now really frantic, he tries to call off the bargain by offering to pay the S.S.S. twice the amount. Oki, in the mean-

CAST:
Edward Abeles....................Ted Ewing
Sessue Hayakawa..........................Oki
Monroe Salisbury.............Sam Parker
Betty Schade...............................Nora
Directed by.........Cecil B. DeMille and Oscar Apfel
Produced by..........................Jesse L. Lasky Feature Play Co.

SESSUE HAYAKAWA.

13

time, attempts hara-kiri. But all ends well when Nora's doting Aunt Diddy offers enough money to call off the "hit."

Oscar Apfel and Cecil B. Demille were co-directors on this Lasky Feature Play Co. movie. The snow scenes that were supposed to be Maine were real and probably shot sometime in late December 1914, or early January 1915, in Big Bear, California. The movie was only received as so-so, with critics calling Abeles "experienced," and Betty Schade (Nora, the ward) as "too theatrical." The only high praise seems to have gone to Hayakawa, whose first name was written as "Succo" in 1915. Edward Abeles continued in movies and on stage, but died of pneumonia five years later. Twenty-one year old, German born Betty Schade left the movies in 1921 after making over fifty films.

Edward Abeles (holding rifle) in a scene from *After Five* (1915) shot on location at Big Bear Lake.

THE CHALICE OF COURAGE (1915)

The winter of 1914-15 was one of the coldest on record in the San Bernardino Mountains. Several movie companies took advantage of these conditions to film snow scenes for their films. The Oliver Morosco Photoplay Company, with a cast and crew of forty, stayed at Pine Knot Resort in Big Bear Lake. Morosco and director Oscar Apfel made at least ten films during 1915, so it is not known what the title may have been.

During that same period, Vitagraph began filming a Cyrus Townsend Brady novel, *The Chalice of Courage: A Romance of Colorado*. It is a convoluted tale of a young prospector named William Newbold (William Duncan) and his bride, Louise, who is fleeing a former suitor, James Armstrong, who has been pestering her. A locket that has a picture of the ex-suitor accompanies her. On a trail in the mountains of Colorado, her horse takes a misstep and she plunges down a precipice. Barely alive, she pleads with her husband to end her misery and he obliges, reluctantly. He flees the gravesite with only the locket and in his grief, he becomes a recluse surviving in the mountains for the next five years.

During this time, Enid Maitland (Myrtle Gonzalez) travels west to visit her Uncle Robert, a wealthy miner, along with her new fiancé—you guessed it—James

CAST:	
William Duncan........	William Newbold
Myrtle Gonzalez...........	Enid Maitland
George Holt...........	James Armstrong
Directed by...........	Rollin S. Sturgeon
Produced by..................	Vitagraph Co.

William Duncan and unknown actor
in a scene from
The Chalice of Courage (1915)
Photo courtesy of The Academy of Motion
Picture Arts and Sciences

Armstrong! While on an outing, she goes off swimming alone and is harassed by a bear, but is fortunately rescued by recluse Newbold. Newbold takes her back to his cabin, but immediately a blizzard strikes and they are snowed in for the winter. True to his late wife, William does not take advantage of the situation and he and Enid become platonic lovers only. When the rescuers arrive, Newbold recognizes Armstrong as the cad in the locket and a fight ensues. Armstrong is unveiled and commits suicide.

William Newbold was played by thirty-six year old William Duncan, born in Dundee, Scotland. Duncan was an actor in over thirty films, a director of thirty-seven films and a writer. He retired from films in 1925 and died in 1961.

Enid was played by twenty-four year old Myrtle Gonzalez, who made only thirteen films. She died in Los Angeles during the great flu epidemic of 1918. The original film may have been made in Colorado, however, it was discovered that over half the film was covered in static and the snow scenes had to be re-shot at Big Bear Lake.

Myrtle Gonzalez in an unknown film
Photo courtesy of The Academy of Motion Picture Arts and Sciences

THE WHITE SCAR (1915)

Around Labor Day, 1915, Universal sent a unit up to Bear Valley to film another Hudson Bay trapper story. No copy of the film exists, but it sounds more exciting than *Call of the North*, and is surely more convoluted in context. Hobart Bosworth was a forty-eight year old actor who wrote, starred and directed *The White Scar*. He even did the titles in rhyme. These were, of course, a big element in silent pictures.

Bosworth plays the part of a trapper called by the Indians, Na-Ta-Wan-Gan (great trapper). He falls in love with young Janet (Jane Novak), the eighteen year old daughter of the trading post's factor. Janet is promised to another (Henri the French trapper), but is secretly attracted to Na-Ta-Wan-Gan. When Janet's brother is accused of the theft of some furs and faces "la long traverse," Na-Ta-Wan-Gan comes to his aid by falsely admitting guilt. Janet then elopes with Na-Ta-Wan-Gan, who is aided by an Indian maiden (Wehnonah). She is also in love with him.

The entire story is told in retrospect to Na-Ta-Wan-Gan's and Jane's twelve year old son many years later by Wehnonah. There are frame-ups by the jilted villain; unrequited love between Wehnonah (Anna Lehr, who was the mother of actress Ann Dvorak) and Na-

CAST:	
Hobart Bosworth	Na-Ta-Wan-Gan
Jane Novak	Janet
Anna Lehr	Wehnonah
Directed by	Hobart Bosworth
Produced by	Broadway Universal Feature

Hobart Bosworth and Jane Novak with unidentified child in a scene from *The White Scar* (1915) filmed at Big Bear Lake.
Photo courtesy of The Academy of Motion Picture Arts and Sciences

Ta-Wan-Gan; and finally, a death bed confession that saves the day. All this is explained by Wehnonah to the boy, as she shows him the knife wound in her neck where she had jumped in front of Na-Ta-Wan-Gan to save him yet again from the evil Henri. It is the "white scar."

The film opened in New York in December of 1915 and was immediately a success with rave reviews, especially about the scenery. One reviewer commented about the authenticity of the location (Big Bear Lake) and the lack of civilization. Hobart Bosworth was a big star in 1915 and made twelve films that year alone. He had a successful career that spanned forty years and one hundred and sixty pictures. Jane Novak also had a successful career in seventy-six films and would return to the San Bernardino Mountains two years later to star in Harold Bell Wright's *The Eyes of the World*. Frank Newberg, who plays Jane's brother in *The White Scar*, was, in fact, her husband in 1915. His career, like so many others, ended when the talkies came in.

Film crew in front of the Pine Knot
Resort in Big Bear, California
Photo courtesy of Tom Core

THE GUSSLE SERIES (1915)

Charlie Chaplin joined Mack Sennett's Mutual Film Corporation in 1913. A year later, Charlie persuaded his half-brother Sydney to join him in Hollywood, because the new motion picture industry needed comedians. Sydney joined the Keystone Film division of Mutual where Charlie had so much success. In April 1915, Mack Sennett arrived in Big Bear with a small group of actors and crew with the express purpose of producing several short comedies. The author was fortunate to have been able to view two of these short films (about ten minutes each) at the Library of Congress, where they are preserved in their paper collection. Each frame was shot and transferred to a sheet of paper and then compiled as a 16mm film.

The antics of Gussle, the protagonist, at first seem quite familiar. It is not until one remembers that Syd Chaplin and Charlie grew up together, that one realizes the similarity of their acting styles.

Syd plays the bumbling, mustached fool in a series of misadventures in the mountains. In one of the films, he is tied to a group of mountain climbers as he is chased around after flirting with a bar maid (*Gussle Tied to Trouble*). He is shot at by his rather frumpy and irate wife played by Phyllis Allen, who happened to be fifty-six years old at the time. Syd, on the other hand, was only thirty years old in 1915. The photography of the mountain snow scenes was lauded by critics at the time.

The second one made at Big Bear and in the river below the dam

Sydney Chaplin
circa 1918

was *Gussle's Backward Way*. Syd plays the hero who is robbed, but foils the bandits by dropping his goods in the river, riding a donkey backwards (some trick photography is used for this) and recounting his adventures to his beer drinking companions at an inn. His use of a Tyrolean long-stemmed pipe to extract the beer from the glass of Phyllis Allen is classic comedy.

Mack Sennett directed the *Gussle* series of seven shorts. In April of 1915, a third film, *A Bear Affair*, the story of a mountain hunting trip, is thought to have been made by the same group at the same time as the two *Gussle* shorts, but has never been corroborated.

Syd Chaplin continued to make movies into the Twenties, but never gained the success nor the fame of his half-brother. Darryl F. Zanuck, who worked for Syd in the 1920s, referred to him as "the greatest ladies' man in Hollywood history." Sydney worked for his brother as his business manager for the rest of his career. Although four years older, he would always be known as "Charlie's brother."

Syd Chaplin made up
as Gussle.
circa 1915

JORDAN IS A HARD ROAD
(1915)

In August of 1915, D.W. Griffith left Mutual to form Fine Arts/Triangle Films. One of the first projects he brought with him was Sir Gilbert Parker's novel, *Jordan Is A Hard Road*. For the exterior shots of the movie, Allan Dwan, the director, created the small town of Askatoon in Big Bear Valley. Filming commenced in mid-September and was completed in two weeks.

Bill Minden (Frank Campeau) is on the verge of arrest for robbery and his dying wife has just given birth. Knowing he can't possibly care for the child, he gives the little girl up to a religious and temperate family who move to Askatoon. The girl, Cora (Dorothy Gish), grows in to a young woman completely ignorant of her father's existence. At a revival meeting, Bill Minden discovers his grown daughter and is morally rehabilitated by finding God. The scenes of the meeting hall are genuine. Allan Dwan hired evangelist Billy Sunday to preach a real-life revival in a tent and then edited Campeau into the film. Cora is in love with penniless Mark Sheldon (Owen Moore), a young mining engineer, who is struggling to open a mine near Askatoon. Attempting to help his daughter by investing in the new mine, Minden deposits some of his ill-gotten gains into a local bank, ironically, only to have it robbed. In those days when a bank was robbed, it was the depositors who lost their money. Minden then decides to pull one more train robbery but is shot in the process. He turns the money over to Mark Sheldon just as he dies in Cora's arms.

Frank Campeau, a dramatic stage actor, made his screen debut in this film at the age

CAST:	
Dorothy Gish	Cora Findley
Frank Campeau	Bill Minden
Owen Moore	Mark Sheldon
Directed by	Allan Dwan
Produced by	Fine Arts Film Co.

Frank Campeau
circa 1915

Owen Moore

of fifty-one. He starred in a few more pictures and then became a character actor with close to a hundred films to his credit over the next thirty years.

Seventeen year old Dorothy Gish was already a screen veteran, with over fifty films to her name by the time she played the temperate daughter. She never gained the star status of her older sister, Lillian, but she continued acting into the 1960s, primarily on stage.

Irish-born, Owen Moore was twenty-nine at the time and he too was an experienced actor who appeared in over two hundred films, most of them before his role in *Jordan*. His career ended with a bit part in *A Star Is Born* in 1937, and he died two years later.

Allan Dwan was also a screen veteran having directed more than eighty films in five years. This was not one of his best efforts since he was criticized for dragging a two-reeler into five. He became a respected director of some great films such as *Heidi*(1937) and *Sands of Iwo Jima*(1949).

Critics faulted the film as too labored and loosely constructed, but Campeau's performance as Bill Minden, the rehabilitated father, was highly praised.

Dorothy Gish
circa 1915

THE BIRTH OF A NATION
(1915)

Probably the most influential movie ever made in the San Bernardino Mountains was the epic Civil War drama *The Birth of a Nation,* filmed in the summer of 1914. This three hour film has been called racist, brilliant, inaccurate and inflammatory. It is all that and more. D.W. Griffith's masterpiece was so far ahead of its time in both pioneering cinematography and content, that it is still taught in film schools to this day. It was screened as *The Clansman* in a preview in Riverside, California, on January 1, 1915. The audience not only stayed the entire three hours, but was left in awe.

In 1915, only fifty years after the Civil War ended, Southerners were still smarting from defeat and this film almost became a rallying cry. There were huge demonstrations and near riots wherever it was shown. Audiences were known to break out in cheers and march up and down the aisles whenever the KKK riders came to the rescue of the heroine. The NAACP protested its very existence and picketed it whenever it was shown.

Griffith, who was a Southerner, was chagrined that it evoked that much controversy. The fact is that it was the box office success of the year, grossing more than $3,000,000. To sooth his critics, Griffith followed up the next year with another epic called *Intolerance* that dealt with bias and racism. Unfortunately for Griffith, it was a financial failure and his career started a downward spiral. He died many years later in almost total obscurity.

Most of the film was shot in what is now Universal City, except for the most dramatic

CAST:	
Lillian Gish	Elsie Stoneman
Mae Marsh	Flora Cameron
Ralph Lewis	Austin Stoneman
Directed by	D. W. Griffith
Produced by	D. W. Griffith

Scene from
The Birth of a Nation
(1915)

Robert Harron and Mae Marsh
in a scene from
The Birth of a Nation (1915)

Lillian Gish
circa 1915

scene of the attempted rape of a white girl (Mae Marsh) by a black itinerant worker (Walter Long, a Caucasian in "black face"). Rather than succumb to the advances of the rapist, the heroine jumped to her death. In order to obtain the hellish, maniacal look of a fiend, Griffith had Long gargle with hydrogen peroxide (creating the foaming-at-the-mouth effect of a mad dog), just before chasing Mae Marsh up the rocks. The cliffs above Big Bear Lake were chosen because of their grandeur for Marsh's fall. It is ironic that these same cliffs, almost to the scene, were also chosen for Tourneau's *Last of the Mohicans* five years later, with the same dramatic effect.

Mae Marsh was a twenty year old screen veteran who had made forty films before *The Birth of a Nation*. It was on this set that she met John Ford, who was an actor and assistant director on the film. Their long friendship would enable her to come back to films over the next three decades, even after she had "officially" retired. Altogether, she was in seventeen of Ford's classic films. It was said that the writer Ernest Hemingway was smitten by her.

Thirty-six year old film veteran Walter Long's career briefly flourished with some lead roles, but then he slipped back to character parts for the rest of his life.

Lillian Gish, the star of the film, was twenty-two at the time and she too was a screen veteran. She became one of Hollywood's most famous celebrities and made more than one hundred movies in the span of eighty years. Gish died in 1993, just months before her one hundredth birthday.

GOD'S COUNTRY AND THE WOMAN (1916)

The word was out — go west and stay west. Vitagraph Company of America, determined not to be left out, returned a crew to Big Bear Lake during the winter/spring of 1915-16. They had obtained the rights to the works of one of the most famous and prolific writers of the time, James Oliver Curwood, noted for his far north adventures. His Alaskan novel, *God's Country and the Woman* (1915), had been extremely popular and it was thought that it would make an excellent movie by director Rollin Sturgeon, who had just filmed *Chalice of Courage* (1915) in Big Bear Lake.

Once more, Sturgeon chose Scottish-born actor William Duncan as his leading man and paired him up with a twenty-four year old Canadian named Nell Shipman. She was better known as a scenario writer and had acted in only one other film. Nevertheless, her portrayal of a young woman who has to carry a terrible secret was acclaimed.

Sturgeon originally tried to talk Vitagraph into sending him to Alaska, but settled for Big Bear Lake. Luckily for them, heavy snows came to the valley and their dog teams happily raced up and down hills with no problems. One of the most dramatic moments came when filming a canoe chase. Just as they began filming, nature cooperated fully and brought down a full-blown storm across the lake to engulf them. Audiences all over America loved it, even though it was one of the longest films made to date (eight reels, whereas the normal was four or five reels for a feature film).

During the Spanish Flu epidemic of 1918 that killed millions, Nell Shipman nearly died. She only made seventeen films, usually

CAST:		
William Duncan	....	Philip Weyman
Nell Shipman	....	Josephine Adare
Directed by	....	Rollin S. Sturgeon
Produced by	....	Vitagraph Co.

William Duncan (left) and Nell Shipman with an unknown actor in a scene from *God's Country and the Woman* (1916)

portraying a strong-willed heroine. Two of her films could be considered sequels to this box office smash: *Back to God's Country* (1919) which was filmed in Canada and *The Girl from God's Country* (1921), which she wrote, produced and directed. The first was a tremendous success (returning 300% to its investors), but the latter a complete and dismal failure. Her retirement came as the talkies arrived. Her last picture, *(The Golden Yukon*-1927), was filmed in the Sierras, which she again wrote, produced and directed. In 1927 Curwood died prematurely at the age of forty-nine, from a suspected but unproved spider bite.

Sturgeon, who was a stickler for authenticity, filmed this feature for a total of six months. Each scene was shot at least three times which probably explains the long length of the movie. Critics faulted him somewhat for this, but in general gave the film a good revue. He returned one more time to Big Bear Lake in 1918 to film *Hugon, The Mighty* with Lon Chaney.

An interesting side note is that after the movie company had wrapped up and departed the area, they did what most crews do—left the set intact. A passing traveler happened upon the set during a rain storm and thinking he had found shelter, lit a fire in the papier-mache fireplace with the inevitable results of burning it down to the ground.

Nell Shipman and William Duncan
at Big Bear Lake filming
God's Country and the Woman (1916).
Photo courtesy of The Academy of Motion
Picture Arts and Sciences

FIGHTING BLOOD
(1916)

In 1916, director Oscar Apfel substituted the San Bernardino Mountains for the green hills of Kentucky in his morality play *Fighting Blood*. This was producer William Fox's first west coast picture and foreshadowed his eventual move to Hollywood.

The plot revolves around Lem Hardy (William Farnum), who comes from a long line of fighters (Bunker Hill, Gettysburg, etc.) He can lick any man, even bigger ones than himself. At a lumber camp he meets and falls in love with Evie (Dorothy Bernard), the owner's daughter. Harry (Henry Herbert), the villain in this melodrama, frames young Lem and then in turn weds Evie, bankrupts her father, and takes to drinking and gambling. Meanwhile back in prison, Lem finds religion and becomes a minister. After his release from prison, he travels out west and stumbles across the evil Harry in a saloon. Of course, there is a tremendous fight in which Lem slays the villain and then rescues the girl from a life of sin by preaching the story of Mary Magdalene. In the end, they marry and live happily ever after in what was beginning to become a Hollywood tradition.

Critics loved the acting, but couldn't buy the story. Nevertheless, it did well at the box-office and Fox Studios established itself in Southern California.

CAST:	
William Farnum	Lem Hardy
Dorothy Bernard	Evie Colby
Henry Herbert	Harry Blake
Directed by	Oscar Apfel
Produced by	Fox Film Corp.

Dorothy Bernard as she appeared in another William Fox movie *Sporting Blood* (1916)

William Farnum
circa 1916

William Farnum was the younger brother of Dustin Farnum and came from a theatrical family. His other brother, Marshall, was a director. William was already a noted Broadway actor and forty years old by the time he began acting in pictures. He signed with Fox the year before and made a series of six pictures with twenty-six year old Dorothy Bernard, a young, bright beauty who was already a veteran of the screen. The South African-born actress made over fifty films before *Fighting Blood*. She left the silent picture industry in 1921, but made a comeback to television in the series *Life With Father* in 1953.

Farnum attained leading man status and at one point in the 1920s, made $10,000 per week. His career faltered after a bad accident on the set of a 1925 movie. Following a long recovery, he had to settle for character roles from then on.

The most interesting character was the villain, Henry Herbert. Is he the same Henry Herbert who sang tenor in many Gilbert and Sullivan operettas for D'Oyly Carte Opera between 1908 and 1913? Henry the actor has no credits before 1915 and Henry the singer disappeared after 1914. Are they one and the same?

Henry Herbert, the
D'Oyly Carte tenor
circa 1909

DAVY CROCKETT (1916)

There already had been five silent pictures made about the bigger-than-life American hero, *Davy Crockett*, before director William Desmond Taylor decided to film Frank Murdock's famous play about him. Pallas Pictures, a division of Paramount, came up to an area near Strawberry Flat (now Twin Peaks) in the spring of 1916 and found themselves in a blizzard. There was a contempary account of the screen hero, forty-two year old actor Dustin Farnum (Davy Crockett), actually rescuing two female hikers from the Arrowhead Springs Hotel directly below Strawberry Flat. He also was credited with saving the heroine, twenty-two year old English-born actress, Winifred Kingston, from a raging stream when she lost her footing.

Dustin and Winifred starred in the immensly popular *The Squaw Man* (1914) and *The Virginian* (1914) two years earlier. In fact, they were to star in nineteen films together, four of them directed by William Desmond Taylor. Taylor took what was called a mediocre script and turned it into a magnificently photographed box office winner. The knee-deep snow scenes and majestic mountains were lauded by critics, who said the director had a bright future in films. Pauliena B. LaFuze (*Saga of the San

CAST:
Dustin Farnum .... Davy Crockett
Winifred Kingston ... Eleanor Vaughn
Directed by .... William Desmond Taylor
Produced by .... Pallas/Paramount

Dustin Farnum and Winifred Kingston in a scene from *Davy Crockett* (1916)
Photo courtesy of
The Academy of Motion Picture Arts and Sciences

Bernardinos, 1971) mentions that "Uncle Billy" Stephen, the bard of Strawberry Flat, was an extra in the picture dressed up as a pioneer.

Taylor, the Irish-born director, went on to direct nearly fifty films. His only hiatus from Hollywood was during 1918-1919 when he served in the British Army. He returned to direct some of the biggest names in Hollywood, but his mysterious murder in 1922 was considered the scandal of the decade. It effectively ended the career of at least three actresses who were associated with him at the time. Many theories of who committed the crime have been offered over time, but the murder remains unsolved.

Dustin Farnum was as much a matinee idol as his brother William, with whom he had starred in a vaudeville act. He made forty films before his untimely death in 1929 of kidney failure at the age of fifty-five. He was considered by some to be a talented but conceited actor. In a dinner exchange with writer Oliver Hereford, he boasted, "I had the audience glued to their seats." To which Hereford replied, "How clever of you to think to do that!"

Winifred Kingston's career ended after the death of her friend Taylor. She eventually married her leading man Dustin in 1924, but they divorced five years later. She had a brief comeback in a remake of *The Squaw Man* in 1931 as an extra. She remains an enigma, as she disappeared for almost thirty years only to arrive on the scene once more as an extra in 1959. She died in La Jolla, California, in 1967 at the age of seventy-two.

Dustin Farnum as he appeared in another Pallas/Paramount movie
David Garrick (1916)

THE HEIR TO THE HOORAH (1916)

The Heir To the Hoorah —it was a strange title for a movie until you understand that the Hoorah was a gold mine and that someone was about to inherit it. Audiences in that day knew the title because it had been a successful stage comedy. In the summer of 1916, Jesse Lasky's Famous Players returned to the Big Bear Lake area for five days, to film the tale of three lonely bachelors.

After the Hoorah made them millionaires they realize that the most valuable gold mine in California would someday revert to total strangers because they had no heirs. They devise a plan to marry off the youngest one, Joe Lacy (Thomas Meighan), so he can sire an "heir to the Hoorah," but the project goes awry because Joe can't seem to find the right girl among the dance hall fillies he has to choose from.

Meanwhile in the East, a conniving mother is trying to wed her young daughter, Geraldine (Anita King), to a repulsive older man for his money. When the daughter rebels, the two travel to the West and meet up with Joe who is found sitting on a hotel lobby floor playing with some children. When the mother learns that Joe is rich, she talks her daughter into snaring him. After the marriage, Joe finds out that he was married for his money and Geraldine returns to the East to get a divorce, not telling Joe that she is pregnant. He exclaims, "You married me for my money." To which she retorts, "you married me for a baby!" Both soon see the foolishness of the situation and all ends well when they get back together.

Thirty-seven year old Thomas Meighan was considered one of the big movie idols of the day. At six feet tall and sporting a strong jaw, he had been a serious stage actor and

CAST:	
Thomas Meighan	Joe Lacy
Anita King	Geraldine Kent
Edythe Chapman	Mrs. Kent
Directed by	William C. de Mille
Produced by	Jesse Lasky Feature Play Co.

Poster for *The Heir to the Hoorah* (1916)
Photo courtesy of
The Academy of Motion Picture Arts
and Sciences

had put off making films as long as he could. However, once he started making films at age thirty-five, he fell into a routine of making several each year throughout the late 1910s and 1920s. He did make the transition to talkies, but by then his star had descended. He made his last film in 1934, the year he learned he had cancer that took his life two years later at the age of fifty-seven.

Anita King was one of the most interesting actresses of her day. At age twenty-two, she was known as "The Paramount Girl" and had actually driven a car solo across the continental United States in 1915 as a publicity stunt. This was in an age when most roads did not exist. She was greeted everywhere she appeared along the way as a true heroine. Her pioneering cross-country trip made the public aware that there was a real need to improve our national highway system. She only completed nineteen films in her lifetime. Why she retired from film acting in 1919 is something of a mystery. By the mid-1920s she was a scenario writer and nothing more is known of her after that.

In her book, *When Silents were Golden*, Evelyn F. Scott recounts how the movie company first traveled to the Mission Inn in Riverside for the night; then lunched in Victorville the following day; and finally motored through sand and cactus before arriving at the Pine Knot Resort in Big Bear Lake via the "back way." There was a direct route (though steeper) from San Bernardino to Big Bear Lake via a road known as the Clark Grade, but it was a one-way road that was regulated by four hours of up traffic and then four hours of down traffic. In 1915, this journey was a two day adventure from Hollywood. The actual film location was an abandoned gold mine (probably the Rose Gold Mine) ten miles from town.

Anita King
circa 1916

Thomas Meighan
circa 1916

[Author's Note: Although I have never seen it, a copy of the film does exist at the Library of Congress and can be viewed there.]

THE STRENGTH OF DONALD McKENZIE (1916)

In the summer of 1916, American Film Company, a division of Mutual Film Corporation, traveled up to what was then called Little Bear Lake, now known as Lake Arrowhead. The film they were shooting was *The Strength of Donald McKenzie*, the story of a lumberman turned poet.

Thirty year old William Russell, son of a well known stage actress named Clara Russell, was chosen for the part of Donald McKenzie. He was cast opposite Charlotte Burton who played the publisher's daughter. The story and the film were of little consequence and critics panned it. What is important, is this is the first picture known to be filmed at the newly formed Little Bear Lake, which was rapidly filling in with water. It is a shame that the film is "lost," as it would have been of great historical significance.

William Russell began on the stage at the age of eight, but was persuaded by his parents to follow a career in law. He briefly practiced in Pittsburgh before returning to the more lucrative profession of acting. He was a very tall, square-jawed actor (the type audiences had come to expect as their heroes) who was extremely athletic. He was an active participant in the New Rochelle Rowing

```
CAST:
William Russell ..... Donald McKenzie
Charlotte Burton ....... Mabel Condon
Directed by .............. William Russell
                    and Jack Prescott
Produced by ....... American Film Co.
```

William Russell
circa 1916

Club, played baseball with the Tanhouser Stars, and became an amateur boxer. He started in moving pictures with D. W. Griffith at Biograph Studios in 1910, and liked to remain independent by moving around to different studios. Russell continued to make films throughout the Twenties, but he died of pneumonia at the age of sixty in 1929.

Charlotte Burton was thirty-four when she played the young daughter and she and William Russell starred together in a total of fifteen films. Amazingly, twelve of them were made in 1916. The year before they had filmed a thirty-two part serial together in Santa Barbara. Being together so much it was probably inevitable that they would marry, which they did in 1917. The marriage lasted four years, but Charlotte's career ended in 1920 — no one knows why.

William Russell and Charlotte Burton
in a scene from
The Strength of Donald McKenzie (1916)
Photo courtesy of
The Academy of Motion Picture
Arts and Sciences

THE DEVIL'S DOUBLE
(1916)

CAST:
William S. Hart .... Bowie Blake
Enid Markey .... Naomi Tarleton
Robert McKim ...... Van Dyke Tarleton
Directed by .... William S. Hart
Produced by .... Triangle Film Corp.

How many silent film actors do we know who were born during the Civil War? Not many, but William S. Hart was one of them. This dramatic actor from Broadway, some called Shakespearean, didn't begin making films until the age of forty-nine. During the next eleven years he starred in, directed and produced some sixty-five films. The stony-faced actor was the most popular western personality of his day.

Although born in New York, Hart actually grew up in Illinois or what was then "the West." According to his own autobiography, he learned Indian tongues and sign language at an early age and his command of these was a source of constant amazement to his fellow actors. (Some critics have questioned this ability and state that this is part of his personal mythology.) Audiences never considered him to be a "drug-store cowboy" (a fanciful dressed up dude), but always the genuine article. It also didn't hurt that he was six foot two or that he had rubbed elbows with real Indians and lawmen, like Bat Masterson. He always held a commanding presence and was known for his two-gun stance and steely-eyed look.

Victorville, California, was used by Hart for many of his pictures and it was just a short jump to the San Bernardino Mountains to the south for his staging of *The Devil's Double*. Although the movie is "lost," scenes from the film look suspiciously like the area around Crestline, especially the Camp Seely area and "Heart Rock." Another Hart film, *Hell's Hinges,* was also probably made in the Victorville area and up into the foothills just south of the town.

The Devil's Double revolves around a painter, Van Dyke Tarleton (don't you love the names?), played by Robert McKim who is frustrated at not being able to paint the Devil. Van Dyke travels west and runs into Bowie Blake

William S. Hart tries to stop Enid Markey from killing herself in a scene from *The Devil's Double* (1916). Photo courtesy of The Academy of Motion Picture Arts and Sciences

(William S. Hart) who is a menacing outlaw, but is not interested in posing—until! Until—Bowie meets Mrs. Tarleton (Enid Markey) and secretly falls in love with her. In order to make Bowie even meaner than he is while posing, Van Dyke berates his wife in front of Bowie. Bowie is not able to stand the abuse and he leaves the camp, only to return in the nick of time to save the heroine from a group of outlaws who have just killed Van Dyke.

Enid Markey, who was considered a beauty, became the silent screen's first "Jane" to Elmo Lincoln's *Tarzan* in 1918. After making thirty-two silent films, Enid retired to the stage and later radio and television, with brief parts in movies in the 1940s and 1960s.

Hart continued as a major star into the 1920s, but faded from the scene after a series of unwarranted paternity suits. Audiences were by then more interested in the younger, more virile heroes like Tom Mix, than the staid and moralistic Hart.

William Hart, Enid Markey and Robert McKim in a scene from
The Devil's Double (1916)
Photo courtesy of
The Academy of Motion Picture
Arts and Sciences

THE CALL OF THE EAST
(1917)

By 1917, the handsome Japanese-born Sessue Hayakawa was a major star. After he finished *After Five* (1915), he made a film called *The Cheat* (1915) in which audiences loved him, but hated his character. Hayakawa took the lead in the Lasky Feature Play named *The Call Of The East*, playing the part of Count Takada, a wealthy nobleman who is fiendishly clever.

The plot revolves around an idol of mercy that Takada's late mother held sacred. Takada has imprisoned, on his island fortress, Alan Hepburn (Jack Holt), the young brother of a woman he admires. The Count hates Alan and has him incarcerated because Alan is a cad and had once shown affection towards a former sweetheart of Takada. Alan's sister, Sheila Hepburn (Margaret Loomis), learns of her brother's plight and travels to the island compound. Takada is smitten with Sheila and makes advances towards her in front of the brother. She becomes frightened and runs away, taking sanctuary at the foot of the idol. Takada pleads with her that he didn't mean to frighten her, only torment Alan, and that he really loves her. She finally realizes her true love for Takada and they embrace.

Meanwhile, Alan breaks loose from his prison and rushes up to save his sister by knocking out Takada. The brother and sister flee the island and in a conversation on the boat, she learns that her real mother was Japanese. She suddenly realizes that was why she has always had "the call" for all things Eastern. She jumps out of the boat and swims back to the island where she is met by Takada on the shore. The last scene is of the two lovers dressed in traditional Japanese wedding costumes in front of the idol.

According to Beulah Marie Dix, the script writer, it took two weeks to shoot the script at Big Bear Lake during July of 1917. She had to fashion a story that would be acceptable to audiences of the

CAST:
Sessue Haykawa	Count Takada
Jack Holt	Alan Hepburn
Margaret Loomis	Sheila Hepburn
Directed by	George Melford
Produced by	Jesse L. Lasky Feature Play Co.

Sessue Haykawa circa 1917

Margaret Loomis circa 1917

Jack Holt

Cast and crew of *The Call of the East* (1917) gathered at Big Bear Lake. Sessue Hayakawa is seated at the left and Mrs. Hayakawa is seated on right. Jack Holt is in the last row with his arm around another crew member.
Photo courtesy of The Academy of Motion Picture Arts & Sciences

day, namely — very biased towards Orientals. Her solution was to make the heroine half Japanese and half Caucasian. The studio chose dark-haired Margaret Loomis, a stage dancer, to pull it off.

At six foot in height, the square-jawed Jack Holt (a former cowboy) was cast as the brother and villain. During one scene that took two days to shoot, he was held over quicksand (actually a stream bed) by Takada's men, which caused some severe bruises and welts on his body, as well as a sprained thumb and a torn ligament. During another scene when he was held in a very cold stream, Holt was allowed liberal shots of whiskey to keep warm. Holt made nearly two hundred films over a period of five decades, usually as the hero during the silent era, and finally as a character actor in later years. It has been suggested by some that the pencil-mustached actor was the model for *Dick Tracy*, the cartoon character created during the Thirties by Chester Gould.

Margaret Loomis was a pupil of the famous dancer Ruth St. Denis and learned to appreciate all things "Eastern" during that period. Between 1917 and 1925 she made twenty-four films.

Sessue Hayakawa continued to play Oriental roles in America, as well as for international companies, over the next fifty years. His career culminated in 1957, when he was nominated for an Oscar for his supporting role in *The Bridge on the River Kwai*. Ironically he lost to Red Buttons cast as an American G.I. stationed in Japan after WWII, who gets the "call of the East" by marrying a Japanese girl in the film *Sayonara*.

NAN OF MUSIC MOUNTAIN (1917)

Late in September, 1917, Beulah Marie Dix, one of the script writers for the Lasky Company, was handed a best selling book by Frank H. Spearman and told to construct a script from it. The book was *Nan of Music Mountain,* illustrated by N. C. Wyeth. The book had been serialized in a popular magazine months earlier. Dix was ordered to return to Big Bear Lake where they would shoot the film, but it was late in the season and Pine Knot Resort had closed. Luckily for the crew of twenty-six men and three women, Knight's Camp was still open for business. In her biography, Dix complained of the food, but said Sunday was a special day because Jack Hoxie, a former rodeo rider, cooked chuck wagon style beans with peppers and onions.

Both Ann Little and twenty-six year old Wallace Reid were acting veterans and part of the stable of actors Lasky and company kept on their permanent payroll. The story is an action-packed Western, with stagecoach robberies, shoot-outs, and of course, romance.

Dix was required to draft a scenario of one hundred and seventy scenes in four days, just barely ahead of shooting each day. Frank Spearman, the author, visited the location shoot and Dix stated that he was pleased with what he observed.

CAST:	
Wallace Reid	Henry de Spain
Ann Little	Nan Morgan
Theodore Roberts	Duke Morgan
Directed by	George Melford
Produced by	Jesse L. Lasky
	Feature Play Co.

Cast and crew from *Nan of Music Mountain* (1917) posing at Big Bear. Seated right to left: George Melford (with open script) , Ann Little, Wallace Reid and writer Beulah Marie Dix (in artists cap) Photo courtesy of The Academy of Motion Picture Arts and Sciences

Twenty-five year old Ann Little was an old hand at Westerns. She was considered a real outdoors girl and had started her film career in Westerns with Thomas Ince and the Bison 101 group in 1911. She retired from films in 1925 after making over fifty-five films.

Wallace Reid was a true matinee idol of the day. He was good looking, but had a boyish charm about him. He had been cast as Jeff the blacksmith in *Birth of a Nation* (1915) and women literally swooned over the tall, handsome man stripped naked to the waist. His addiction to morphine scandalized the movie industry in the early 1920s and his premature death in 1923 led to the first attempts to curb the drug culture in Hollywood.

In addition to Little and Reid, a thirty-three year old actor by the name of James Cruze was cast as a cowboy. Months earlier he had been a Japanese henchman in *The Call of the East*. He later became one of Hollywood's leading directors with over seventy-five films to his credit.

Wallace Reid (holding rifle) and Ann Little (next to him) being directed by George Melford (consulting script) atop some rocks at Big Bear Lake in a scene from *Nan of Music Mountain* (1917).
Photo courtesy of The Academy of Motion Picture Arts and Sciences

EYES OF THE WORLD
(1917)

In the summer of 1916, the Clune Film Producers created a set in Mill Creek Canyon near Forest Home (Forest Falls today) for *Eyes of the World*, written by Harold Bell Wright. They had just finished filming the successful *Ramona* (1916) near Riverside, with Monroe Salisbury in the lead and Donald Crisp as director. Using the same team, they came into the mountains to film the hugely popular morality book, written by the minister who once had a congregation in Redlands.

The names of some of the characters seem out of place today, but at that period (pre-WWI) were timely: Salisbury was Civilization; Jack Livingston was Art; Jane Novak was Nature; Edward Peil was Sensuality; Jack McDonald was Materialism; etc. The story involves tales of a small city's inhabitants. Adultery, betrayal and illegitimate children are at the core of this snobbish little group of hypocrites. One critic summed it up, "a sweet little girl who plays a violin, a hero who paints pictures, a villain who endeavors to ravish the heroine and a villainess who is equally unsuccessful in her lecherous designs on the hero."

The book (1914) sold over a million copies. The movie broke all box office records and was well received all over the nation, except for one town—Redlands. There, the citizenry felt that they were being ridiculed. Wright traveled with the Clune Film group as they filmed in different locations to lend authenticity to the production. One scene called for a fight between Salisbury and another man on the edge of a cliff. Sphinx Rock, a craggy outcrop near Arrowhead Highlands, was chosen for its stunning vistas. Wright was staying at the Squirrel Inn at the time and came out to watch the stunt being performed, along with a group of local residents and guests at the inn. Using a stunt double, the villain took a

CAST:	
Monroe Salisbury	Civilization
Jane Novak	Nature
Writen by	Harold Bell Wright
Directed by	Donald Crisp
Produced by	Clune Film Producers

Monroe Salisbury
circa 1917

Jane Novak and Eva Novak
circa 1917

fall over the spectacular Sphinx Rock into a net, all to the delight of those who watched from a safe distance.

Critics raved about twenty-one year old Jane Novak and cited her work in the picture. A true beauty, she was the sister to the equally beautiful Eva Novak. Jane starred in *The White Scar* (1915) with Salisbury and she continued in films for the next forty years. She made over seventy-five films and died in 1990 at the age of ninety-four.

The forty year old Monroe Salisbury was no stranger to the mountains. He had made *After Five* in 1915 and returned to make a total of six films in the San Bernardino Mountains. Over six feet tall and weighing two hundred pounds, he was ideal for the rugged mountain men he portrayed. He made over forty films in a brief period and retired to his ranch near Hemet in 1922. Ironically, he died at the foot of the San Bernardinos after a fall at Patton State Hospital, a mental institution, where he was a patient in 1935. He was fifty-nine years old.

Scottish-born Donald Crisp, the director, had a long history with the Lasky Players as both actor and director, but broke away to direct the two Clune productions *Ramona* in 1916 and *Eyes of the World* in 1917. He would best be remembered for his parts in the *Lassie* movies of the Forties, but his crowning achievement came when he won the Academy Award for Best Supporting Actor for his role in *How Green Was My Valley* in 1942. His body of work includes acting in over one hundred and thirty films and directing more than sixty films. He, too, died at age ninety-four in 1974.

Although the movie was extraordinarily long for the time (ten reels), it played to packed houses all over the country. At Clune Auditorium in Los Angeles, a thirty piece orchestra accompanied the panoramic sets that were part of the staging for the film. Clune Production Company only made the two highly successful movies and this author never has discovered why they did not continue in business.

Donald Crisp as he appeared later
in character roles

Director Donald Crisp (in white hat with script in hand)
giving directions to cast and crew in a scene from
Eyes of the World (1917).
Photo courtesy of The Academy of Motion Picture
Arts and Sciences

BROADWAY ARIZONA (1917)

CAST:
Olive Thomas .... Fritzi Carlyle
George Chesebro .... John Keys
George Hernandez .... Uncle Isaac
Directed by .... Lynn Reynolds
Produced by .... Triangle Film Co.

Broadway Arizona—What a marvelous title! It tells the complete story in two words. Arizona rancher (George Chesebro) vacations in New York and meets Broadway showgirl (Olive Thomas). He proposes marriage and she accepts, only she has done it for a publicity stunt and recants the next day. Heartbroken, he returns to his ranch and she goes back to whatever chorus girls do. Eight months later she suffers an illness and somehow, he learns of it. He goes back to Broadway, kidnaps her and takes her back to Arizona to recuperate. The posse follows and just as they are about to arrest the "villain," she announces that she arranged the whole kidnaping as a publicity stunt and that they are actually engaged to be married. All that is left out is the ride into the sunset. Someone in Hollywood once said that there is only one movie plot— boy meets girl, boy loses girl, boy gets girl!

George Chesebro, who spelled his name at least seven different ways, was one of the most prolific actors in the business. Over the next fifty years, he made close to four hundred films. Starting off as the tall, handsome hero, he would best be known for his "bad" guy portrayals in "B" Westerns and serials during the 1930s and 1940s.

Olive Thomas was considered one of the leading beauties of early films. She actually had been on Broadway in the Ziegfeld Follies and met her future husband, Jack Pickford (Mary Pickford's brother) in 1916. After only twenty-three films, her death in Paris in 1920 of an overdose of mercury bichloride (a medicine used for syphilis) was considered the first of the great scandals to rock Hollywood

Olive Thomas
circa 1917

during that era.

The writer and director of *Broadway Arizona* was Lynn Reynolds and he too was cast into the public limelight ten years later. During a snowstorm, he and his cast almost perished. Supposedly, he was so traumatized by the event that he took his own life.

According to the American Film Institute, exterior shots were filmed at Big Bear Lake. A copy of the film exists in The George Eastman House, Rochester, New York and another exists in Archives du Film et du Depot Legal du Centre National de la Cinematographie, in Bois d'Arcy, France.

George Chesebro and George Hernandez (seated with chaps) in a scene from *Broadway Arizona* (1917)
Photo courtesy of The Academy of Motion Picture Arts and Sciences

HELL HATH NO FURY (1917)

CAST:
Melbourne MacDowell
Grace Davison
Joe King
Directed by .... Charles Earl Bartlett
Produced by .... Anchor Film Corp.

Melbourne MacDowell
Photo courtesy of the
Library of Congress

One of the many mystery films supposedly made in the San Bernardino Mountains is *Hell Hath No Fury* (1917). According to the American Film Institute, the exterior shots were made in the mountains around Big Bear. However, little else is known of the film or its star Grace Davison. We do know that Anchor Film Corporation did come out to California from New York for their first film and brought with them a highly respected sixty-one year old Shakespearean actor, Melbourne MacDowell. This was MacDowell's first picture, as well as that of Davison.

Filming also occurred in Santa Cruz and their daily paper picked it up in January, 1917. The six reel film was released in March of that year.

London-born MacDowell had a successful career on the stage and with his first film must have caught the "Hollywood bug," because he then made nearly sixty films over the next fifteen years. He retired in 1932 and died at the age of eighty-five in 1941.

The other lead in the film, thirty-four year old Joe King, was a screen veteran and made almost one hundred and fifty movies during his career. But the real mystery is Grace Davison, who was known as the Cameo Girl. Other than knowing she made ten films in five years, her age and other pertinent data including photographs have not been found. The AFI has suggested that the movie *When Destiny Wills* is the same movie, but there is some disagreement with experts on this.

THE HIDDEN CHILDREN
(1917)

Late in the fall of 1916, Oscar Apfel returned to the San Bernardino Mountains to film *The Hidden Children* based on a novel by Robert W. Chambers. The filming took place around the Pine Crest Resort (original spelling). One of the most attractive screen couples at the time, Harold Lockwood and May Allison, starred in the Yorke Film production. The five reel adventure tale centers around Colonial days, when it was a practice for Indians to give their children to foster parents until maturity. Thus two white children are given for various reasons to someone else until they become of age. There are the obligatory fights between Colonial troops and the Indians and the love affair between the two adult "hidden children."

Critics liked the background scenery and the acting, but faulted the story as being too choppy. Certain scenes just popped up and made no sense. This was in an era when the director usually was the film editor, so the failing falls on the shoulders of Apfel. He was one of the pioneers of Hollywood, coming west with Cecil B. DeMille and Jesse Lasky in 1914. His collaboration with them ended in 1916 when he went over to Fox Studios and later did work with many independents. He directed over seventy films and as an actor participated in one hundred and fifty movies.

Harold Lockwood was the strong silent type and head-turning handsome. He began his acting career with Selig Company playing bit parts in 1911. By 1913, he was a major star and the heartthrob of women nationwide. Between 1915 and 1917, he and May Allison were teamed in twenty-three films. Sadly, the worldwide flu epidemic of 1918 killed him at the age of thirty-one. He leaves a legacy of one hundred and twenty

CAST:	
Harold Lockwood	Evan Loskiel
May Allison	Lois de Contrecoeur
Directed by	Oscar Apfel
Produced by	Yorke Film Corp.

May Allison
circa 1917

movies in eight years.

May Allison was considered a real beauty and in 1915 she began acting in pictures at age twenty-five. She was devastated at the death of Lockwood, but continued making films until her retirement in 1927. She died at the age of ninety-nine in 1989.

May Allison and Harold Lockwood in a scene from
The Hidden Children (1917)
Photo courtesy of The Academy of Motion Picture
Arts and Sciences

THE EAGLE (1918)

In the summer of 1918, Bluebird Photoplays persuaded Monroe Salisbury to star in another one of their features, *The Eagle* filmed at Big Bear Lake. This time Salisbury takes on the role of an avenging son (John Gregory) whose family has been unjustly robbed of their fortune by an unscrupulous mining company. After the death of his mother, John takes on the disguise of an Indian and becomes "The Eagle," a thief determined to get even for past injustices. When he finally does get into the main office of the mine, he finds that the company has already been robbed and a night watchman killed.

The story then becomes very twisted. John's sweetheart, Lucy (played by Edna Earle), has a younger brother, Bob, who is accused of the robbery as well as the other crimes of "The Eagle." John confesses to Lucy that he is really "The Eagle" and she forces him to go to court where he declares that he was the actual bandit and saves the younger brother for his sweetheart's sake. With another turn, Bob then commits suicide and leaves a note confessing that he really did rob the company and commit the murder. Lucy frantically rides to the hanging site and saves her lover, John, just in time.

Some of the tag lines for advertising the movie were quite inventive: " . . . have a man in Indian dress driven through the streets by a girl in western costume who holds a pistol on him. On her back place a sign, 'If you want to see why I'm driving my sweetheart to jail, see *The Eagle* at (theater and date)'." By the middle of 1918, audiences were getting particular about their movies and were looking for something better than the quickies that were produced in earlier years.

Salisbury liked playing Indian roles. He was strong and tall and for his make-up he used just a slightly darker shade to portray the Indi-

Contemporary ad for *The Eagle* in the Redlands Review, July 14, 1918

Monroe Salisbury
circa 1918

ans. He had a genuine interest in the Indian way of life and their well being and vowed he would write a book about them one day. No such book was ever written, however.

Edna Earle is a true mystery. There is no date of birth nor death. She made four films in 1918, each at a different studio and then dropped out of sight until she is listed, but not credited, with a bit part in 1934. This author has never found a picture of her and all of her films are presumed to be lost. It is just a guess, but the name Edna Earl, which she is sometimes credited with (without an "e"), was a common first and middle name during the first part of the twentieth century. It is just possible that she added the last "e" to Earl for theatrical reasons.

[Note: *The Eagle* is presumed to be lost.]

THE GUILT OF SILENCE
(1918)

A blinding snow storm leaves a man without a voice in the Bluebird Photoplays production of *The Guilt of Silence*, Ethel Hill's story set during the Alaskan gold rush era. Monroe Salisbury ("Silent" Smith) returned to the Big Bear Lake area as the lead, but this time opposite Ruth Clifford (Mary), as the daughter of the a miner who has saved "Silent" from the storm. When the miner's wife Amy (Betty Schade) gives birth to a child, she falsely accuses "Silent" of being the father and the miner shoots him, wounding him in the shoulder. Mary, although disgusted with "Silent," nurses him back to health wherein he regains his voice and sets things right by exposing Amy's lie. She and her partner, Gambler Joe (Sam De Grasse), are exposed and the miner finds that he has been duped into a phony marriage.

Salisbury was forty-two when he made *The Guilt of Silence* and was highly popular with movie audiences. This was the seventh picture he made with the eighteen year old Ruth Clifford and they made one additional film together the following year. After his success in *Ramona* (1916), Salisbury purchased property in the Hemet Valley near the Soboda Indian Reservation and

> CAST:
> Monroe Salisbury ...... Mathew Smith
> Ruth Clifford .... Mary
> Betty Schade .... Amy
> Sam De Grasse .... Gambler Joe
> Directed by .... Elmer Clifton
> Produced by .... Bluebird Photoplays

Ruth Clifford
circa 1918

there he created his own ranchero. He was active in the Indian affairs of the reservation for many years and was truly interested in their well being.

Clifford was a stunningly beautiful young girl who started in pictures just two years earlier. She was an active actress over the next fifty years with more than one hundred films to her credit. Her lead parts ended with the talkies and in later years she settled for bit parts. She was known as being very "dependable" by her fellow actors. She died at the age of ninety-eight in 1998.

The "vamp" was played by Berlin born Betty Schade who entered American pictures in 1913, but nothing is known of her earlier career. She made almost sixty films before she retired in 1921.

As is usually the case, a good villain can make a movie successful and Canadian-born Sam De Grasse looked the part. Douglas Fairbanks, Sr. was so taken with his villainous looks that he offered him many parts in his films. Not being blessed with good looks, De Grasse made the best of it and had a noteworthy career making over a hundred pictures before his retirement in 1930.

[Note: This film is presumed to be lost.]

This photo of Monroe Salisbury is dated "December 1919" on the back.

HE COMES UP SMILING
(1918)

Who better to play the part of the affable bank clerk with time on his hands than one of the most popular film actors of his day, Douglas Fairbanks? When Jerry Martin (Fairbanks) is asked to take care of a pet canary for his boss, the bird escapes and is chased by the hero until they both stumble upon the "good life" and the freedom of a camp of hobos. Following a mix-up in clothing after a swim, Jerry becomes "Batchelor," a stock broker and with Batchelor's blessing takes on his guise while visiting a wealthy business man. When Jerry discovers Batchelor's real intent is to ruin the businessman, he steps up and rescues him, thereby gaining a partnership and the hand of the businessman's daughter (Marjorie Daw).

Allan Dwan who directed the film was considered to be a pioneer and a real workhorse in the industry. He again worked with Fairbanks in *Robin Hood* (1922), considered to be one of Fairbanks best efforts. Dwan enjoyed the climate of Big Bear Lake and the San Bernardino Mountains so much that he returned often over the next fifty years, filming such classics as *Heidi* (1937) and *Here We Go Again* in 1942.

Marjorie Daw was sixteen when she made *He Comes Up Smiling* with the thirty-five year old Fairbanks and evidently he liked her work because they did six pictures together that year. She was considered to be cute as opposed to beautiful and played the fresh-faced ingenue in her films. Her stardom continued throughout the Twenties until her retirement in 1927.

Fairbanks also liked working with Frank Campeau, a great character actor, who took on the role of the stern older man. Fairbanks and Campeau combined

CAST:	
Douglas Fairbanks	Jerry Martin
Marjorie Daw	Billie
Frank Campeau	John Bartlett
Directed by	Allan Dwan
Produced by	Artcraft/Paramount

Marjorie Daw
circa 1918

Frank Campeau
circa 1918

their efforts in a total of fourteen pictures. Campeau began his career in pictures with *Jordan Is a Hard Road* (1915), filmed in the San Bernardino Mountains, and he would end it with an uncredited role in a Royal Mountie picture, which was also filmed in those same mountains.

The part of Jerry Martin came easily to Fairbanks, as he had appeared on stage in the original play by the same name in 1914. The five foot ten, athletic actor is credited with doing most of his own stunts during his career in films. Fairbanks is often thought to not have made the transition to talkies because of his high pitched voice, but that is not true. He made at least ten talkies before his retirement. Some film historians blame a Hollywood producer with "speeding" up his talking films, in order to give the illusion of a higher pitch. Fairbanks died at the age of fifty-six in 1939.

Douglas Fairbanks (left) and two unknown actors in
a scene from *He Comes Up Smiling* (1918)
Photo courtesy of
The Academy of Motion Picture Arts and Sciences

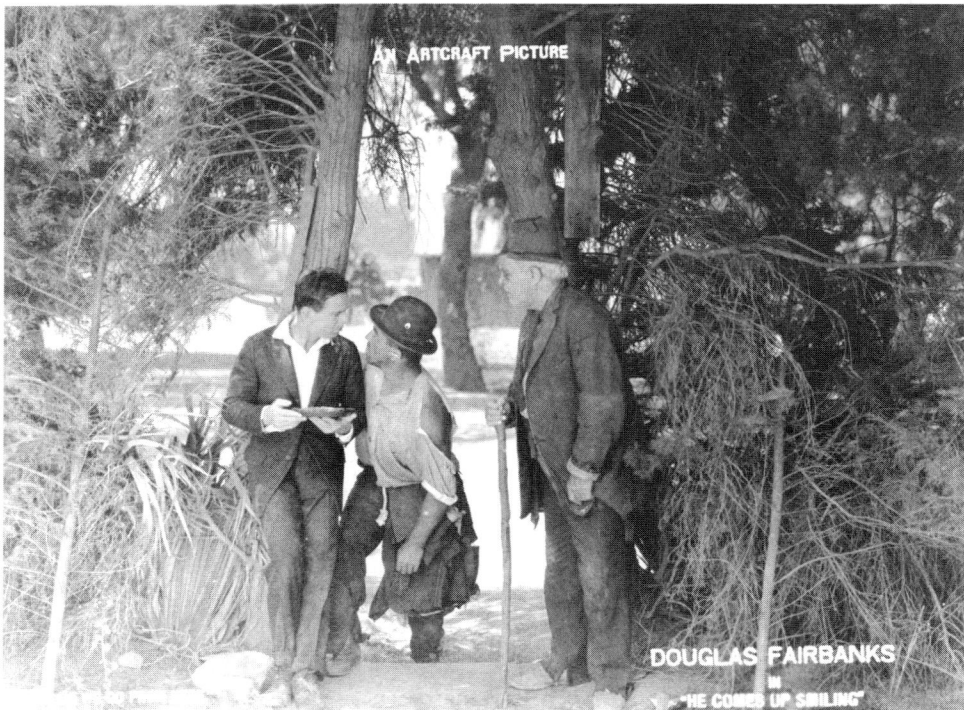

REVENGE (1918)

By 1918, movie studios were churning out scenarios by the hundreds, but the written novel was still their best source of material. In the spring of that year, the Metro Pictures group sent veteran director, Tod Browning, along with a cast and crew up to Pine Crest Resort to film Edward Moffat's novel, *Hearts Steadfast*. This became the first of many films to be titled *Revenge*.

Alva Leigh (Edith Storey) arrives in a mining camp, from back East, just as her fiancé, Donald (Charles West), is murdered. Alva swears vengeance on the murderer so "Sudden" Duncan (Ralph Lewis), the real killer, accuses Donald's partner, Dick Randall (Wheeler Oakman), of the crime. "Sudden" knows that Dick is about to make a trip into the desert, so he fills Dick's canteen with poison. This is unbeknownst to Alva who also wants to avenge her late lover. She hears about the trip, so she drills a hole in the canteen so that Dick will die of thirst. Only when Dick has left does Alva learn the truth of the real killer from "Tiger Lil" (Alberta Ballard), a dance hall girl, who is jealous of "Sudden's" attention towards the newcomer. The desperate Alva races to save Dick, who she recognizes as her true love, while "Tiger Lil" shoots "Sudden" in a barroom quarrel.

Twenty-six year old Edith Storey was one of the most celebrated actresses of her day. She began in movies with the New York based Vitagraph Company at their Flatbush studio (New York) when she was fifteen. By the time she filmed *Revenge*, she already had been in over one hundred roles. Because of her diminutive

CAST:
Edith Storey .... Alva Leigh
Wheeler Oakman .... Dick Randall
Ralph Lewis .... "Sudden" Duncan
Directed by .... Tod Browning
Produced by ... Metro Pictures Corp.

Theater advertisement
circa 1918

B.A. ROLFE
presents
Edith Storey
in
REVENGE
From Edward Moffat's
Famous Novel
"HEARTS STEADFAST"
Directed by Tod Browning
A 5-Act METRO
All Star Series Play

size, she had been able to play the part of Charles Dickens' *Oliver Twist* in the first film version by that name produced in 1909. But the real story about Edith Storey began during WWI. While many actresses were filmed with wounded soldiers and talked about becoming nurses and ambulance drivers, Edith Storey really did become one. She dropped out of acting in the fall of 1918 and ferried wounded soldiers returning from France around to hospitals in New York. During the flu epidemic, she worked twelve hour shifts in New York hospitals. The hiatus proved to be self satisfying to her personally, but her film career never revived. She made a couple of films in the early Twenties and then retired from the screen in 1921.

Handsome Wheeler Oakman, who also appeared in *Mickey* in 1918, was a stage actor before entering films. He, too, was a veteran actor by the time he made these two films in the

Alberta Ballard, Edith Storey and Ralph Lewis in a scene from *Revenge* (1918)
Photo courtesy of
The Academy of Motion Picture
Arts and Sciences

San Bernardino Mountains, with more than forty films to his credit. During the time he made *Revenge,* the tall, twenty-eight year old actor was married to Priscilla Dean, one of the leading actresses of her day. His career spanned four decades and he is credited with over two hundred films, usually playing the "heavy" in later years.

Forty-six year old Ralph Lewis played the part of "Sudden" in this mining melodrama. His part in *The Birth of a Nation* (1915) as Austin Stoneman had won him many fans and accolades. Over the next three decades, he appeared in over one hundred films, equally able as a stern judge or kindly grandfather.

Director Tod Browning was thirty-six and also a veteran of the silver screen by the time he filmed *Revenge.* His best works were yet to come in the Twenties and Thirties, with critical acclaim for his films, *The Unholy Three, The Road to Mandalay* and *West of Zanzibar,* all shot with Lon Chaney as the lead. He would best be remembered for his horror films of the 1930s, *Freaks* and *Dracula,* which were to star Chaney, but Lon's untimely death forced Browning to cast an unknown Hungarian actor, Bela Lugosi in the role of Count Dracula. By the late Thirties, Browning no longer was considered an "A" director after making a string of mediocre movies and he retired in 1939. To his credit though, there are regular film festivals dedicated to his works as a director.

Edith Storey
circa 1918

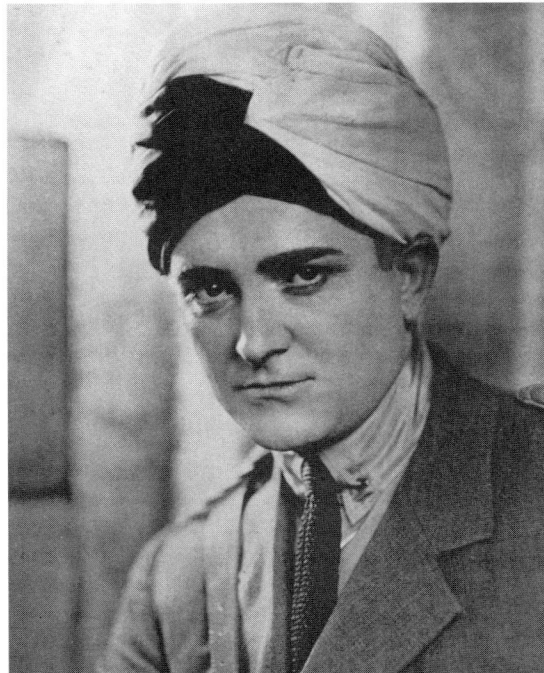

Wheeler Oakman
circa 1920

MICKEY (1918)

Mabel Normand as she appeared in
Mickey (1918)
Photo courtesy of
The Academy of Motion Picture
Arts and Sciences

Fortunately, *Mickey* was one of the most popular movies of the late 1910s and thus it has survived and can be seen and studied by film historians. It is a tale of a gritty little girl, Mickey (Mabel Normand), who is to inherit her father's gold mine. Greedy relatives entice her back East to the monied life, only to find her ways too rustic for their taste. When they learn that she is really penniless, that is the last straw and they send her packing back West. Wheeler Oakman plays the part of the visiting surveyor who reluctantly falls in love with her, despite her tomboy attitudes.

Critics and fans both adored *Mickey*, which was filmed in the San Bernardino Mountains (one historian credits Big Bear Lake and another Lake Arrowhead) and no wonder, it is as delightful to watch today as it must have been in 1918. It has been called Normand's best film and box office receipts prove it. Studios had learned that the key to any movie's success was publicity and publicity was what *Mickey* received. A special song was created for it and there were contests and novel stunts arranged whenever it was shown. It was heralded that even the inmates at Sing Sing, the notorious prison in New York State, had voted it "best picture of the year."

Because of her comedic nature on and off the screen, the diminutive Mabel Normand was known as the female "Charlie Chaplin." She probably made over three hundred films in her lifetime, most of which were one reel quickies and their titles lost forever. For instance, in 1913, she made sixty-four movies and in 1914, she appeared in seventy-three. Audiences loved her and eagerly awaited her weekly adventures. She gained true star recognition after partnering with Fatty Arbuckle in 1915 and brought her production of films down to a more reasonable twenty per year.

Born Vivian Eichelberger, it is no wonder that he changed his name to Wheeler Oakman for stage purposes. The tall, handsome twenty-eight year old Oakman began with the Selig organization and moved from supporting roles to star in a short time. But he will best be remembered for playing a hundred villains in various Westerns, spy thrillers and action movies over a span of thirty-five years.

Normand had a longtime association with the domineering Mack Sennett which almost ended in 1916, until he agreed to provide her with her own production company. *Mickey* was the only production it ever produced and the backers made sure that even though the film was a tremendous success, neither Normand or Sennett ever realized any great gains. Does this sound familiar?

Unfortunately for Normand, her star soon faded and her association with the murder of William Desmond Taylor (she was the last person to see him alive) effectively ended her career. She died at the age of thirty-eight in 1930, from complications of drug use (denied by many contemporaries and confirmed by others) and tuberculosis.

Wheeler Oakman
Circa 1918

THE GODDESS OF LOST LAKE (1918)

Louise Glaum vamping circa 1918

In January 1919, local citizens of San Bernardino and the mountain communities were treated to a movie shot near Strawberry Flat and Pinecrest Resort. The previous summer, Louise Glaum Productions had traveled by auto stage up the new high gear road through Waterman Canyon to Pinecrest to make *The Goddess of Lost Lake*. This is another "lost" movie so we will never know if Glaum ever found the Lost Lake or if there are any scenes of it. Presumably, they would have used Little Bear Lake (Lake Arrowhead) for reasons of convenience. The lake in the summer of 1918 was close to its capacity and was used by fishermen and duck hunters. The village was yet to be built and the background would have lent itself to being very rustic.

The story itself was very racy for the times and involved an attempted rape. Mary Thorne (Louise Glaum), who is a quarter Indian, returns home after earning a degree at a prestigious Eastern college. At her father's cabin, she decides to dress as a squaw and pretend to be a full-blooded Indian princess. When two hunters arrive in the area, she vamps it up with them and is later attacked by the villainous Chester Martin (Hayward Mack), but then rescued by the handsome Mark Hamilton (Lawson Butt). Mary's father, who has been prospecting for gold in the Lost Lake area, is killed by an Indian guarding the lake's treasure, thus fulfilling an ancient prophesy of the stolen gold. Because of her Indian blood, Mary is allowed to inherit the fortune and she then marries Mark.

Louise Glaum was the Marilyn Monroe of her day. Her films were well attended by young men who knew they would get their money's worth of sex and then more sex. This was very tame stuff compared to today's films, but it was then the fulfillment of men's fantasies. The diminutive Glaum was twenty-four when she made "Goddess" and was known for her seductive looks. Even the titles of her films would elicit some prurient interest: *Shackled* (1918), *Love Madness* (1920), *Love* (1920), *The Leopard Woman* (1920) and finally — *Sex* (1920). Glaum started out as a bit player with Thomas Ince and then progressed to playing "the other woman" and finally to starring status. By 1921, when she made *I Am Guilty*, audiences had become more sophisticated and had moved away from "vamp" films. Glaum tried once more in 1925 to revive her film career but realized her type of films had had their day and finally retired at the age of thirty.

Lawson Butt was born on the Isle of Jersey, an English enclave just off the coast of France. He came to America at the turn of the century and began acting in films at the age of thirty-two. His best work came in the following years when he worked with Lon Chaney in *The Miracle Man* (1919), as Philip Vanderdecker in *The Flying Dutchman* (1923), and in the DeMille classic *The Ten Commandments* (1923). He retired from films when the talkies arrived, with a final appearance in *The Lady of the Lake* (1930).

Louise Glaum and unknown actor in a scene from
The Goddess of Lost Lake (1918)
Photo courtesy of
The Academy of Motion Picture
Arts and Sciences

HUGON, THE MIGHTY (1918)

CAST:

Monroe Salisbury	Hugon
Marjorie Bennett	Marie
Directed by	Rollin S. Sturgeon
Produced by ...	Bluebird Photoplays

Monroe Salisbury must have loved the San Bernardino Mountains after his fourth appearance in a Universal Bluebird production, *Hugon, the Mighty*. This tale of the northwest revolves around Hugon (Monroe Salisbury), a Canadian backwoodsman, who is the strongest man in the territory. His unspoken love for little Marie (Marjorie Bennett) knows no bounds as he unsuccessfully attempts to make a man out of Gabriel (Antrim Short), her fiancé. Meanwhile, Roque (George Holt) and his gang of crooked surveyors try to cheat Hugon out of his property. After a tremendous brawl, Hugon is wounded. Intensely ashamed that he was not strong enough to thwart his enemies, he retreats into his cabin to mend. When the fickle Gabriel loses interest in Marie, she realizes her love for Hugon and nurses him back to health and consoles him by stating "that even the lowly spider must dig down deep to rebuild its web when it is torn."

Monroe Salisbury was at the pinnacle of his career when he made *Hugon, The Mighty*. As a boy growing up in Buffalo, New York, he dreamed about one day becoming a cowboy and going west to shoot Indians. Later when he was in the West, and witnessed the appalling conditions many of them lived in, he became their friend and built his home near a reservation in the Hemet Valley to be close to them. By the late Twenties, however, he had to accept smaller and smaller character roles and finally faded from sight. His death came after a fall in a mental institution where he had

Marjorie Bennett and Monroe Salisbury in a scene from *Hugon, The Mighty* Lobby card circa 1918

been an inmate in 1935.

Australian-born actress Marjorie Bennett came to the United States in 1917 at the urging of her older sister, Enid, who was already a star in the silent era. In two years she made only three films and then abruptly left the screen for thirty years. Her next appearance occurred in 1947, in a film partially filmed in Lake Arrowhead, *Monsieur Verdoux*. Over the next thirty years she carved out a career as a character actress in more than a hundred film and TV appearances. Because of her lusty, deep throaty voice, she will long be remembered as the Duchess in Disney's animated version of *101 Dalmatians* (1961).

Little is known of George Holt, who played the villainous character by the name of Rogue. He had been in two previous films made in Big Bear, *Chalice of Courage* (1915) and *God's Country and the Woman* (1916). He did bit parts in the 1920s, then tried a comeback in the Thirties and made one final appearance in 1948, as a German in an uncredited role in *Berlin Express*.

Monroe Salisbury
circa 1918

63

THAT DEVIL, BATEESE (1918)

Lon Chaney
circa 1918

Once more in the summer of 1918, Bluebird Photoplays returned to the Big Bear Lake area with Monroe Salisbury, but this time they brought with them a character actor by the name of Lon Chaney to play the villainous part of Louis Courteau, the town bully. Ada Gleason was cast as the innocent schoolmarm who was molested by Courteau and in turn saved by Salisbury's character, Bateese Latour, better known to the inhabitants of the village as "That Devil, Bateese."

Unfortunately, this film did not survive but the scenes of the canoes on the lake must have been as stunning as those shot four years earlier in *The Call of the North* (1914). Charles Seeling, the cinematographer, was cited by critics for his spectacular scenic shots. Earlier that year, he had just completed another film shot at Lake Tahoe.

Thirty-five year old Chaney's career started in 1913 with bit parts. As his expertise in guises progressed, better roles came his way. He was the unsurpassed character actor for the next two decades and made over one hundred and fifty films in eighteen years. His portrayals in *The Hunchback of Notre Dame* (1923) and *The Phantom of the Opera* (1925) are silent screen classics. Although he never won any awards, he was selected by the United States Postal Service to appear on a stamp depicting the best of the silent screen. His film, *Tell It To The Marines* (1926) was considered the definitive film about drill sergeants and earned him an honorary title of "Marine," the only non-military person ever so named. Chaney died from throat cancer in 1930 at the age of forty-seven.

Ada Gleason had worked with Salisbury previously in the production of *Ramona* (1916) and had played the part of Ramona to his Alessandro. Because critics loved *That Devil,*

Bateese, they didn't exactly pan her performance, but only called it "acceptable." When the talkies arrived her star power had faded and she was consigned to bit parts and uncredited appearances. She made twenty-eight films in the span of thirty-five years and died at the age of eighty-three in 1971.

Critics also liked the strong, virile Salisbury in this role and his smiling personality won the audiences over immediately. He was at the pinnacle of his success the following year when he would star in seven productions for the Bluebird/Universal Pictures companies. After he left Universal in 1921, he only made three more pictures. He died in 1935 in total anonymity.

Monroe Salisbury
circa 1918

Monroe Salisbury and Ada Gleason
as they appeared in an ad for
That Devil, Bateese (1918)

TYRANT FEAR (1918)

CAST:
Dorothy Dalton .... Allaine Grandet
Thurston Hall .... Harley Dane
Melbourne MacDowell .... James Dermot
Directed by .... Roy William Neill
Produced by ...Thomas H. Ince Corp.

Thomas Ince returned to the San Bernardino Mountains to film sequences of *Tyrant Fear* in late 1918. Although he was not the director, he was in charge of the production for Universal Pictures. There was a great deal of consolidation going on in the movie industry at this time, and Universal brought in several of the independents under their banner, including Ince.

The tale revolves around a woman's fear and the men who cause it. First, she fears her father and secondly, the man her father forces her to marry and, finally, the greedy dance hall owner. The fact that it was supposed to be in the Canadian wilds is almost irrelevant. The majority of the film was made in Santa Cruz amongst the giant redwoods. For the winter scenes, however, the company trooped back to the Big Bear Lake area and filmed the exterior shots. Critics had a field day with this one. "Not convincing; Nativity scene completely inappropriate; completely theatric," were some of the comments made at the time. But Dorothy Dalton stood out and was praised for her gritty role as a wife turned dance hall girl. This author hopes to someday review this film, as it still exists at the Library of Congress in Washington, D.C.

Noted for her exotic good looks, Dorothy Dalton made fifty-five films in the span of ten years. At the height of her career, Dalton was earning $5,000 per week. Her marriage to Arthur Hammerstein in

Dorothy Dalton as a dance hall girl circa 1918

1924 ended her film days. Remarkably, at least five of her films survived and can be seen on video.

Handsome Thurston Hall played the young man that Dalton eventually married in the film. This was their sixth collaboration together in two years and audiences loved them playing opposite each other. Later in his career, because of his very distinguished looks and blustery deep voice, six foot tall Thurston Hall was best remembered for playing the part of the old, gruff, bumbling senator, governor or judge in his movies. The thirty-six year old actor originally played on the legitimate stage, including three years in England, before entering into his long partnership with motion pictures. He made over two hundred screen appearances in the next forty years.

Melbourne MacDowell, who played the evil dance hall owner, was born four years before the Civil War. The sixty-two year old Shakespearean actor started his film career only three years earlier in *Hell Hath No Fury* (1915), also filmed in the San Bernardino Mountains. He made almost sixty films before his retirement in 1932 at the age of seventy-six.

Producer Thomas Ince did not escape the scandals that rocked the movie industry in the early Twenties. The handsome playboy director/producer was supposedly shot and killed aboard the luxury yacht owned by William Randolph Hearst. No one has ever been able to unravel exactly what happened that night, but it has been strongly suggested that Hearst had something to do with the murder. Ince's official death certificate indicates that he died of heart failure on November 24, 1924.

Thurston Hall circa 1918
Photo courtesy of The Academy of Motion
Picture Arts and Sciences

Thomas H. Ince
circa 1920

WILD YOUTH (1918)

Louise Huff and Jack Mulhall in a scene
from *Wild Youth* (1918)
Photo courtesy of
The Academy of Motion Picture
Arts and Sciences

Once more, in 1918, Jesse Lasky sent his Famous Players unit to film *Wild Youth* in the Big Bear Lake area. This time they needed shots of ranches and woods where they could "lose" their married heroine, Louise (Louise Huff), among the tall timber. The story was a bit racy for the times. Huff played the young wife who is forced into a loveless marriage because of debts. Her older, overbearing and cruel husband Joel was played by Theodore Roberts. The neighboring rancher just happens to be a young, handsome chap named Orlando Guise (Jack Mulhall).

When Orlando is wounded, Joel warily agrees to allow the young man to recuperate at his ranch. With spring in the air, Orlando and Louise fall hopelessly in love, much to Joel's chagrin. Later, when Louise disappears, Joel accuses Orlando of stealing his wife which he denies. When Orlando does find her injured after a fall from her pony, he reluctantly returns her to Joel who beats her mercilessly. At this point, her Chinese servant, Li Choo (James Cruze), jumps to her rescue and kills Joel. Orlando is charged with the crime, but with Li Choo's confession, Orlando is left free to marry Louise.

Two important things are brought to bear in this story. First, it was not unusual at this time to find newspaper ads from husbands indicating that their wives had run off with another man, which was a crime. Secondly, the killing was done by an Oriental and there was a strong racial bias against them at this period of history.

Louise Huff was well known to audiences and well liked. She already had made twenty films in five years before *Wild Youth*. She continued in silents for another four years, but abruptly quit the screen in 1922 after making a total of thirty-seven films.

Theodore Roberts loved playing the heavy. He was fifty-seven when he made *Wild Youth* and had appeared in over forty films by that time. He began acting on stage and in vaudeville in the 1880s, with his biggest success as Simon Legree in the stage play *Uncle Tom's Cabin* at the turn of the century. His screen career began with the Lasky company's *Call of the Wild* in 1914, also filmed in Big Bear. He died in 1928 of uremic poisoning after a long and colorful career.

Theodore Roberts
circa 1919

The affable thirty-four year old James Cruze supposedly began his acting career selling "snake oil" in traveling medicine shows, before starting in films in 1911. Cruze was no stranger to the Big Bear area having been in two previous films, *Call of the East* and *Nan of Music Mountain* the prior year. In 1918, Cruze was elevated to director by Jesse Lasky and he stepped behind the cameras for the rest of his screen life directing over seventy films in the next two decades. His big budgeted epic, *Covered Wagon* (1923), set the standard for westerns for years to come. Cruze returned one last time to film in Big Bear in 1936 when he filmed portions of the film *Sutter's Gold* (1936).

James Cruze
circa 1920

Jack Mulhall was a screen heartthrob by 1918 and reportedly the first actor to receive $1,000 per week in salary. In the hectic days of early film making, it was not unusual for Mulhall to star in a film in the morning and then be dragged into a DeMille picture that afternoon for the bit part of a priest. One of the most enduring actors of his day, Mulhall's screen and television life spanned fifty-three years with almost three hundred and fifty film and TV appearances.

THE HEART OF YOUTH (1919)

CAST:
Lila Lee .... Josephine Darchant
Tom Forman .... Russ Prendergast
Directed by .... Robert Vignola
Produced by .... Famous Players
Lasky Corp.

Lila Lee
circa 1919

Beulah Marie Dix specifically wrote the screenplay *The Heart of Youth* for Lila Lee, the young star she admired at Paramount Pictures. She adapted it from her novel, *Friends in the End*, during the flu epidemic of 1918 by sitting for hours in her house with a mask covering her face.

The Romeo/Juliet story involves two feuding families, a spring, a dam and a cat that goes missing. Critics called it a real "cream puff" with little plot. The most interesting feature of the film was that the mountain lodge was constructed on the Lasky lot in Hollywood. Trees from the local mountains were brought in and situated so they appeared to be at high altitudes. However, cast and crew did go on location and the scenes of Lila Lee in a car plunging into the cold waters of Big Bear Lake are real.

Tom Forman plays the young and wealthy scion of the neighboring family, who have been fighting for years over water rights to a spring. Forman began his acting career with the Universal Pictures group at the age of twenty-one in 1914. Within four years he was playing the boy-next-door leads. In 1920, he convinced Universal to allow him to direct films. Meeting with moderate success, he left Universal and joined Budd Schulberg at Preferred Pictures Company. In the span of twelve years he acted in forty-six films and directed twenty-seven. His last directorial effort screened to poor reviews in October, 1927, and a month later he committed suicide—one more juicy Hollywood tale in a scandal-riddled era.

Lila Lee was born Augusta Appel in 1901 into a vaudevillian family. She began acting at an early age and made her screen debut at sixteen. Although her face was one of the most recognizable during the silent era, she never truly hit star status. Her best role came later that year when she played opposite Thomas Meighan and Gloria Swanson in *Male and Female*. She made almost one hundred films over the next twenty years and retired in 1937. Her comeback efforts a few years later were in vain and she was relegated to minor bit parts. Her son from her first marriage was writer James Kirkwood, Jr., best known for his 1985 play *A Chorus Line*.

Tom Forman
circa 1919

Lila Lee and Tom Forman in a scene from
The Heart of Youth **(1919)**
Photo courtesy of
The Academy of Motion Picture
Arts and Sciences

A FIGHT FOR LOVE
(1919)

CAST:
Harry Carey .... Cheyenne Harry
Neva Gerber .... Kate McDougal
J. Farrell MacDonald .... The Priest
Directed by .... John Ford
Produced by .... Universal Film Co.

Harry Carey circa 1930s

Neva Gerber circa 1919

NEVA GERBER

A Fight For Love could more aptly have been called *Many Fights For Love*, because of the series of fights between: the hero and villain (twice), priest and villain, and finally, villain and Indian. Cheyenne Harry, a persona that Harry Carey created in many movies, has just crossed over into Canada ahead of a posse. He sits upon his winded horse and calmly rolls a cigarette as he looks back over his shoulder at the frustrated American posse. The scene described is pure John Ford, the man who directed this feature filmed in the mountains around Big Bear Lake in May of 1918. This series of fights, as all good Westerns must have, culminated in a cliff-hanging scene which was created on a two-story high boulder perched above the lake. Naturally, the villain goes over the side into the frigid waters below and our hero triumphs.

By 1919, six foot tall, forty-one year old Harry Carey had the quintessential features of the ideal, rugged cowboy that would serve him well over the next forty years. His stony demeanor and gravelly voice was what the "West" was all about. In the late 1910s, Carey influenced Universal Studios into hiring John Ford as a director and their long association resulted in twenty-eight films together. Ford's gratitude extended to Harry's son, Harry Carey, Jr., as well. There is hardly a John Wayne/John Ford movie that does not list Harry Jr. in its credits.

Neva Gerber was perfect as the daughter of the factor (overseer) of the Hudson Bay Company. The twenty-five year old star was a seven year veteran by the time she filmed *A Fight For Love*. In the next decade, she became the serial queen of films and as well known to audiences as any of the bigger stars. Her career expanded into the talkies and then in 1930, she disappeared completely from the movie industry. Film historians traced her through a series of marriages until her death at age seventy-nine in 1974 in Palm Springs, California, just ninety minutes away from Big Bear Lake.

J. Farrell MacDonald, who played the (fighting) priest in *A Fight For Love*, was one of the most interesting character actors of his time. The forty-four year old actor began films in 1911 and by the end of his career had credits in over three hundred movies. The gruff looking actor was also a director and directed one of the first *Wizard of Oz* films. John Ford loved MacDonald's work and over the next thirty-five years they collaborated on twenty-seven films together, including one of this author's all time favorites, *My Darling Clementine* (1946).

J. Farrell MacDonald
circa 1928

Harry Carey being accused in a scene from *A Fight for Love* (1919).

WHEN DOCTORS DISAGREE (1919)

CAST:
Mabel Normand .... Millie Martin
Walter Hiers .... John Turner
Directed by .... Victor Schertzinger
Produced by .... Goldwyn Pictures

With the success of *Mickey* (1918) a year earlier, Mabel Normand could pick and choose her parts. When she was offered the role of Millie Martin in the Goldwyn Pictures' comedy *When Doctors Disagree*, she jumped at the chance to play the erratic daughter of a miserly old man.

During a train trip, Millie is enamored with a man posing as a doctor (Walter Hiers). She feigns a toothache to get his attention, but her father intervenes and feeds her chewing tobacco as a cure and to avoid paying a doctor's bill. The tobacco does more harm than good and when they stop the train at a sanitarium, the phoney doctor orders an operation. Millie panics and escapes to the maternity ward where Hiers finds her with a baby and mistakenly thinks she has just given birth. All is explained away shortly and the two fade out, hand in hand.

After Mabel Normand completed *Mickey (1918)*, Sam Goldwyn offered her $3,500 per week to join his organization. *When Doctors Disagree* was one of five comedies Normand made for Goldwyn in 1919. She made an additional three films with the Goldwyn company before a disagreement sent her back to her tempestuous friend, Mack Sennett, the following year. With the death of her lover at the time, William Desmond Taylor in 1922, her career spiraled downward until her death in 1930 at the age of thirty-eight.

The overweight Hiers was Goldwyn Pictures answer to one of the top comedians of the day, Fatty Arbuckle, with whom Normand had co-starred in many earlier pictures. His jovial good looks played well with audiences and he made over eighty films in the span of seventeen

Mabel Normand
circa 1919

years before his untimely death in 1933 from pneumonia.

Critics at the time cited the cinematographer for his excellence in picking scenic waterfalls, streams and deep valleys to shoot the exterior shots of the film in the San Bernardino Mountains. A copy of this film still exists in Bruxelles, Belgium, at the Cinematheque Royale, but can not be viewed due to its extremely fragile condition.

Walter Hiers circa 1919

Mabel Normand and Walter Hiers in a scene
from *When Doctors Disagree* (1919)
Photo courtesy of
The Academy of Motion Picture
Arts and Sciences

THE EXQUISITE THIEF (1919)

CAST:
Priscilla Dean .... Blue Jean Billie
Thurston Hall .... Algernon P. Smythe
Directed by .... Tod Browning
Produced by .... Universal Film Co.

Blue Jean Billie (Priscilla Dean) is attractive, sophisticated and a thief. She has successfully pulled off a series of jewel thefts so the local police set a trap for her. The marriage of an English nobleman (Thurston Hall) to a rich American heiress is enough to draw out the infamous girl bandit. The plan goes awry and she makes off with the gems and the Englishman, who falls in love with her and makes her see the error of her ways. Critics loved the Dean/Hall combination and also gave credit to an up and coming director by the name of Tod Browning, praising his unusual plot twists.

Thirty-seven year old Browning began as a bit player with D. W. Griffith and started directing films in 1914. Always considered a little quirky, he made his mark in the industry with classics like *London After Midnight* (1927), *Dracula* (1931) and an MGM film classic, *Freaks* (1932).

Priscilla Dean began life on the stock stage before the age of ten and was a seasoned professional of twenty-three when she played the part of Blue Jean Billie. Audiences loved the beautiful winsome girl who always managed to get out of scrapes. She made more than fifty films in the span of twenty years and retired in the mid-Thirties.

Thurston Hall, who had appeared in *Tyrant Fear* a year earlier, was thirty-seven at the time he made *The*

Thurston Hall as he appeared in later films

Exquisite Thief. His leading role days continued for another couple of years and then he retired from screen acting to pursue the legitimate stage. In 1935, Hall returned to the movies and revitalized a screen and television career that lasted another twenty-three years.

The Exquisite Thief is a film that almost did not make the list of movies made in the San Bernardino Mountains. The story and settings have nothing to do with mountains, but at least two sources place at least one scene in the mountains. When the movie was recently shown in the United States (the copy belongs to the Musee d'Orsay, France) at a Tod Browning Film Festival, this author contacted a film historian, James Cozart, for verification. Unfortunately, the film was not complete and complete verification was still not forthcoming.

Tod Browning
circa 1922

Priscilla Dean
circa 1919

THE WAY OF THE STRONG (1919)

CAST:
Anna Q. Nilsson .... Audrie Hendrie/
Monica Norton
Joe King .... Alexander Hendrie
Directed by .... Edwin Carewe
Produced by .... Metro Pictures

Anna Q. Nilsson
circa 1918

ANNA Q. NILSSON

It didn't happen often, but the crew of Metro Pictures was asked to pack up once more and traveled to a cold clime in February, 1919. In order to finish some snow sequences that they lacked for their film *The Way of the Strong*, Anna Q. Nilsson and company motored up to Big Bear Lake. They had just returned to the balmy weather of Hollywood from the freezing rains of Truckee, California, and were once more plunged into a cold climate.

Greta Garbo was not the first Swedish actress to have a cool demeanor; that distinction goes to Anna Q. Nilsson (the Q. stands for Saint Quirinus' Day, March 30, her birth date). Nilsson played a dual role of step-sisters in this Alaskan tale of betrayal in a gold mining camp, based on the popular Ridgwell Cullum novel of the same name (published in 1914).

In order to play the dual roles convincingly, the thirty-one year old Nilsson was required to dye her natural blonde hair to brunette, to play the weak-willed wife, Audrie Hendrie, who deserts her husband and is killed in a snow storm. As blonde step-sister Monica, she falls in love with Audrie's ex-husband, Alexander, played by Joe King. There are some plot twists and critics found the tale both fascinating and satisfying as did audiences.

Joe King, who appeared in *Hell Hath No Fury* in 1917, began his career with Thomas Ince six years earlier. The tall, good looking actor was thirty-six when he made *The Way of the Strong* and was a screen veteran with numerous screen appearances. His film career continued for another thirty years and he was credited with over one hundred and forty roles before his death in 1951.

Anna Q. Nilsson, who began working with the Kalem Company in 1911, was also a seasoned actress. Taller than most actresses, at five foot seven inches she required leading men who were at least as tall as she. Nilsson was one of the most productive actresses of her day, appearing in almost two hundred features over a period of forty years. Oddly, she and Joe King did not appear together again until twenty-two years later in the film *They Died With Their Boots On* (1941), when they played bit parts in this Errol Flynn classic. Nilsson returned to the mountains one more time in 1938 for the movie, *Prison Farm* shot in Crestline.

Joe King
circa 1913

THE LAST OF HIS PEOPLE (1919)

CAST:

Mitchell Lewis .... Lone Wolf
Yvette Mitchell .... Na-ta-le
Edward Hearn .... Reynard Lacey
Directed by .. Robert North Bradbury
Produced by ... Select Pictures Corp.

In August, 1919, Mitchell Lewis and a cast and crew of twenty-three others traveled up to Big Bear Lake to film *The Last of His People*. For this, his company erected an elaborate hunting lodge near the lake. Critics called it the "usual story of the White villain . . . taking advantage of the Indian maiden." Lewis played the part of Lone Wolf, revenging brother to Na-ta-le, the heartbroken maiden (Yvette Mitchell). The love interest was provided by Katherine Van Buren who is engaged to the villain, Reynard Lacey (Edward Hearn). Like all good Indian features of its day, there had to be a knife fight—on top of a rock, but this time the Indian wins and the villain plunges over the side.

At six foot two, Mitchell Lewis was well known to audiences in that day and his characterization of an ethnic part fit well with his fans. He had just completed two other "far North" films that year, one of which may also have been made in the Big Bear Lake area, but has never been confirmed (*Faith of the Strong*).

Lewis had been making pictures since 1914 and his career spanned the next four decades and included one hundred and seventy plus credits.

Katherine Van Buren is one of those silent ladies that is a complete mystery. This was her third film in two years and she made four more before dissolving from the scene completely the following year.

Yvette Mitchell is much the same story. She made nine films in five years, none of which survived, and finally disappeared.

Thirty-one year old Edward Hearn was a veteran actor when he started playing opposite Mitchell Lewis. Because

Edward Hearn
circa 1920

of his good looks, the six foot athletically built Hearn was picked to play the part of Jack Dempsey, the heavyweight champion of the world, in a serial called *Daredevil Jack* for Pathé Films. His career would also span the next four decades and he was credited with more than two hundred and fifty films over that period.

The director of the film was a thirty-three year old writer by the name of Robert North Bradbury. He too had a long and illustrious career in Hollywood, writing, directing and producing films over the next three decades. His son, who took the name Bob Steele, was a very prolific actor in Westerns, some of which were also shot in the Big Bear Lake area.

Mitchell Lewis in unconfirmed film *Faith of the Strong* (1919) which was probably filmed in the San Bernardino Mountains (note the trees and lake).

Mitchell Lewis dressed for his role in *The Last of His People* (1919). Photo courtesy of The Academy of Motion Picture Arts and Sciences

HEART O' THE HILLS (1919)

CAST:
Mary Pickford .... Mavis Hawn
Harold Goodwin .... Jason Honeycutt
Directed by .... Joseph De Grasse/
Sidney Franklin
Produced by .... Mary Pickford Co.

Five-foot tall Mary Pickford and Harold Goodwin in a scene from *Heart o' the Hills* (1919)

It was inevitable that the most recognizable actress in the world would eventually make a movie in the San Bernardino Mountains. "America's Sweetheart," Mary Pickford, brought her production company up to Forest Home (now Forest Falls) in the summer of 1919 to film John Fox, Jr.'s popular saga of moonshine, murder and romance, *Heart o' the Hills*. Amazingly, this film survives and one can witness today the talent and appeal Canadian-born Pickford had on audiences of her day.

The story itself is simplistic by today's standards. Thirteen year old Mavis Hawn (Mary Pickford) is a wild and tomboyish mountain lass. When her father is mysteriously murdered, she vows revenge. With the help of her youthful friend, Jason Honeycutt (Harold Goodwin), she practices sharpshooting with a rifle. She inadvertently kills a man, but during the trial she is freed when the whole jury and town admit to the shooting. Mavis is sent away to be educated and returns six years later and finds out her father was murdered by Jason's stepfather, played by Sam De Grasse.

Playing opposite seventeen year old Harold Goodwin, the youthful looking twenty-seven year old Mary Pickford was still able to do what she had been doing for the past ten years — play the part of a younger person and still have audiences believing it. Critics didn't dare not like a Pickford film, but found this one too long. They did praise her energy while dancing in what was called a "shindig."

By 1919, Mary Pickford could practically name her own price and she did, $350,000 per picture! This was an extraordinary amount of money for the times. But she was well worth it, and the box office receipts proved it. One year later, she and her new husband, Douglas

Fairbanks, along with Charlie Chaplin and D.W. Griffith formed United Artists. By this date, Pickford had already made over two hundred movies and wanted to do less film starring and more film producing.

Over the next decade Pickford still managed to star in eighteen more films, culminating in her first Oscar in 1930 for her role in *Coquette* (1929). She retired in 1935 and received a second honorary Oscar in 1976 (in recognition of her unique contributions to the film industry and the development of film as an artistic medium), three years before her death.

Harold Goodwin never attained the star power of Pickford, but he did co-star with her the following year in *Suds* (1920). Over the next four decades he worked in more than one hundred and eighty film and television roles.

In the supporting cast was a bit player named Jack Gilbert, who played the city son who wanted to marry Mavis. This was considered his big break and within five years, Jack became John Gilbert, one of the biggest stars and heartthrobs of the silent cinema.

Again, Sam De Grasse got the honor of playing the nasty villain. Of course, it didn't hurt to have his brother, Joseph De Grasse, as one of the directors.

Mary Pickford
circa 1919

Mary Pickford on location at Big Bear
in *Heart o' the Hills* (1919)
Photo courtesy of
The Academy of Motion Picture
Arts and Sciences

THE RED LANE (1920)

```
CAST:
Frank Mayo ............. Norman Aldrich
Lillian Rich ................ Marie Beaulieu
Jean Hersholt ........... Vetal Beaulieu
Directed by .............. Lynn Reynolds
Produced by ........ Universal Film Co.
```

In the early summer of 1920, a group of actors and crew arrived at Big Bear Lake to film *The Red Lane*, based on the Holman Day novel, *The Red Lane: A Romance of the Border* (1912). Heading the cast was Frank Mayo, Lillian Rich, James Mason (not the British actor by the same name) and Jean Hersholt.

Marie Beaulieu (Lillian Rich) returns to her father, Vetal (Jean Hersholt), after spending her childhood in a convent, only to find that her father, who is a leader of a gang of Canadian smugglers, is about to marry her off to one of his henchmen, Dave Roi (James Mason). Repulsed by the idea, she flees with the help of Norman Aldrich (Frank Mayo), an American customs agent, to the sanctuary of a small town. The father is enraged at her deception and kidnaps her back across the border. The custom agent follows and somehow the father is killed in the struggle. Aldrich is blamed and is about to be jailed for murder, until a half-witted shepherd admits to the killing to avenge an old grudge. Exonerated, Aldrich becomes an elected official of the town and vows to wipe out the smugglers,

Frank Mayo and Lillian Rich in a scene at
Big Bear Lake (1920)

FRANK MAYO
IN
THE RED LANE

which he does and wins the hand of Marie.

Critics hated it, except for the spectacular scenery of Big Bear Lake. The story was padded and Universal was accused of cutting a lot of financial corners to produce it. Unfortunately, we will never know because the film is presumed lost.

London-born Lillian Rich was nineteen when she played Marie. The dark-haired beauty started out the year before in bit parts before starring opposite Frank Mayo. Over the next three years, they co-starred in another three films. In 1925, Rich was picked by Cecil B. DeMille to play the femme fatale in his extravaganza, *The Golden Bed*. Critics lauded her performance in a blonde wig, but her vamping days were nearly over. Rich continued to play supporting roles throughout the 1930s and she retired in 1940. She died in 1954, after making sixty-five films in her twenty plus years before the cameras.

Thirty-four year old Frank Mayo was also a screen veteran who had debuted in films in 1911. He continued to star for a few more years and then gradually was relegated to minor roles. In the 1930s and 1940s, his career faded and he appeared in many films, but always as either a bit part or uncredited.

Danish-born Jean Hersholt came from an acting family and was a seasoned professional by the time he arrived in America. During his early silent years, he was cast as the heavy. Even though he had a thick European accent, he made the transition to talkies. In the Thirties, he created the character of Dr. Christian, the kindly family doctor, for both radio and film audiences. Hersholt's character and his own persona of kindness were real. He founded the Motion Picture Relief Fund to help fellow actors. In order to honor his memory, The Academy of Motion Picture Arts and Sciences created the Jean Hersholt Humanitarian Award in 1956. Periodically, the Academy awards the honor to a deserving indivdual during the Oscar ceremonies.

Lillian Rich circa 1920

Frank Mayo circa 1920

DOLLAR FOR DOLLAR (1920)

CAST:
Frank Keenan .... Marcus Gard
Kathleen Kirkham .... Mrs. Marteen
Directed by .... Frank Keenan
Produced by ..... Frank Keenan Prod.

Frank Keenan
circa 1920

The author has not determined when the Pathé Movie unit came to Big Bear Lake, but it probably was in the late fall of 1919 to shoot a camping sequence for the film, *Dollar For Dollar*. The story was written by playwright and novelist, Ethel Watts Mumford, and is a morality play exposing the evils of Wall Street and the men who made their money there. The moneyed tycoon was played by Frank Keenan. His rival is just as wealthy and ruthless, but also a bigamist. The plot sounds strangely benign by today's standards, but in 1920 these were the scandals of the day. True to the fashion of a play, there is a little murder, blackmail by a society lady (Kathleen Kirkham) and true love between two young people caught up in the whole corrupt mess (Katherine Van Buren and Jay Belasco). The film is lost to us, but the camping scene appears out of place for the rest of this highly theatrical movie.

Frank Keenan was a venerable stage and silent screen actor who was born before the Civil War in 1858. He began amateur acting in his twenties and earned the princely sum of nine dollars a week. His film career began in 1909, working for the Vitagraph Company in New York. He was one of the highest paid stars of early films, acknowledged by Photoplay Magazine in 1916 when he signed for $1,000 per week with Ince Productions. The serious-faced actor made forty films in the span of seventeen years and he died at the age of seventy-one from complications of pneumonia. His grandson was actor Keenan Wynn.

Twenty-five year old Kathleen Kirkham played the high society, blackmailing femme fatale. The pretty and tall actress had already made two movies in the San Bernardino Mountains before making this film, *Eyes of the World* in 1917 and *He Comes Up Smiling* in 1918. Considered too thick-waisted to play leading roles, the versatile actress had played the mother of Tarzan in the first movie made of that genre. During her brief ten year career, she made fifty-six films and retired in 1926.

Katherine Van Buren is a silent star mystery. From 1918 to 1920, she made seven films and then nothing more is mentioned of her. She had appeared opposite Mitchell Lewis the year earlier in *The Last of His People*, which was also filmed at Big Bear Lake.

Jay Belasco was the cousin of the famous playwright and producer, David Belasco. He never attained the fame of his cousin and because he could not make the transition to talkies, he left films in 1927. His comeback ended with minor bit parts in the 1930s.

Kathleen Kirkham
circa 1920

THE SAGEBRUSHER (1920)

CAST:

Roy Stewart .... Dr. Barnes
Marguerite De La Motte .... Mary
Noah Beery .... Sim Gage
Directed by .... Edward Sloman
Produced by .... Great Authors Pictures

Writers in the 1910s were looking for a new name to call cowboys and they came up with the term "sagebrusher." Emerson Hough's 1919 novel, *The Sagebrusher: A Story of the West*, was a typical Western saga that readers loved and producers brought to the silent screen. *The Sagebrusher* was filmed in the Santa Ana Canyon just below Big Bear Lake.

In this slice of western life, there is an unkempt cowboy, Sim (Noah Beery), whose buddy advertises, on Sim's behalf, for a mail order bride, Mary Warren (Marguerite De La Motte). Mary's eyesight is bad and even before she arrives, she goes blind. Before the wedding, Mary is accosted by the villainous Big Aleck and she shoots him with Sim's gun. Fleeing to the mountains, she finds herself blind and alone in a forest fire. Fortunately, she is saved by Dr. Barnes (Roy Stewart) whom she mistakes for Sim. On the day of the wedding, Sim realizes he is not good enough for Mary and asks Barnes to take his place when asked to kiss the bride. The inevitable operation to regain her sight is performed and then Sim obligingly drowns, allowing Barnes to really take his place. Critics called it wholesome family fare that no theater would be ashamed to show.

Roy Stewart began acting in comedies when he joined Hal Roach Studios in 1915. The good looking, lanky Stewart quickly attained star status and began a career of being a screen "sagebrusher." His production of over one hundred movies in eighteen years attests to his staying power, but during the Twenties he gradually relinquished star status to supporting roles. Stewart died of a heart attack at the age of fifty in 1933.

Marguerite De La Motte, who was trained as a dancer, began acting in Westerns in 1915 at the age of thirteen. By 1920, she was well established and later that year she starred opposite Douglas Fairbanks in one of his greatest roles,

Roy Stewart rescues the lady

A popular post card from the 1920s.

Zorro, in *The Mark of Zorro*. She continued to star into the Thirties and then retired in 1934. Her comeback in the early Forties failed and she quit films in 1942. A true dark-haired beauty, the diminutive star with over sixty films to her credit died of cerebral thrombosis at the age of forty-seven. In her last film, *Overland Mail* (1942), she once again played opposite Noah Beery.

Six foot Noah Beery was two years older than his more famous half-brother, Wallace Beery. He successfully carved a niche for himself in early films as a character actor and familiar heavy. His perceived screen persona allowed him to remain in movies for almost thirty years, with over two hundred screen credits. Noah worked up to the day he died from a heart attack in 1946, and his brother followed him in the same manner three years later.

Noah Beery, Marguerite De La Motte, Betty Brice and Roy Stewart in a scene from *The Sagebrusher* (1920)
Photo courtesy of
The Academy of Motion Picture
Arts and Sciences

THE LAST OF THE MOHICANS (1920)

Finally, Hollywood got one right. This was the third filming of James Fenimore Cooper's novel and is considered by critics to be the best of the thirteen versions to date. Recently restored, this silent classic embodied the genius of French director Maurice Tourneur and foretold the coming talent of the assistant director, Clarence Brown. This was to be French-born Tourneur's masterpiece, but an illness and subsequent injury on location in Big Bear sent him to bed for three months and he was replaced by Brown, thus giving them both equal credit for its timelessness.

It is interesting to note that thirty-five year old Wallace Beery, who played the "bad guy" in numerous films up to that time, was given top billing as Magua, the crafty and evil Huron Indian. It was not until later films that "Hawkeye" emerged as the central character. Critics questioned the use of Caucasian Beery to play the role of an Indian, but praised his work nevertheless. Beery, who had been making films since 1913, felt more comfortable in comedy and went on to make over two hundred films in his lifetime. He almost didn't make the transition to talkies because of his gravely, folksy voice. Fortunately, MGM saw this as an attribute and signed him to star in some great classics, like *Viva Villa* (1934) and *Treasure Island* (1934). He won the Oscar for best actor starring opposite Jackie Cooper in *The Champ* (1931).

Harry Lorraine (Hawkeye) confronts Wallace Beery (Magua) in a scene from *The Last of the Mohicans* (1920).

Barbara Bedford, who played the ill-fated Cora, was seventeen in her debut year in films. She was given star billing for the next couple of years and then gradually slipped into accompanying and bit parts for the next two decades. In all, she made over one hundred and fifty films in a span of twenty-five years, but none as memorable as *The Last of the Mohicans*.

Handsome and tall, thirty-two year old Alan Roscoe played the romantic lead of Uncas, whose devotion to Cora led to the fight with Beery on top of the Big Bear cliffs. Roscoe and Bedford made five films together and became husband and wife in 1922. He made nearly one hundred films, but his career faded rapidly in the 1920s. He died at the age of forty-five in 1933.

English-born Harry Lorraine was thirty-four when he played the almost minor role of Natty Bumpo or "Hawkeye." During his career he made a total of forty-two films, but did not make the crossover into the talkies. He died at the age of forty-eight in 1934.

Tourneur had been making silents in the United States since 1913 and was considered to be one of the best directors in Hollywood. He never again found another film as good as *The Last of the Mohicans* to prove his talents. Tourneur left Hollywood to direct in his native Paris in 1926, but his son Jacques stayed on in Hollywood and became a successful director in his own right.

Clarence Brown became one of the most successful directors in Hollywood and garnered six Oscar nominations during his lifetime. Unfortunately, he never won any of them. He returned to the San Bernardino Mountains many years later to film the movie classic *The Yearling* in 1945.

One of the extras who played an Indian in the masterful massacre scene was an Englishman named William Henry Pratt, who would later change his name to Boris Karloff.

A scene from *The Last of the Mohicans* (1920) at Big Bear

Maurice Tourneur circa 1920

Alan Roscoe (Uncas) holds Barbara Bedford and Lillian Hall seeks shelter in the arms of Harry Lorraine (Hawkeye) in *The Last of the Mohicans* (1920).

UNDER NORTHERN LIGHTS (1920)

```
CAST:
Virginia Faire .... Suzanne Foucharde
Leonard Clapham ................ Jacques
                                 Foucharde
William Buckley ... Douglas MacLeod
Directed by ............. Jacques Jaccard
Produced by ........ Universal Film Co.
```

There is not much good to say about Universal Film's *Under Northern Lights* other than it was beautifully photographed, but because it is "lost" we will never know. Critics absolutely hated this movie. They called it substandard fare and best shown as the second feature of a double bill, so long as the first feature "delivered the goods."

No biography or picture of William Buckley has ever been found by this author. Even critics of the day, who called him handsome, acknowledged that he was an unknown actor. Even with this anonymity, he does have film credits in twenty-five pictures and must have been associated with the film industry for the next two decades because his last credit is as a technical advisor in the James Cagney prison film *Each Dawn I Die* in 1939.

At some point in his colorful career, Leonard Clapham changed his name to Tom London and Western fans will remember him as the grizzled character actor they saw in hundreds of "B" Westerns during the Thirties and Forties. He alternated back and forth from good guy to the heavy in his over five hundred films and TV appearances spanning six decades. From his first Western, *The Great Train Robbery* (1903), to his last TV episode of *Laramie* (1959), London was known as the consummate cowboy actor.

Leonard Clapham and Virginia Faire in a scene from *Under Northern Lights* (1920) filmed at Big Bear Lake.
Photo courtesy of Northeast Historic Film

Sixteen year old Virginia Brown Faire, who was born Virginia Labuna in Brooklyn, N.Y., was considered one of the most beautiful girls of the era. She attracted scores of fans wherever she went. Her work in the Rin-Tin-Tin films assured her an instant success and acceptance by audiences, even though critics were not as kind about her acting abilities. Between 1920 and 1935, when she retired, she had played in sixty-six films, none of them memorable however.

THE RIVER'S END
(1920)

During the winter of 1919-20, director Marshall Neilan, who happened to have been born in San Bernardino and was familiar with the area, insisted that First National send the cast and crew to Big Bear Lake to film the snow sequences of *The River's End*. When they arrived, they got more than they had bargained for because Big Bear experienced one of their worst winters in a decade.

Forty-one year old Lewis Stone played the dual lead of suspected killer (John Keith) and pursuing Royal Mountie (Constable Conniston) in this James Oliver Curwood thriller set in the north woods of Canada. Led by a tracker, Conniston locates Keith in a cabin during a blizzard. Keith convinces the Mountie that the killing was justified and agrees to return, but before they do Conniston becomes ill and dies. Because of the resemblance between the two (they might have been twins), the tracker suggests that Keith assume the trooper's identification and agrees to help him. When Keith/Conniston returns to the post, he is accepted as the dead trooper and when Conniston's sister Mary (Marjorie Daw) arrives, Keith finds himself in love with her. After many twists and turns, including a Chinese cook who tries to seduce the true killer's sister (Jane Novak), Keith and Mary are united.

Known for his military bearing and stand-up style, theatrically trained Lewis Stone actually had been in the military, both Spanish American War and World War I. He was prematurely grey at the age of twenty-one. During the following decade, he continued to play romantic leading roles opposite most of the leading ladies of that era, including Florence Vidor, Alice Terry, Greta Garbo and Norma Shearer. He is best remembered for his character role of the kindly Judge Hardy in the Andy Hardy series produced by M-G-M, where he was a fixture from 1924 until his death in 1953.

CAST:	
Lewis Stone	Derwent Conniston/ John Keith
Marjorie Daw	Mary Josephine
Jane Novak	Miriam Kirkstone
Directed by	Marshall Neilan/ Victor Heerman
Produced by ...	Marshall Neilan Prod.

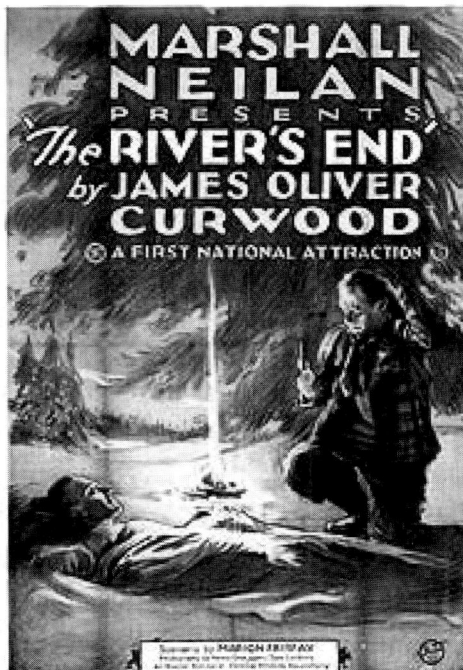

Lobby card for *The River's End*
circa 1920

MARSHALL NEILAN PRESENTS *The* RIVER'S END *by* JAMES OLIVER CURWOOD
A FIRST NATIONAL ATTRACTION

Jane Novak
circa 1920

Marjorie Daw, Jane Novak, and Lewis
Stone (white hat) with two unidentified
actors at Big Bear Lake
Photo courtesy of The Academy of Motion
Pictures Arts and Sciences

Stone loved the mountains and was one of the first home owners at the newly formed Lake Arrowhead in 1922.

Eighteen year old Marjorie Daw was an acting veteran with more than twenty screen credits when she made *The River's End*. She continued to play leads throughout the 1920s, but abruptly quit films in 1927. She is reported to have been married to David Selznick's brother, Myron, who was also a home owner in the San Bernardino Mountains.

Twenty-four year old Jane Novak played the part of the blackmailed sister. Jane and her equally beautiful younger sister Eva, were film icons well known to audiences of the Twenties. *The River's End* began a series of Northwest dramas for Jane, some of which may also have been filmed in the San Bernardino Mountains, but never verified. She followed up with the *Golden Trail* (1920), *Kazan* (1921), *Belle of Alaska* (1922), *Colleen of the Pines* (1922) and finally *Snowshoe Trail* also in 1922. Jane made over seventy movies from 1915 to 1954, when she retired. She died at the age of ninety-four in 1990. She outlived her younger sister by two years.

[NOTE: *The River's End* was remade twice, once in 1930 and again in 1940. The 1930 version was supposedly made in Lake Arrowhead, however, the film was reviewed by the author at the UCLA film archives and there are no lake scenes and neither it nor the 1940 version were filmed in the San Bernardino Mountains.]

THE COURTSHIP OF MILES STANDISH (1923)

Charles Ray, the barefoot boy with cheeks of tan, could also be called "America's Sweetheart" —the male version. By 1923, Ray, who usually played the fair-haired hero, was tired of the same roles, for he had already been in close to one hundred films by that time. That year his new production company embarked upon one of the most costliest projects to date, Henry Wadsworth Longfellow's *The Courtship of Miles Standish*. This nine reel epic proved to be his undoing.

Ray's headstrong attitude alienated producers which forced him to put up his own money to begin production. His team constructed one of the most elaborate sets ever built in Hollywood, including a floating replica of the Mayflower whose mast and sails could be seen for miles around. In the newly formed community of Lake Arrowhead, they erected three complete log cabins for all the exterior scenes. Around Christmas, 1923, Ray released his film to great critical acclaim, but unfortunately audiences didn't agree and stayed away. Again, we will never know because the film is lost to us.

The three cabins were so well built that they were able to be dismantled. Later they were sold and eventually relocated to Rustic Canyon near Pacific Palisades, where they have survived to this day. Ray never recovered from his misfortunes and by the 1930s he was lucky to get even bit parts. He died of an impacted tooth infection in 1943 at the age of fifty-two.

Australian-born Enid Bennett, who had just played Maid Marian in Douglas Fairbanks' very successful *Robin Hood* (1922), was chosen to play the pivotal part of Priscilla Mullens. Bennett, whose

CAST:
Charles Ray .... John Alden
Enid Bennett .... Priscilla Mullens
E. Allyn Warren .... Miles Standish
Sam De Grasse .... John Carver
Directed by .... Frederick Sullivan
Produced by .... Charles Ray Prod.

Contemporary Advertisment for
The Courtship of Miles Standish
circa 1923

Charles Ray (on right) and unidentified
actor in a scene from *The Courtship of
Miles Standish* (1923)
Photo courtesy of
The Academy of Motion Picture
Arts and Sciences

stage career launched her into movies, was one of the most popular and recognizable silent stars of her day. She had married the director of her first film, Fred Niblo and, after three children, she decided to slow down her acting career and devote more time to her family. She left the movies permanently in 1940 after appearing in over fifty movies.

Sam De Grasse was once more cast as a heavy in this melodrama. The Canadian-born actor had also been in *Robin Hood* (1922) with Bennett, where he portrayed the evil Prince John. His career spanned sixteen years and over one hundred movies.

One of the interesting side notes to this film is that it had already been parodied before it was released. *The Courtship of Miles Sandwich* (1923) starred comic Snub Pollard. It was said to be a delightful spoof on the Miles Standish story, with Snub attempting to tell his son the origin of Thanksgiving.

The Marco Hellman house circa 1925, one of three log cabins moved from Lake Arrowhead.
Interior of the Marco Hellman House (below)
Photos courtesy of Betty Lou Young from the Young Collection

THE OREGON TRAIL (1923)

CAST:
Art Acord
Louise Lorraine
Directed by .... Edward Laemmle
Produced by .... Universal Pictures

In the winter and spring of 1922-23, a large group of Universal players and crew descended upon Big Bear Lake to make a cliff-hanging serial called *The Oregon Trail*. In all, they shot thirty-seven reels and divided them into eighteen episodes. The film featured one of the most popular Western serial stars in his day, Art Acord. His leading lady was twenty-two year old Louise Lorraine, who also was a popular actress of the silent screen. Over the next four years they starred together in a total of six features and eventually married.

Because the films are lost, not much is known of the series. One old timer remembered years later that some good horseplay went on amongst the cast. One night at Knight's Camp, he recalled, one of the actors was accused of not wearing a genuine Stetson, an unpardonable sin among real cowboys. He was put on mock trial and found guilty and sentenced to a chapping (a man is held down and his bottom spanked with a pair of chaps). It was reported that it was all in good fun and everyone shook hands afterwards.

Art Acord and Louise Lorraine in a scene from *The Oregon Trail* (1923)

Thirty-three year old Art Acord had arrived early on the scene of cowboy movies, working for the Bison 101 Company. Born in the Indian Territory, later Oklahoma, he was the real thing—an authentic cowboy who loved to ride and rope. Acord was the World's Champion Steer Bulldogger in 1912 and again held the title in 1916 by beating challenger Hoot Gibson. His series of serials in the early Twenties made him one of the most recognizable faces on the screen. Unfortunately, Acord had a serious drinking problem which led to his divorce from

Lorraine in 1928 and a reduction of roles in the late Twenties. According to some sources, he was murdered by cyanide poisoning after an affair with a Mexican politician's wife.* John Wayne sent his personal nurse to retrieve the body for burial in California. Acord's drinking may have started after his experiences in WWI when he served eighteen months in the military and was awarded the Croix de Guerre for bravery.

Louise Lorraine had gained fame as a damsel in distress in serials before *The Oregon Trail* series, and always insisted on doing her own stunts until she witnessed an automobile accident in which the actors were killed. With the advent of talkies, her lead roles diminished and she retired from the screen in 1932.

The Oregon Trail was directed by thirty-six year old Edward Laemmle, nephew of Carl Laemmle, founder of Universal Pictures. He had already directed thirty films by 1923 and had a world of experience, literally. In 1917, he had been sent to Siam, Java, and New Guinea to film documentaries. Whether he was fortunate or not, Laemmle found himself shipwrecked on the islands and spent two years filming the natives. *Shipwrecked Among the Cannibals* (1920) was the first film to gross more than $1,000,000 for Universal Pictures.

* Mexican authorities in Chihuahua, Mexico, listed his death as suicide.

Louise Lorraine
circa 1923

Cast and crew from
The Oregon Trail
circa 1923

STEELE OF THE
ROYAL MOUNTED (1925)

CAST:

Bert Lytell .... Philip Steele
Charlotte Merriam ...... Isobel Becker
Stuart Holmes .... Bucky Nome
Directed by .... David Smith
Produced by ..... Vitagraph Company

**Bert Lytell comforts Charlotte Merriam
in a scene from
Steele of the Royal Mounted (1925).**

Vitagraph Company, one of the first of the movie companies and one which later merged with Warner Brothers, sent a crew to Lake Arrowhead in the spring of 1925 to film yet another Royal Canadian Mounted Police film, *Steele of the Royal Mounted*. This story, though, was better than the average script produced in Hollywood, as it was an adaptation of a James Oliver Curwood novel by the same name. At the time, Curwood was one of the most widely read authors in America and his books probably account for more screen plays than any other writer's before or since.

With the idea of arousing jealousy in Philip Steele (Bert Lytell), Isobel Becker (Charlotte Merriam) persuades her father to permit himself to being introduced as her husband.*

Unfortunately for Isobel, the scheme doesn't work on the stoic Steele and he takes off for the Canadian wilds where he is attracted to service in the RCMP. Not deterred, Isobel follows with her father in tow on the pretense that her father would like to get into the fur business. In the meantime, Steele has distinguished himself and earned a promotion. He is sent after the notorious Bucky Nome (Stuart Holmes) who has broken out of jail and hooked up with his band of cutthroats. Bucky and his cohorts wreck the train Isobel is on and she and her father are taken captives. Steele, of course, comes to the rescue, falls in love and resigns from the force when he realizes that his true place is next to Isobel in the social world.

Forty year old Bert Lytell was at the top of the acting world in 1925. He began as a

*This same plot would be used again and again over the years with the latest being *My Father the Hero* (1994) starring Gerard Depardieu.

stage actor and was in a starring role in his first picture released in 1917. Over the next fifteen years he appeared in more than fifty films, usually as the star. His detective movies as the "Lone Wolf" were copied by dozens of producers from that time forward. Because of his stage training, Lytell had a strong speaking voice and opted to go into a career in the fast emerging field of radio dramas. He continued his acting on Broadway throughout the Thirties and Forties, but his real love was still radio where he hosted the *Stage Door Canteen* series during WWII. In 1925, he married Claire Windsor, yet another starlet who had been associated with William Desmond Taylor's murder in 1921.

Stuart Holmes (seated) is confronted in a scene from *Steele of the Royal Mounted* (1925).

Charlotte Merriam was nineteen when she made "Steele," and had been in films since the age of thirteen. She did make the transition to talkies, but her career peaked in the early Thirties and she retired after a string of forgettable pictures in 1934.

One of the memorable character actors in the cast was Stuart Holmes who played the dastardly Bucky Nome. His career spanned five decades and he is credited with more than three hundred screen appearances. He was equally comfortable playing the "Captain of the Guard" or the crook on the run.

THE HIGH HAND (1926)

CAST:
Leo D. Maloney .... Sandy Sands
Josephine Hill .... Edith Oaks
Murdock MacQuarrie .... Martin
Directed by .... Leo D. Maloney
Produced by ... Leo D. Maloney Prod.

In 1926, Leo Maloney brought his production company up to the Skyland area of the San Bernardino Mountains with the expressed purpose of purchasing several acres with a small lake for a western studio and town. The cost of this was supposed to be more than $100,000 according to an article in *Motion Picture World* in August of that year. The intention was to film year-round with a permanent group of thirty-five actors and crew. His partner was Ford Beebe, the writer, and the films were to be released by Pathé Pictures. *The High Hand* was their first venture and was released on the 12th of September.

The exact location where he located his town has never been established. Today Skyland is an area at the crest of the ridge that separates Highway 18 and present day Crestline. There is no place in that area that could hold a small lake and it is believed by this author that the real location was down in what was then called Huston Flat (Lake Gregory).

Leo Maloney holds the gun in a scene from *The High Hand* (1926).

Maloney began his film career with Thomas Ince and Broncho Productions in 1912 and continued making films up until his death in 1929. A contemporary of Tom Mix and William S. Hart, he never quite gained their fame or fortune, yet theatergoers loved the winsome cowboy and looked forward to his off-beat comedic Westerns. It is known that at least three films were made directly in the Crestline area: *The High Hand* (1926); *Outlaw Ex-*

press (1926); and *Long Loop on the Pecos* (1927). There are probably more, but this author has not been able to verify them. The other films include: *His Own Law; Don Desperado* (1927); *The Man From Hard Pan* (1927); *and Without Orders* (1926). In all, his production company made thirteen "oaters" between 1926 and 1929, when he died. Unfortunately, the Hollywood life had not been kind to Maloney. He developed a drinking problem and died in New York City, November 2, 1929, of acute and chronic alcoholism.

Twenty-seven year old Josephine Hill played the female lead in *The High Hand* and from 1924 through 1927, she starred in twenty Westerns with Maloney. During that time she was married to another equally famous cowboy actor, Jack Perrin, with whom she occasionally co-starred. In a period of fifteen years she made close to sixty films before retiring in 1934. She died at the age of ninety in 1989 in Palm Springs, California.

Writer Ford Beebe was Maloney's best friend and when Maloney's alcoholism became too severe, Beebe would step in and direct the films. In the span of forty plus years, Beebe was producer, writer, and director of close to one hundred films, before his retirement in 1959. He too would die at the age of ninety in Lake Elsinore, California.

One of the most colorful character actors who worked with Maloney and Beebe was forty-eight year old Murdock MacQuarrie, who was also a writer and director. In fact, he was one of the founding members of the group that eventually became the Directors Guild. From 1913 to 1942, MacQuarrie wrote, starred in, or directed nearly two hundred films, usually playing the mild-mannered sheriff or politician.

Leo D. Maloney
circa 1926

Murdock MacQuarrie
circa 1920

Eugenia Gilbert circa 1926

Gilbert's film career spanned two decades (1921-1945). She played opposite Leo Maloney in seven films including: *Long Loop on the Pecos* (1927); *The Man from Hard Pan* (1927); and *Don Desperado* (1927).
Photo courtesy of
The Academy of Motion Picture Arts and Sciences

Leo Maloney directs the posse in this exhibitor's campaign book.
circa 1926

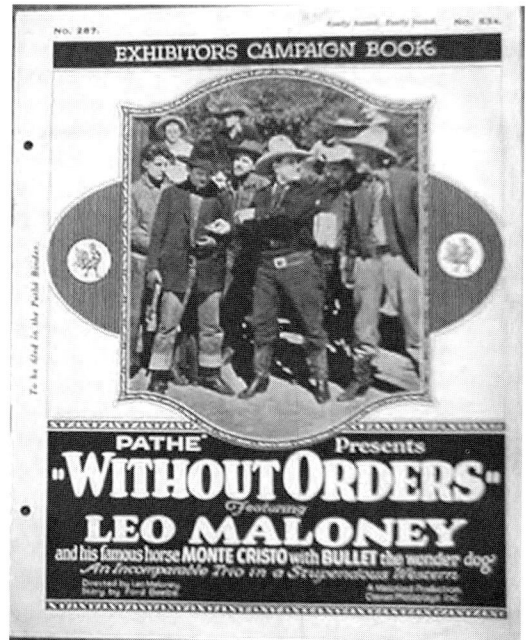

Eugenia Gilbert and Bullet, the Wonder Dog (standing on hind legs), cavorting in a snow scene from the movie *Don Desperado* (1927) believed to have been made in the Crestline area.

LAZY LIGHTNING
(1926)

Rance Lighton (Art Acord) is arrested for being a lazy, itinerant vagrant and taken to a ranch owned by a wheelchair bound Dickie Rogers (Bobby Gordon) and his sister Lila (Fay Wray). An unscrupulous uncle, who stands to inherit the ranch if Dickie dies, has a gambling problem and is heavily in debt. He nicknames the lazy stranger Lightning as a joke. When the uncle sees Dickie sliding down a cliff toward the lake, he turns his back and does nothing to help. Dickie is saved in the nick of time by "Lazy" Lightning who dives his horse over a cliff into the lake to rescue him.

Dickie becomes seriously ill due to the exposure and requires a serum which the uncle is sent to retrieve. Lightning is suspicious and follows the uncle, who has no intention of delivering the serum. The big fight scene is between the uncle, a gambler and Lightning with Lazy coming out on top. Lightning then races back through a driving rainstorm and saves Dickie and marries the grateful sister.

Old-time residents recalled the thrill of seeing Art Acord dive his horse off one of the cliffs near Emerald Bay in Lake Arrowhead during the filming. Thirty-six year old Acord was a genuine cowboy who had started in films from the very beginning in Southern California. In his first films, he rode as an extra and did stunts for Nestor, Biograph, Selig, and Bison. Notable was his appearance in Lasky's *The Squaw Man* (1914), considered to be the first full length feature made in Hollywood. Acord's drinking was legendary as were his barroom brawls. He died in Mexico in 1931. His death was attributed to cyanide poisoning, either by himself or by

CAST:
Art Acord .... Lance Lighton
Fay Wray .... Lila Rogers
Bobby Gordon .... Dickie Rogers
Directed by .... William Wyler
Produced by .... Blue Streak Films

Lobby card with a scene from
Lazy Lightning (1926)

Fay Wray
circa 1926

Art Acord
circa 1926

strangers (see p. 99). As a member of the horse-drawn 144th Field Artillery during WWI, he was allowed full military honors at his burial in Glendale, California.

Nineteen year old Canadian-born actress Fay Wray began acting in films as an extra while still a teenager. Her bit parts did little to further her career, until she was named one of thirteen starlets who would most likely succeed in motion pictures in 1927 by WAMPAS (see P. 121). The Western Association of Motion Picture Advertisers list also included Mary Astor, Joan Crawford, Dolores Costello, Dolores Del Rio, and Janet Gaynor. Unfortunately, it did little for Wray because she was working for Universal at the time. It was not until Universal released her from her contract that she began to get better roles. *The Wedding March* (1928) with Erich von Stroheim was the most noteworthy. In 1933, she was offered the part of the heroine in *King Kong*, a role that would make her forever world famous.

Born in Alsace, France, in 1902, William Wyler was asked to come to the United States during the Twenties by his cousin, Carl Laemmle, head of Universal Studios. He began learning his skills as a director in low budget Westerns, but eventually became one of the pillars of the American film industry. Over the next fifty years he was nominated for twelve Oscars and awarded Best Director three times for *Mrs. Miniver* (1942), *The Best Years of Our Lives* (1946), and *Ben-Hur* (1956). Even in the early years he was famous for demanding endless takes from his actors, with his inability or unwillingness to explain exactly what he required of them. His stubbornness paid off with his being the director most responsible for Oscar-winning performances (fourteen) and Oscar-nominated performances (thirty-five).

Bobby Gordon had been acting in films since the age of ten. The thirteen year old actor gained some fame a year later when he played the part of Al Jolson as a child in the first all talkie, *The Jazz Singer* (1927). He drifted through bit parts during the Thirties and then left the industry in 1936.

MANTRAP (1926)

From the opening shot of Lake Arrowhead to the final frame, Sinclair Lewis' successful novel *Mantrap* was a cinematic home run. From a historical view, it is one of the most important films shot at the newly formed lake. Almost the entire movie was shot on location at what would later be called Movie Point and now is referred to as Point Hamiltair.

Exuberant manicurist Alverna (Clara Bow) has hastily married folksy, good-natured backwoodsman Joe (Ernest Torrence), who has taken her out of the rat race of city life to the rustic wilds of Mantrap, Canada. Unaccepted by the local women because of her coquettish ways, Alverna realizes she may have been too hasty in accepting marriage to Joe and longs for something to happen in her life. The happening is the arrival of city lawyer Ralph Prescott (Percy Marmont), who has just traveled fifteen hundred miles to get away from women. Joe senses that his wife is unhappy, but is unable to figure out what to do. Prescott, uneasy with the flirtatious girl, leaves on a hunting expedition. Alverna quickly follows in a canoe, finally catching up to the exasperated Prescott. She pertly pleads with him to help her escape back to the city and he reluctantly agrees. At this point, Joe arrives by motor boat and instead of a bloody confrontation, Joe and Prescott sit around and discuss the wayward girl they both obviously can't stop adoring. Disgusted with both, Alverna launches the motor boat leaving the two stranded on the beach. When Joe yells that she is carrying his good name she smartly turns around in the boat and says, "So's your old man!," a popular retort of the day.

Critics loved it, audiences loved it and the movie made the already popular actress one of the biggest stars of the day. She definitely had "It" (sex appeal), observed one critic who stated

CAST:
Ernest Torrence .... Joe Easter
Clara Bow .... Alverna Easter
Percy Marmont .... Ralph Prescott
Directed by .... Victor Fleming
Produced by ..... Paramount Pictures

Clara Bow and Ernest Torrence as they appeared on the lobby card for *Mantrap* (1926)

Percy Marmont decides to get away from the ladies in a scene from *Mantrap* (1926)

Set of *Mantrap* fishing village at Lake Arrowhead (1926)
Photo courtesy of
The Academy of Motion Picture
Arts and Sciences

that, "she could flirt with a grizzly bear." By 1927, Clara Bow was receiving 45,000 pieces of fan mail a month.

After winning a popular beauty contest, Brooklyn-born Clara Bow came to Hollywood and made a series of "flapper" movies. Her sweet but devilish persona came through as she built up bigger and better roles for herself. An instant scene stealer, she was twenty-one when she made *Mantrap* for director Victor Fleming, one of the big loves of her life. Women loved her for her liberation and men loved her for her angelic look and wayward way (a typical Madonna/whore complex). The following year, at the height of her career, she was chosen to play the only female lead in the Academy Award winning film *Wings*. Her off-screen romances were legendary and included the biggest names in Hollywood. It was suggested the "morals clause" in all actors' contracts to this day was a direct result of her shenanigans back then. Her output of movies declined noticeably as the talkies arrived, because she was deathly afraid of sound with her strong Brooklynese accent. She married cowboy actor Rex Bell in 1931 and retired permanently from the screen in 1933.

Forty-eight year old Scottish-born Ernest Torrence was a stage actor when he was picked to play the heavy in *Tol'able David* (1921) opposite Richard Barthelmess. At six foot four inches, he was as comfortable playing a menacing bad guy or a " big softie" as in *Mantrap*.

Usually the supporting actor, Torrence seldomed played the lead. Amazingly, more of his silent pictures survive to this day than some of the more popular actors of the time. In thirteen years, he was cast in more than fifty films. Sadly, he died shortly after making *I Cover the Water Front* in 1933 at the age of fifty-five.

A leading actor of his day, English-born Percy Marmont was never a true star. In four decades he made eighty-three films, none of them memorable, with the exception of *Lord Jim* (1925) which led to his being chosen by Victor Fleming for the part of the harassed lawyer in *Mantrap*. Because of his rich baritone voice, Marmont easily made the transition to talkies and was in much demand. In the late Thirties he returned to his native England to make several films. He died in London in 1977 at the age of ninety-four.

Considered to be a man's man, the good-looking forty-three year old Victor Fleming was a director everyone liked and wanted on their set. His torrid on-again/off-again love affair with Clara Bow was a feast for gossip columnists. However, Fleming's best work was yet to come. With *Treasure Island* (1934), *Captains Courageous* (1937), and *Test Pilot* (1938) under his belt, he was chosen to replace Richard Thorpe in M-G-M's musical fantasy *The Wizard of Oz* (1939). Next he was asked by David O. Selznik and Clark Gable to replace George Cukor on *Gone With the Wind* (1939), because Cukor was paying more attention to Vivian Leigh than the rest of the film. Ironically, he too was later replaced on the film by Sam Wood when he suffered a nervous breakdown, but Fleming's name alone was credited and he won the Oscar for Best Director in 1940 for GWTW. Shortly after completing his forty-seventh film, *Joan of Arc* (1948), he died of a heart attack at the age of sixty-five.

To make a good movie a producer needed a lot of different talents: acting, directing, staging, and filming. When Mr. Edison first introduced his moving picture camera, it was a hand-cranked affair that varied in speed with each operator and projectionist. By the mid-Twenties, mechanical cameras had not been totally perfected, and it still required a good cinematographer to get the right shots. One of the best was James Wong Howe. Twenty-seven year old Howe was born in Canton, China, and immigrated at an early age with his parents. Howe

wanted to be a boxer and never considered being in the photography business, but his first job was as an assistant to a photographer. He began his movie career as an assistant in an editing room and moved up to "slate boy"(a person who holds a clapboard up before a scene) with C. B. DeMille. Eventually, his talents behind a camera emerged and he was noted for his pioneering work with lights and shadows. *Mantrap* is an excellent example of his early work. Howe overcame a strong prejudice against Orientals and became an icon in his field, with a career that spanned almost six decades. His list of 130 films reads like the What's What of Hollywood, and includes: *Viva Villa!* (1934); *Body and Soul* (1947); *Picnic* (1955); *Hud* (1963); and his last film, *Funny Lady* (1975). Howe earned nine nominations from the Academy and won two Oscars, one for *Hud* and the other for *The Rose Tattoo* (1955). His Oscars attest to the fact that his best work was always in black and white, the medium that first launched him.

The "It" Girl—Clara Bow
circa 1926

SUNRISE (1927)

CAST:
George O'Brien .... The Man
Janet Gaynor .... The Wife
Margaret Livingston ....The Woman
from the City
Directed by .... F. W. Murnau
Produced by .... William Fox

Without a doubt, the most important film ever shot at Lake Arrowhead was F. W. Murnau's *Sunrise* in the summer of 1926. Not only has this film been named as one of the most influential films of the 20th Century by the American Film Institute, but it has the distinction of being called the first talkie.

German-born F. W. Murnau was an internationally recognized director of some of the 1920s greatest films when William Fox asked him to direct *Sunrise*. His *Nosferatu* (1922) is the classic horror film of all time according to some film critics. Murnau planned *Sunrise* while still in Germany. After he arrived in Hollywood, he began constructing a huge stylized European village at Lake Arrowhead. Its odd angles and narrow streets generated the dark shadows needed for the story. But the real strength of this impressionistic film was that it could have stood on its own without dialogue or title cards. Murnau's unusual use of camera tracking created an illusion of depth and limitless space. One of his most inventive sets, which was crucial to the story, was a long electric streetcar track constructed through the forest. Its seamless blending from dark woods to glaring city lights is extraordinary. Because there was no electricity at the site, the streetcar was actually pushed down a small grade through the woods by men who were hidden behind it.

The story is by German Hermann Sudermann and was subtitled "A Song of Two Humans." The advertising at the time called it a "timeless story of two hearts." Viewing the film seventy-five years later one can be impressed by all of the technical innovations, but the story is far too simplistic by today's standards. The Man (George O'Brien) is literally carrying

Margaret Livingston, George O'Brien and unidentified man carrying Janet Gaynor in an art deco lobby card for *Sunrise* (1927).

the world on his shoulders. The Wife (Janet Gaynor) is just trying to make it meekly through life day by day with her child. Thrown into the mix is Margaret Livingston, known simply as "The Woman from the City." Livingston vamps her way into The Man's heart and suggests he "accidently" drown his wife, sell the farm, and live comfortably the rest of their life in the fast track of the city. Emotions run deep as Murnau cuts back and forth through a series of tender, motherly shots of wife and child and the seduction scene between O'Brien and Livingston.

In order to make O'Brien slow and plodding throughout the film, Murnau had constructed special boots with lead weights for O'Brien to wear. The same technique would again be used for Boris Karloff's monster four years later in *Frankenstein* (1931). The six-foot actor towered over the diminutive Gaynor, making her look even more weak and himself even more hulking.

Twenty-seven year old O'Brien was a true athlete (he had been the Pacific Fleet Boxing Champ during WWI) and had begun acting in bit parts and stunt doubling five years earlier in Westerns with John Ford. He played leads into the Thirties, but eventually wound up in a slew of "B" movies. Enlisting again in the service during WWII, he returned to a Hollywood that had changed. He found a few small parts, thanks to his old friend John Ford, but retired from films in 1951. He made one final appearance in Ford's *Cheyenne Autumn* (1964) and a few television appearances before his death in 1985.

Twenty-one year old Janet Gaynor belonged to what was known as the "Irish Mafia" at Fox studios that consisted of John Ford, Charles Farrell and George O'Brien among others. Together, the group made a series of Irish-themed movies during the 1920s. In the first year of awarding Oscars (actually a banquet on May 16, 1929, at the Hollywood Roosevelt Hotel), Gaynor was picked as best actress for her work in *Sunrise* as well as *Seventh Heaven* (1926) and *Street Angel* (1928). The diminu-

George O'Brien relaxing on the set of *Sunrise* (1927) at Lake Arrowhead. (Note that the tower is in the background and that he is wearing only one of the leaded shoes).

George O'Brien and Janet Gaynor in a scene from *Sunrise* (1927)

tive actress did make the transition to talkies and her small voice is said to have matched her size. She effectively retired from the screen in 1938 and married the famous dress designer Adrian, the following year. She briefly flirted with television, but never truly made a comeback. Her death in 1984 was attributed to complications from a horrific taxi cab accident two years earlier in San Francisco. Mary Martin was also a passenger and sustained injuries along with her agent who died.

Margaret Livingston began her career at the age of sixteen in 1916 in a film shot on location in Havana, Cuba. Over the next decade she played a few leads, but was generally cast as the "other woman." The dark-haired beauty left the film industry in 1934 after making close to eighty films.

F. W. Murnau was born in Germany in 1888 and studied art and literature at the University of Heidelberg. He began as an assistant director in films in Germany in 1919 shortly after WWI, in which he flew as a combat pilot. His groundbreaking and still spine-chilling tale of Dracula, *Nosferatu* (1922), and the sweeping epic film *Faust* (1924) guaranteed his place among the all-time great directors. Even though *Sunrise* was critically acclaimed by some and badly panned by others, it was a commercial failure. Murnau continued to make films with William Fox, but never again with the freedom he had to make *Sunrise*. Ironically in 1931, he too died in a car accident near Santa Barbara, California.

Sunrise is credited with being the first talkie because of the sound of bells peeling, cars honking and a distinct voice yelling during a traffic jam on the sound track of the film. It was nominated in four categories by the Academy and won three Oscars: Best Actress, Janet Gaynor; Best Picture, Unique and Artistic Production; and Best Cinematography. Strangely, it did not win for one of its strongest points, Best Art Direction, nor was the man most responsible for its greatness, F. W. Murnau, even nominated.

F. W. Murnau (with megaphone) directs George O'Brien in a scene from Sunrise (1927) at Lake Arrowhead.

Elaborate European set built at Lake Arrowhead for the film Sunrise (1927)

All photos on p.111, 112, and 113 are courtesy of The Academy of Motion Picture Arts and Sciences

WHERE THE NORTH HOLDS SWAY (1927)

CAST:

Jack Perrin .... Rance Raine
Pauline Curley .... Gambler's wife
Lew Meehan .... Jules Landeau
Directed by .... Bennett Cohen
Produced by ... Rayart Picture Corp.

In the summer of 1927, director Bennett Cohen brought a small group of actors and cast up to the San Bernardino Mountains to film some quickie "oaters" for Rayart Picture Corporation. One of these, *Where the North Holds Sway*, miraculously survives to this day.

Northwest Mounted Policeman, Rance Raine (Jack Perrin) sets out to find who murdered his brother. Unbeknownst to Rance, the gambler, Jules Landeau (Lew Meehan) shot the brother because of the brother's interference into the gambler's treatment of his wife, played by Pauline Curley. Vowing revenge, Rance and his steadfast stead, "Starlight" (billed as The Wonder Horse), travel to the gambler's lair. After an accident, Rance finds himself under the care of the gambler's wife and the story switches to a cat and mouse game with the killer. Actually, Starlight is rather good, which can't be said about the rest of the cast, except for poor Pauline Curley who had to put up with a lot of phony fisticuffs.

Thirty-one year old Jack Perrin had been in the movie business since the mid 1910s when he worked with Mack Sennett and the Keystone Kops, although uncredited. One biographer stated that he was in the U.S. Navy during WWI, however, it must have been a short enlistment as his film credits give him little time to have served. By the time Perrin filmed *Where the North Holds Sway*, he had already appeared in more than eighty films and was a recognized cowboy star. His career spanned the next three decades, usually in Westerns, and he is one of the very few silent cowboys to have made the transition to talkies. Perrin's last role was in 1960, seven years before his death.

Jack Perrin and Billy Lamoreaux in a scene from *Where the North Holds Sway* (1927)

Considered a real beauty, Pauline Curley had been acting since she was a child. She appeared on Broadway and played opposite some of the biggest names in Hollywood: Douglas Fairbanks, Harold Lockwood, and John Gilbert. During the early 1920s, she was the cliff-hanging heroine in dozens of Vitagraph serials. By the late Twenties, near the end of her career, she was being cast in mediocre Westerns and seeing the handwriting on the wall, retired in 1929. She was twenty-six years old and had been in more than forty films. Her marriage to cinematographer Kenneth Peach kept her close to the industry, but she never returned to the movies. She died in 2000 at the age of ninety-seven.

One must feel sorry for Lew Meehan. In more films than he cared to recall, his name in the credits listed him as "henchman." The thirty-seven year old character actor had the permanent looks of a bad guy. Short, stocky and with a swarthy face, Meehan played the heavy from day one in the business. However, his looks bode well for the next twenty years and he acted in more than one hundred and sixty films before his death at the age of sixty-one in 1951.

Pauline Curley
circa 1927
Photo courtesy of John Drennon

Jack Perrin, Billy Lamoreaux, and Pauline Curley as they appeared together in *Thunderbolt's Tracks* (1927)
Photo courtesy of John Drennon

HAWK OF THE HILLS (1929)

CAST:

Allene Ray .... Mary Selby
Walter Miller .... Laramie
Frank Lackteen .... The Hawk
Directed by .... Spencer Gordon
Bennet
Produced by .... Pathé Exchange

Frank Lackteen
circa 1930s
Photo courtesy of Les Adams

During the Twenties and Thirties, producers needed gimmicks to get their audiences back to theaters each week. One of the best ways they found was the fast paced cliff-hanging serial and the "King of the Serials" had to be producer/director Spencer Gordon Bennet. In 1927, he directed the very successful ten-episode thriller, *Hawk of the Hills* for Pathé. Two years later he re-cut it and possibly added some scenes of the San Bernardino Mountains to produce a five reel mishmash. The big question is why? The story is evidently the same, but we will never know because the movie survived and the serial did not. Serials continued until the Forties, at which time audiences became more sophisticated and demanding. Still the serial didn't die out, producers just called it by another name—the sequel.

The Hawk (Frank Lackteen) is the leader of a renegade band of outlaws, thieves and Indians. They attack prospectors, young maidens in distress, entire towns and the 5th Calvary in this chaotic film. Walter Miller plays the dual role of Laramie, a man on the run from the law, and Captain Bradley Fiske, a member of the 5th Calvary on special duty. When Mary Selby (Allene Ray) is kidnaped by the Hawk's henchmen, it is Laramie who comes to her rescue—not once, but twice. There is also an episode between "good" Indians and "bad" Indians, which depended upon what tribe they belong to.

If Spencer Bennet was King of the Serials, then Allene Ray had to be the Queen. From her earliest film, the radiant beauty was a star. In 1924, she began a collaboration with Bennet and they made thirteen films together. Of her twenty-eight films made before 1931, when she retired, almost half of them were thrilling nail-biting serials. Ray made the transition to talkies, but evidently not well as she only did three before leaving pictures in 1931 at the age of thirty. She did attempt a comeback in 1949 in a low-budget Western called *Gun Cargo* and then quietly left the industry for good.

One of the great character actors of his day was Lebanese-born Frank Lackteen. The thirty-five year old's shifty-eyed looks and high cheek bones made him the ideal nemesis of every white-hatted hero the screen had to offer. Very few actors possessed the ability to look exotic, but Frank Lackteen was just as able to play an American Indian as a Mongolian camel driver or for that matter, a French gendarme. When the talkies arrived, his accent lent itself to an indeterminate foreign land. His five-decade career earned him credits in more than one hundred and sixty films, many of which were the white-knuckle serials of Spencer Bennet.

Walter Miller began acting in pictures with the Biograph Company and D.W. Griffith in 1911 at the age of nineteen. Later, as part of the Bennet crew, handsome and tall, Miller got to wear the white hat in most of his early movies. When talkies arrived, he was able to make the transition and continued making films up to his death in 1940 at the age of forty-eight. By that time he had amassed a film resumé of close to two hundred films.

Allene Ray
circa 1927

Walter Miller as he
appeared in
Hawk of the Hills (1927)

O'MALLEY RIDES ALONE (1930)

CAST:
Bob Custer .... Sergeant O'Malley
Phyllis Bainbridge .... Joyce McGregor
Bud Osborne .... Bull Sampson
Martin Cichy .... Sled Sassoon
Directed by .... J. P. McGowan
Produced by .... Syndicate Pictures

Sgt. O'Malley (Bob Custer) is sent to join Trooper Dan Calhoun (Perry Murdock) to investigate a series of robberies involving miners. At the same time, Sled Sassoon (Martin Cichy) delivers a letter to Joyce McGregor stating that her father has struck it rich and is taking the notorious "inland route." When Joyce spurns Sled's suggestion of marriage, he plots to rob the father of his gold. The two Mounties arrive just as the attack occurs and although wounded, McGregor is rescued and secreted away by O'Malley. Sgt. O'Malley instructs Trooper Dan to proceed into town, as he intends to "ride alone" in order to switch identities and become one of the bad guys and infiltrate the gang.

Director J.P. McGowan picked Lake Arrowhead to film a good portion of the movie, and it may have been serialized from the look of it. The photography is actually very good, but the story is pure melodrama and was shot as a silent.

Great changes were coming to the country after the Wall Street crash in October 1929 and even more so in the motion picture industry that depended upon front money to make movies. After working for Film Booking Office, a prolific production and distribution company run by Joseph P. Kennedy (JFK's father) in the 1920s,

Bob Custer (on left) as he appeared in
Riders of the North (1931)
Photo courtesy of Les Adams

Bob Custer ended up filming with "poverty row" producers in 1930 (see p. 120). His earlier work in silent films was considered very good, but he never received the recognition that other cowboy stars did. Born at the turn of the century in Kentucky, he graduated with an engineering degree and eventually ended up working in Hollywood under his real name, Raymond Glenn. Unfortunately when talkies arrived, Custer, who was by then considered a second rate actor, didn't have many roles come his way. He retired in 1937 and became a building inspector with various city governments around Southern California.

Perky and winsome, blonde Phyllis Bainbridge made two films only, *Covered Wagon Trails* and *O'Malley,* both with Bob Custer and Martin Cichy, as well as J.P. McGowan and Perry Murdock. Mysteriously she disappeared totally from the industry in 1931. The two films came out within a month of each other and must have been shot at the same time, because she makes the mistake in *O'Malley* of calling Sled, "Brag," a character in *Covered Wagon Trails*.

Martin Cichy and Phyllis Bainbridge in a scene from *O'Malley Rides Alone* (1930)

Thirty-eight year old Martin Cichy was the consummate villain. With a swarthy look and piercing eyes, the six foot pock-marked Cichy was a match for any hero. It is amazing that producers didn't use him more often, as he only made nineteen films in a span of twenty-five years.

Australian-born J. P. McGowan could almost be called the "king of workaholics." Known for his low-budget thrillers, McGowan began acting in films in 1910 at the age of thirty. His directorial debut in films was three years later. When he wasn't acting, directing or producing films, he was either editing them or writing them. In his forty plus years in the industry, he acted in one hundred and thirty-one films; directed another one hundred forty-five; and produced ten. His last writing assignment was for *Show Boat* in 1951, a year before he died.

One of the bad guys in this film was Bud Osborne who had one of the most enduring careers in Hollywood. Osborne was known as a real horseman or teamster, who could handle large numbers of horses in stagecoach scenes. He is often seen as the grizzled, weather-beaten old timer in countless Westerns. From 1912 until 1966, Osborne has an astounding number of screen and television credits — five hundred and thirty.

J. P. McGowan
circa 1930s
Photo courtesy of Les Adams

THE MYSTERY TROOPER (1931)

CAST:
Robert Frazer .... Jack Logan
Blanche Mehaffey .... Helen Holt
Directed by .... Stuart Paton
and Harry S. Webb
Produced by .... Guaranteed Pictures

At the beginning of the 1930s depression, audiences were looking for escape and a slew of motion picture companies sprang up in Hollywood along a couple of streets known as "poverty row." Sometimes they only made one film and then faded into history. Such was the case of Guaranteed Pictures who produced *Mystery Trooper* in 1931. Other than this film having some great outdoor scenery in the San Bernardino Mountains, there is not much to recommend it today. But audiences in the Thirties loved serials and this edge-of-your-seat, ten chapter film was a real hoot. Stuart Paton directed the cast and crew in the serial about a hunt for a lost gold mine.

Scottish-born Stuart Paton started as an actor in 1914, but quickly found working behind a camera was more satisfying than posing in front of it. From 1915 until he retired in 1937, he directed more than fifty films. In 1916, he co-produced, directed, and wrote the screenplay to Jules Verne's *20,000 Leagues Under the Sea*, a film that critics loved and still survives to this day. The film was a tremendous success and assured Paton's future as a director. After working at Universal in serials, his career waned and he became an independent director working for whichever studio needed him. After directing his last picture in 1937, Paton returned to Europe and was stranded there during WWII. He died in Monte Carlo in 1944 at the age of sixty-one.

Forty year old Robert Frazer was the handsome leading man in many a silent film. His career started with Universal Pictures in 1912 on the East coast and he came west three years later to act in a string of sentimental love stories. When the talkies arrived, his voice

Robert Frazer in a scene from
The Mystery Trooper aka
Trail of the Royal Mounted (1931)

was good enough to keep him working, but by that time his age was a factor. Frazer found himself, more and more, being cast as a "general purpose" actor and even the bad guy. Now comes the crazy part. He is supposed to have died in Los Angeles in 1944, yet his film credits continue for five more years. The credits again resurface in a TV movie in 1966 and again in another 1990 TV movie, which would make him ninety-nine years old! Still, considering just his films through 1944, he would have had a remarkable career of one hundred and eighty plus films.

Like all true stars, Blanche Mehaffey fudged on her age. Various biographies list her birth year as either 1906 or 1907 or 1908 — take your pick. Nevertheless, she was considered to be a really stunning beauty and was a WAMPAS Baby Star in the year 1924, the same year Clara Bow made the list.* Mehaffey was a former Ziegfeld Follies dancer, and she began her movie career with Hal Roach in a string of comedies in 1924. Two years later, she was cast in a series of Westerns, which seemed to be her lot from that point forward. Her off-screen romances kept the gossip columnists busy at their typewriters. Her whirlwind courtship by big-game hunter George Joseph Hansen and subsequent ten-week marriage/divorce was juicy news in 1928. In 1934, she changed her stage name to Janet Morgan and finally retired in 1938 after making almost forty films. Her comeback in 1946 in a film called *Devil Monster* (called by some the worst movie ever made) was a disaster and she was never seen on the screen again.

Blanche Mehaffey
circa 1930

*A WAMPAS Baby Star was the title the Western Association of Motion Picture Advertisers gave thirteen Hollywood actresses they considered as most likely to succeed, from 1922 through 1934. WAMPAS awards were extremely popular. The interest they generated was equal to that which the Oscar would later achieve.

McKENNA OF THE MOUNTED (1932)

Greta Granstedt
circa 1930s
Photo courtesy of
Jason Fabbri

What do you do with one of your most popular cowboy stars when you run out of ideas for a Western story? You dress him up in a Royal Canadian Mounted Police uniform, put him back on his horse and recycle old stories. That's exactly what Columbia Pictures did with forty-three year old Buck Jones in *McKenna of the Mounted*. Jones was one of the most recognizable cowboy stars of the Twenties and Thirties and as popular as Tom Mix or Hoot Gibson. The six foot actor has been described as: "Ruggedly handsome, solidly built, a man's man in every way, with an unswerving embodiment of fair play." This made him the idol of just about every boy in the country. At one time in the 1930s, he received more fan mail than any other actor.

Although born in Indiana, Jones grew up on a ranch in what was then called Indian Territory (Oklahoma). He enlisted in the U.S. Army and saw action along the U.S.-Mexican border and again in the Philippines during the Moro uprisings in the early years of the Twentieth Century. He joined the Miller Brothers 101 Ranch Wild West Show, moved onto Ringling Brothers Circus and eventually came to California. He began his film career with bit parts in westerns and was put under contract by William Fox in the mid-Twenties. Born Charles Frederick Gebhart, he began to go by Charles Jones, then Charles Buck Jones, and finally, just plain Buck Jones.

When WWII broke out, Jones enlisted once more, but the Army saw more of an advantage in using him to raise money in their bond-selling drives. In November 1942, Jones was asked to go to Boston where he was the guest of the local citizens at the famous Cocoanut Grove nightclub. With almost a thousand guests in attendance, many of whom were in uniform and due to be sent overseas shortly, a fire broke out and spread quickly amid the colorful crepe decorations. There were two revolving doors in front and a couple of other "fire exits." It has been called one of the worst fire disasters in history. Almost five hundred people died that evening, including Buck Jones. His wife of twenty-seven years, Odelle, whom he had met during his circus days, was not at his side. One of the most beloved cowboys had been in more than one hundred and fifty films when he died at the age of fifty-three.

Strikingly beautiful, Swedish-born Greta Granstedt was twenty-five when she filmed *McKenna* and had been in the business for only four years, but had already been in twenty films. Her career began with nondescript secondary roles and she only starred in a couple of films before again falling back into the same type of minor parts for the rest of her career. During the height of the depression she was able to find work, usually with the "poverty row" producers. By 1940, she was lucky to get walk-on parts. (She is described as just "a Babe" in the Hope/Crosby classic *Road to Singapore*.) Granstedt entered television early, but her career ended in 1958 after some seventy film and TV credits. She did have a strange hobby — collecting husbands, she had seven, some of whom forgot to get divorced before marrying her. Her one comeback film in 1970 finished her career and she died at the age of eighty in 1987.

Buck Jones (leaning over) in a scene from
McKenna of the Mounted (1932)
Photo courtesy of The Academy of Motion
Picture Arts and Sciences

THE DRIFTER (1932)

CAST:

William Farnum .... The Drifter
Noah Beery .... John McNary
Phyllis Barrington ... Ronnie McNary
Directed by ..... William A. O'Connor
Produced by .... Willis Kent Prod.

Charles Sellon and William Farnum smile at Ann Brody in a scene from *The Drifter* (1932).
Photo courtesy of
The Academy of Motion
Picture Arts and Sciences

The Drifter (William Farnum), a carefree French-Canadian wanderer, searches for his little brother who ran away at an early age. His reputation as a fighter is tempered by his philosophical espousals. When two competing lumber companies get into a war, the Drifter intervenes by stopping the hired gun, Montana (Russell Hopton), and later killing him in self-defense. Paul La Tour (Bruce Warren), the superintendent of the Northern Lumber Company, is sweet on Ronnie McNary (Phyllis Barrington), the daughter of the rival lumber company's owner. When John McNary (Noah Beery) is killed, Paul is accused of the murder but saved by the Drifter, who finds out that his ex-partner is the real culprit. The Drifter then learns that Paul is really his long lost brother.

Beautiful blonde Phyllis Barrington, a twenty-something actress, had been a dancer from childhood. When she won a local beauty contest, she was awarded a screen contract with "poverty row" producer Willis Kent. Kent produced *The Drifter*, along with eight of her eleven films made between 1930 and 1933, that showcased her special talents. Kent was known for his racy titles that somehow eluded the censors. Nothing is known of Barrington after 1933. Amazingly, three of her films survive to this day.

Willis Kent was famous for hiring silent screen actors who were well past their prime. William Farnum was fifty-six when he made

The Drifter, and had been on the stage since he was ten years old. He was once one of the highest paid stars in Hollywood, earning $10,000 per week at Fox Studios. In his four decade career, Farnum is credited with almost one hundred screen appearances. He was so beloved in the industry, that at his funeral in 1953, his pallbearers included C.B. DeMille, Jesse Lasky, and Clarence Brown. His eulogy was read by Pat O'Brien.

Another actor who had seen better days was fifty year old co-star Noah Beery. At six foot one inch, Beery was still a striking character with a strong speaking voice. Noah was the older brother of the more famous Wallace Beery, and the father of Noah Beery, Jr., an equally competent character actor in later years. Noah, Sr. carved out a niche for himself over the next decade playing the "heavy." He died in 1946 at the age of sixty-four.

The most interesting role in the film is played by thirty-five year old Russel Hopton (Montana—the gunfighter). One cannot but be surprised to note the similarities between his walk and talk with that of the great John Wayne. One has to ask: Who copied who? Hopton's career spanned twenty years from 1926 to 1945, when he committed suicide (Wayne's career began in 1926 as well). Curiously, Wayne and Hopton did appear together in two films, *Idol of the Clouds* (1937) and *Tall in the Saddle* (1944).

Although not credited, it is possible that Margaret Hamilton (the wicked witch in *The Wizard of Oz*-1939) is the shrewish townswoman who throws sticks at the Drifter in one scene.

Noah Beery
circa 1930s

William Farnum, Phyllis Barrington and Noah Beery (Charles Sellon in rear) in a snow scene from *The Drifter* (1932)

TO THE LAST MAN (1933)

CAST:
Randolph Scott .... Lynn Hayden
Esther Ralston .... Ellen Colby
Jack La Rue .... Jim Daggs
Shirley Temple .... Mary Stanley
Directed by .... Henry Hathaway
Produced by ..... Paramount Pictures

Jack La Rue in a scene from *The Last Man*
filmed at Cedar Lake
Photo courtesy of
The Academy of Motion Picture
Arts and Sciences

To the Last Man is Zane Grey's classic Romeo and Juliet tale of a bitter feud between two unforgiving factions, the ranchers on the one side, and a band of cattle rustlers on the other. In the grip of a relentless code of loyalty to their own people, they fight the war of the Tonto Basin, desperately, doggedly, to the last man, neither side seeing the futility of it until it is too late. In this volatile environment, young rancher Lynn Hayden (Randolph Scott) finds himself hopelessly in love with Ellen Colby (Esther Ralston) the daughter of the rustler leader. Thrown into this cast of colorful characters is the oily henchman Jim Daggs (Jack La Rue — later known as Lash La Rue), who has designs on young Ellen and double crosses his boss to marry her. Paramount Pictures had filmed the same story at the Grand Canyon in Arizona, as a silent in 1923 with Richard Dix and Lois Wilson in the leading roles. In the 1923 cast was Noah Beery, who again appears, but this time as the head of the rustlers in the 1933 version. In addition, John Carradine, Barton MacLane, Buster Crabbe, Fuzzy Knight and a very young Shirley Temple also appear in this better than average "oater." The 1923 version probably came closer to the book, at least they used the same names as Grey. The 1933 version, which was filmed at Big Bear Lake and Cedar Lake, has the annoying habit of continually introducing actors as the film progresses, instead of at the beginning of the film.

Randolph Scott started as an extra in films in 1928 at the age of thirty. By 1933, the handsome, lanky actor was one of the hottest stars on the Paramount lot. His charming ways would play equally well in either dramas or comedies during the Thirties and Forties, but his real success did not come until he starred as the stoic loner in many later Westerns. The six foot four inch Scott was not born to the saddle, but he made the most of it by the end of his career. By shrewdly investing in real estate, it was estimated that Scott was a multimillionaire by the time he retired in 1962 with more than one hundred film credits.

Thirty-one year old Esther Ralston was born into a stage family and had been acting since the age of two. Her screen debut was in 1915 at the age of thirteen. By the time she made *To the Last Man*, she was already known as the "American Venus," after the successful 1926 picture by the same name. Alternating between blonde and brunette, she too was considered to be equally good in either dramas or comedies, but preferred the latter. Unlike Scott, she did not do well with money and lost most of her picture fortune to unwise business ventures. She left the screen in 1941 after some ninety pictures, briefly came back in 1946 and made some television appearances in the 1960s before finally calling it quits. She died in 1994 at the age of ninety-two.

Sometimes billed as her debut film, *To the Last Man* was actually Shirley Temple's fourteenth film, although she was only five years old. In the film she is seen being carried around and has her doll's head shot off. By 1933, the studios were beginning to recognize Temple's abilities to attract audiences' attention. Paramount featured her the next year in *Now and Forever*, another film made in the San Bernardino Mountains.

Esther Ralston
circa 1930s

By 1936, Shirley Temple was a depression era phenomena and mothers all over the country dressed their little girls up to look like her. She was the most recognizable star in the late Thirties and the most popular box office star, beating out the likes of Clark Gable, Bing Crosby, Robert Taylor and Joan Crawford. She loved the mountains and returned to make *Heidi* (1937) and *The Blue Bird* (1940), as well as making a guest appearance in a mountain community parade.

Randolph Scott as he appeared in1933

TRAILING NORTH (1933)

Born at the beginning of the Depression, Monogram Pictures was known for their "quick and dirty" films, meaning low-budget thrillers. In 1935, Monogram and a couple of other studios merged to form Republic Pictures, famous for their Westerns. *Trailing North* is just another Western dressed in the guise of the Royal Canadian Mounted Police.

When Ranger Jim Burns (Fred Burns) is shot, his dying words to his partner, Lee Evans (Bob Steele) are: "look for a girl named Mitzi." Mitzi (Doris Hill) is a saloon singer who has hooked up with a bad element in the form of Lucky the gambler, who is headed north by dog sled. Ranger Evans disguises himself as Curly the Kid and pursues the killer into the snows of the Northwest Territories, only to be unmasked by dapper Flash Ryan (George Hayes), a henchman of Lucky's gang. Things turn nasty, but Evans' fast fists win the day and the girl.

Twenty-six year old Bob Steele was the son of writer/director Robert North Bradbury (*Last of His People*–1919). He and his twin brother Bill had been acting in one form or another since the age of three. His screen career began with a series of shorts (*The Adventures of Bob & Bill*) that his father wrote, directed and produced in their hometown of Glendale, California, in 1920. By 1927, Bob Bradbury, Jr. had changed his name to Bob Steele and began a career as a leading cowboy hero. Although he gained a certain audience, especially among his peers, Steele was never ranked with the great cowboys of the era. In later years, Steele contented himself with character roles, usually playing the

CAST:	
Bob Steele	Lee Evans (Curly)
Doris Hill	Mitzi
George Hayes	Flash Ryan
Directed by	John P. McCarthy
Produced by	Monogram Pictures

Bob Steele
circa 1930s

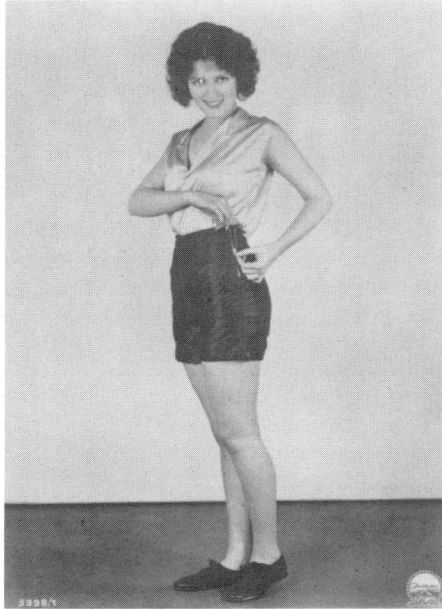

Doris Hill
circa 1930s

George "Gabby" Hayes
circa 1940s

heavy. When television arrived, he made the transition and for the first time played comedy in the TV series *F Troop*. His career spanned fifty plus years with over two hundred screen and televison credits.

Doris Hill began acting in movies in 1926 at the age of twenty-one. Within three years, she had attained enough fame and roles to be named a WAMPAS Baby Star of 1929. Unfortunately, she was saddled with a contract with a studio known for its low-cost Westerns and melodramas and her career never flourished as she had hoped. Her first talkie was the disastrous *His Glorious Night* (1929) with John Gilbert. In the film his declarations of love to her were met with howls of laughter because of his high-pitched voice. Gilbert defended himself later by saying the studios deliberately altered the sound tracks to make his voice appear higher than normal. Nevertheless, Hill's career suffered and she was doomed to continue in minor roles and pictures for the next several years. She retired in 1934 after thirty-five films.

One of the most beloved character actors of all time was George Hayes, better known as "Gabby." A former burlesque, vaudeville and stock player, Hayes began his movie career in the 1920s playing clean-shaven roles, but then retired in his forties. The stock market crash of 1929 is said to have wiped him out and he was forced to begin acting in films once more. Hayes found a niche as the lovable sidekick to many of the famous cowboy stars of the Thirties and Forties, including Hopalong Cassidy and Roy Rogers. Consistently ranked in the top ten as a box office favorite with audiences in the Forties, Hayes found fewer and fewer roles by the time television arrived in the Fifties. He made the transition to TV, but retired after he hosted *The Gabby Hayes Show* for six seasons. In 1999, Hayes attained a bit of fame when he was named by the American Film Institute as one of a very select few cowboys included in the 100 Greatest Screen Legends, along with Roy Rogers, William Boyd, and Gene Autry.

HER SPLENDID FOLLY
(1933)

It is not often that this author is thrilled to see some of these "not so" magnificent mountain movies, but *Her Splendid Folly* is a big exception. This is the earliest film I have found that was shot in the original Lake Arrowhead Village, along with footage of autos making the climb up Highway 18 from San Bernardino.

At the height of the depression, Jill McAllister (Lilian Bond) and her mother (Beryl Mercer) face eviction until Jill finds a job with International Studios as a double for snooty star Laura Gerard (also Lilian Bond). When Laura is injured in an auto accident before a big film's production, Jill is asked to impersonate Laura. Reluctantly she does and falls in love with the leading man Wallace Morley (Theodore von Eltz). Meanwhile, Laura's unknown husband surfaces and accuses Jill, who is on her honeymoon at Lake Arrowhead, of bigamy. Jill's mother comes to the rescue by tearing Jill's dress to reveal an old scar on her back, thus proving she is not Laura but Jill.

English-born Lilian Bond was a favorite of the independent and major studios during the 1930s, because of her good looks (she had won a beauty contest in England in 1926) and refined British accent. She began acting in films at the age of twenty-one, just as they were transiting into the sound era in 1929. In 1932, she was named a WAMPAS Baby Star, but the honor did little to secure the big roles that never seemed to come her way. After 1935 the roles dried up and she worked sporadically over the next twenty years, averaging a film per year. Her most memorable role was that of Lily Langtry, the object of Judge Roy Bean's affection in

CAST:	
Lilian Bond	Jill McAllister
Beryl Mercer	Jill's Mother
Theodore von Eltz	Wallace Morley
Directed by	Willam A. O'Connor
Produced by ...	Progressive Pictures

Lilian Bond
circa 1933

the Gary Cooper classic *The Westerner* (1940). Bond died at the age of eighty-three in 1991.

Because of his deep, rich baritone voice and stage acting experience, Theodore von Eltz was able to make the transition in the 1930s from clean-shaven leading silent man to mustachioed supporting character actor, usually playing the suave society patron. Besides his onscreen movie experience, he also narrated films and had an extensive radio career. The son of a Yale language professor, von Eltz began acting in films in 1915. Over the next forty years he amassed more than one hundred and eighty movie credits, culminating with his oily depiction of a smut peddler in Humphrey Bogart's *The Big Sleep* (1946).

Beryl Mercer, who plays the long-suffering mother was born in Spain to British parents in 1862. Much too short to ever be considered for leading roles, she contented herself with playing the fragile matronly roles that were her staple over four decades of film making. From the grieving mother in *All's Quiet on the Western Front* (1930) to the feisty portrayal of Queen Victoria in *The Little Princess* (1939), Mercer was considered one of the true professionals of the screen. She continued to work in films until the day she died at the age of seventy-seven in 1939.

Theodore von Eltz
circa 1933

THE RICHEST GIRL IN THE WORLD (1934)

By the height of the 1930s depression, audiences weren't interested in films about their humdrum lives, they longed to know more about how the wealthy were surviving. Norman Krasna's romantic screenplay, *The Richest Girl in the World*, was exactly the escapist movie fans were looking for. Krasna probably got his idea from the real life tragedy of Barbara Hutton, dubbed "Poor Little Rich Girl," who had inherited fifty million dollars in 1933.

Supposedly "Richest Girl" Dorothy Hunter (how close can a name get?), played by Miriam Hopkins, is sure she can never find a man who wants her for herself and not her money. She persuades her friend and secretary Sylvia (Fay Wray) to front for her, since no one, not even the press, knows what she looks like. Inevitably, Dorothy falls for a penniless but promising Tony Travers (Joel McCrea). Through a series of adventures, Dorothy tests whether his love is true or if he is like all the other gold diggers after her money. In the end he proves his merit by marrying her, still thinking she is the poor secretary to the world's richest girl.

The screenplay was hot property in 1934 and there was spirited bidding for the rights to it. RKO Radio Pictures finally outbid M-G-M and paid Krasna $4,000 for the play. Originally, Ann Hardin was to play Dorothy, but RKO finally had to "borrow" Hopkins from Paramount Studios, where she was under contract, and Fay Wray from Twentieth Century. The screenplay was nominated for an Academy Award in the category of best original screenplay, but lost to *Manhattan Melodrama*.

Because this film is seldom screened today, this author was fortunate to have viewed an archival copy

CAST:
Miriam Hopkins .... Dorothy Hunter
Joel McCrea .... Tony Travers
Fay Wray .... Sylvia Lockwood
Directed by .... William A. Seiter
Produced by ..... RKO Radio Pictures

Lobby card from
The Richest Girl in the World (1934)

at the UCLA Film Archives and found that the story has stood the test of time. It is as fresh today as it was in 1934. The scenes on Lake Arrowhead are breathtaking and the acting first class.

Miriam Hopkins was born in Georgia to wealth and privilege. She attended the best schools before settling on a career in the theater. In 1930, the twenty-eight year old actress was brought to Hollywood because it was thought that stage actors were better suited to the new age of the talkies. After a poor start, Hopkins then began a string of successful films that lasted out the decade. She and McCrea starred together in another four films during the mid-1930s, including *Splendor* (1935), which was also filmed in the San Bernardino Mountains. Hopkins was a big star, but never a super star, and the roles dried up for her in the 1940s. She made thirty-five films in the span of thirty-eight years. Ironically, her last film called *The Comeback* (1969) was never released.

Twenty-nine year old Joel McCrea stood a foot taller than the five foot two Hopkins, so their kissing scenes sometimes look a bit awkward. Born in Southern California, he had been exposed to the film world for all of his younger years. McCrea attended the famous Pasadena Playhouse and began with some stunt work in films after graduating from USC. His down-home, boyish looks went well with the product Hollywood had to offer in the late Twenties and early Thirties. He had hoped for a career in Westerns, but the studios liked him better in romantic comedies. He finally got his chance in Westerns with the lead in *Wells Fargo* (1937). Over the next four decades, McCrea became the epitome of the stoic cowboy hero. He died in 1990 at the age of eighty-five.

Although born in Canada, Fay Wray had been brought up in Southern California and

Miriam Hopkins
circa 1933

entered the film industry at the age of sixteen in 1923. By the time she made *The Richest Girl in the World*, Wray had more than fifty screen credits, many of them two reel "oaters" like *Lazy Lightning* (1927), also filmed at Lake Arrowhead. Instantly recognizable due to her role a year earlier in *King Kong*, Wray was at the top of fan popularity charts. Over the next twenty plus years, she continued in character roles in more than forty films and made regular television appearances.

Joel McCrea and Fay Wray in a scene from
The Richest Girl in the World filmed at
Lake Arrowhead.
Photo courtesy of
The Academy of Motion Picture
Arts and Sciences

FORSAKING ALL OTHERS
(1934)

CAST:

Joan Crawford .... Mary Clay
Robert Montgomery ..... Dylan Todd
Clark Gable .... Jeff Williams
Directed by .... W. S. Van Dyke
Produced by .... M-G-M Pictures

Robert Montgomery
circa 1934

Dylan Todd (Robert Montgomery), Jeff Williams (Clark Gable) and Mary Clay (Joan Crawford) have been friends since childhood. Upon returning from Spain, Jeff finds that Dylan and Mary are engaged, much to Jeff's disappointment. Playboy Dylan gets drunk the night before the wedding and elopes with his old girlfriend, Connie. Jilted, Mary tries unsuccessfully to forget her love and is tempted when Dylan steps back into her life, although he is still married to Connie. Dylan and Mary find themselves alone together in a mountain cabin owned by her Aunt Paula (Billie Burke). Faced with scandal, Jeff covers for Mary when Dylan's wife, Connie, reappears. Later Mary realizes it is really Jeff she loves and she races to catch him as he returns to Spain.

In 1934, the lot of M-G-M looked like the who's who of Hollywood. Three of their biggest stars were in this romantic comedy that was adapted from a successful Broadway play and it paid off for M-G-M in big box office receipts despite the depression era. Gable had filmed *It Happened One Night* earlier in the year and audiences were clamoring for more of him. Crawford was at the top of the fan charts as was Montgomery. The only objection to the film was the hated Hays Office which told M-G-M to tone down the innuendoes or else. Words such as "tramp," "sex appeal," and "nudist wedding" were considered objectionable and subsequently dropped from the dialogue.

Robert Montgomery was born into wealth and position. When his father died and the family fortune lost, Montgomery found himself drawn to the stage. Tall (six foot one inch) and handsome, Montgomery took to Hollywood where he began playing the young upper-class sophisticate in a string of romantic comedies. When WWII began, he enlisted in the Navy and saw action in both the Atlantic and Pacific theaters of war. His Navy experiences bode well for his directorial debut in the John Wayne classic, *They Were Expendable* (1945). Finding himself behind the camera more to his liking, Montgomery accepted fewer acting assignments and when television arrived, he began directing and producing his popular *Robert Montgomery Presents* series starting in 1950, where his daughter, Elizabeth Montgomery got her start.

The son of a wildcat oil driller, Clark Gable quit school and worked in a tire factory. After seeing a play, he became interested in acting and went to Broadway where he attracted the attention of audiences and producers. Hollywood moguls were reluctant to hire the tall, gangly youth with big ears. Finally hired by M-G-M, he distinguished himself in a series of confrontational films, usually playing the heavy. As punishment for turning down a role, M-G-M loaned him out to Columbia Pictures for the romantic comedy, *It Happened One Night.* This earned Gable his first Oscar and assured his future career. In 1935, he was again nominated for an acting Oscar (*Mutiny on the Bounty*), but lost out to Victor McLaglen. When the part of Rhett Butler was offered to him, Gable was reluctant to accept until convinced to do so by then third wife, Carole Lombard. This earned Gable his third and final Oscar nomination, but once again he lost, this time

Clark Gable and Joan Crawford in a scene from *Forsaking All Others* (1934)

to Robert Donat. When his wife, Carole Lombard, was killed during a war bond junket, Gable entered the service in the U.S. Army Air Force and flew dozens of missions over Nazi Germany. Hitler had a price on Gable's head and his orders were to have him captured alive. Gable died in 1960 at the age of fifty-nine, several months before the birth of his only son by then fifth wife, Kay Spreckles.

Twenty-nine year old Joan Crawford was already a consummate M-G-M veteran of both silent and talking pictures, with more than fifty roles to her credit by the time she made *Forsaking All Others*. She got her start as a dancer and began her Hollywood career in the mid-Twenties. Although she was considered a super star during the Thirties, she was never nominated for an Oscar until she had left M-G-M and was considered to be "washed-up." In 1945, she was nominated for *Mildred Pierce* and won the Oscar for her portrayal of a rags-to-riches woman, a part she had perfected in her earlier years. Off screen, her marriages were the fodder that kept the gossip tongues wagging. It wasn't until her adopted daughter's autobiography, *Mommy Dearest* was published, that her true nature was revealed. Crawford's later screen appearances were probably the best of her career. She retired in 1970, after making *Trog*, a film she considered dreadful and should never have been made.

Robert Montgomery and Joan Crawford in a scene from *Forsaking All Others* (1934)
Photo courtesy of
The Academy of Motion Picture
Arts and Sciences

NOW AND FOREVER
(1934)

Adapted from the Jack Kirkland story, *Honor Bright*, director Henry Hathaway captivated audiences with the romantic drama that brought three of the top stars of Paramount together in *Now and Forever*. Con artist, Jerry Day (Gary Cooper) and his grifter girlfriend, Toni Carstairs (Carole Lombard), are stranded in a Chinese hotel until he devises a scheme to get their back room rent paid by posing as the hotel auditor and bilking unwary residents. Thus freed, he returns to the U.S. to be reunited with his daughter, Penny (Shirley Temple), whom he has never seen. His late wife's brother, who has been taking care of Penny, seeks custody and offers to pay Jerry $75,000. However Jerry, like the audiences of the day, is so taken by the cute little dimples and golden ringlets, that he succumbs to her charms and takes her with him bent on a life of crime. When he tries to go legit for the sake of his daughter, he finds himself making the wrong decisions and is once again seduced into the life of a thief. In the end he has to make a decision that separates him from his daughter and has audiences both cheering and weeping.

Originally, the script called for both Cooper and Lombard to die in a fiery crash over a cliff, but Paramount nixed the idea and gave it a softer ending. Temple's play acting with Cooper on a pirate island was filmed on Lone Pine Island in Lake Arrowhead. All three actors would make more sojourns to the San Bernardino Mountains, both professionally and as welcomed visitors.

Thirty-three year old Cooper was raised on a ranch in Montana and

CAST:	
Gary Cooper	Jerry Day
Carole Lombard	Toni Carstairs
Shirley Temple	Penny Day
Directed by	Henry Hathaway
Produced by	Paramount Pictures

Carole Lombard
circa 1934

Studio publicity shot for
Now and Forever (1934)

was a natural for stunt work in Hollywood during the Twenties. Producers quickly noted the shy gangling, six foot three youth with the boyish looks and began to cast him in bigger and better roles. His real break came with a role in *Wings* (1927) and from then on audiences demanded more of him. One of the true Hollywood legends, Cooper was nominated for Best Actor five times by the Academy and won an Oscar twice for his performances in *Sergeant York* (1941) and *High Noon* (1950). He also won an Honorary Oscar for a lifetime of memorable films in 1961, the year he died of lung cancer at the age of sixty.

Twenty-six year old Carole Lombard began in silent pictures as Jane Peters, her real name, in 1921 at the age of twelve. In 1926, she was badly scarred in an automobile accident that cost her a contract with Fox Studios. In many of her earlier films she was cast as the other woman until she was co-starred with William Powell, later to be her husband, in *Man of the World* (1931). By 1934, Lombard was on top of the fan charts and playing the young sophisticated but sometimes scatterbrained blonde in romantic comedies, a role she perfected during the Thirties. In 1941, she completed another one of her signature comedies with Jack Benny, *To Be or Not To Be* (1942). She never saw it screened as she died in a plane crash outside Las Vegas while on a WWII war bond tour just a month and a half after the attack on Pearl Harbor. Her husband, Clark Gable was so bereft that he enlisted in the U.S. Air Corps. The five foot two actress was thirty-three years old at the time of her death.

Always a crowd pleaser, six year old Shirley Temple was also a scene stealer whether she wanted to be or not. Many actors shied away from playing opposite her because of it, but once they did accept roles, they too were smitten with the doll-like features and winning smiles she exuded. Thrust into movies at an early age by a true stage mother, Temple enjoyed play acting and soon became the most famous child star in the world. Depression weary children craved any thing to do with her, be it dolls, coloring books or clothes. In 1938, she was slated to be Dorothy in M-G-M's fantasy, *The Wizard of Oz* (1939), but Fox refused to lend her out and so the role went to teenager Judy Garland. Unfortunately, critics have not been kind to her over the years, citing the opinion that she was never an actress and her later teenage films proved the point. Nevertheless, her films brought joy and smiles to millions of fans. She retired from screen acting in the late Forties and did some television work in the 1950s and 1960s before finally quitting acting. In later years she became a Delegate to the United Nations and our country's Ambassador to several smaller nations.

Gary Cooper and Shirley Temple in a scene from *Now and Forever* (1934) filmed on Lone Pine Island in Lake Arrowhead. Photo courtesy of The Academy of Motion Picture Arts and Sciences

FIGHTING TROOPER & others (1934-1936)

Studio photo card for
Fighting Trooper (1934)

In the very depths of the Depression, Maurice Conn formed Ambassador Pictures along "poverty row" (an area in Hollywood where inexpensive films were shot) and filmed a series of northwest adventure pictures utilizing stories from author James Oliver Curwood. He teamed up with Kermit Maynard, popular cowboy star Ken Maynard's younger brother. In a string of low-cost Royal Canadian Mounted Police movies, beginning in 1934 and ending in 1937, Conn and Kermit Maynard made at least nine of them in the San Bernardino Mountains. Two of them (*Fighting Trooper*, 1934, and *Northern Frontier*, 1935) were made at the City of Los Angeles' recreation park, Camp Seely, near the town of Crestline. *Northern Frontier* is especially fun to watch because we get a first glimpse of a very young Tyrone Power, who within a year would be a star in *Lloyd's of London*. For his leading ladies, Conn used a chain of beautiful and young unknown actresses, but none of them twice. None of these leading ladies ever distinguished themselves, except for a gorgeous twenty year old redhead who had been lent to Ambassador Pictures from Paramount Studios. Her name was Clara Lou Sheridan, later changed to Ann Sheridan, who became known to millions of servicemen during WWII as the pin-up "Oomph Girl."

At the urging of his popular brother Ken, Indiana-born Kermit Maynard arrived in Hollywood in 1927 as "Tex" Maynard. At first he doubled for his brother and loved to do stunt work, especially if it involved riding horses. After a series of low-budget Westerns where he played bit roles, he was cast in the lead of *Fighting Trooper* in 1934. Buster Crabbe, his longtime friend, said the difference between Kermit and his brother Ken was like night and day. Kermit was the better horseman, always a gentleman who never had a bad word to say about anyone and always sober. It was a backhanded way of saying Ken was just the opposite. Ironically, the younger brother who abstained from spirits and was the embodiment of good health, died two years earlier than the friendless and alcoholic brother, Ken. Kermit never attained the star status of his older brother, but because he was so well liked he never lacked work. From 1927 to his retirement in 1960, Kermit amassed nearly two hundred and fifty screen and television credits.

Beautiful twenty-eight year old Barbara Worth had been an actress in the silent film era, but retired from acting in 1935 with seventeen screen credits. In the Forties she returned to Hollywood, but this time as a screenwriter when she collaborated with her former producer, Maurice Conn, in three films. She died at the age of forty-nine in 1955.

Barbara Worth
circa 1934

It is sad to see in two of these films, *Code of the Mounted* (1935) and *Wildcat Trooper* (1936), an older Native American who is dissipated, overweight and dispirited. The Indian is none other than one of the greatest athletes ever born, Jim Thorpe, who had fallen on bad times and was obviously alcoholic at that time and needed work. An all-around Olympic champion, he later played baseball, football, and even tried his hand as a wrestler, but he was never an actor. Regardless, Thorpe continued to accept bit roles in the movies until 1950. He died at the age of sixty-five in 1953.

Kermit Maynard with "hands up" in a
scene from *Northern Frontier* (1935)
filmed in Crestline.

CAST OF NORTHERN FRONTIER:
Kermit Maynard .... Trooper McKenzie
Eleanor Hunt .... Beth Braden
J. Farrell MacDonald .... Inspector
Stevens
Tyrone Power .... Trooper Joe
Directed by .... Sam Newfield
Produced by .... Ambassador Pictures

Kermit Maynard punishing the bad guys
while Eleanor Hunt looks on in a scene
from *Northern Frontier* (1935).

Fuzzy Knight, Billie Seward and
Kermit Maynard in a scene from
Trails of the Wild (1935) filmed at Big Bear.

CAST OF TRAILS OF THE WILD:
Kermit Maynard .... McKenna
Billie Seward .... Jane
Fuzzy Knight .... Windy
Directed by .... Sam Newfield
Produced by ..... Ambassador Pictures

Kermit Maynard (riding the white
horse with a white hat) in a scene
from *Trails of the Wild* (1935)

Kermit Maynard (holding man above) must prove he's capable of being a "Mountie" when he infiltrates a gang of thieves in a scene from *His Fighting Blood* (1935) filmed at Big Bear Lake.

```
CAST OF HIS FIGHTING BLOOD:
Kermit Maynard ................ Tom Elliott
Polly Ann Young ......................... Doris
Directed by ..................... John English
Produced by .... Ambassador Pictures
```

Polly Ann Young
circa 1930s

CAST OF RED BLOOD OF COURAGE:
Kermit Maynard .... Jim Sullivan
Ann Sheridan .... Beth Henry
Directed by .... John English
Produced by ... Ambassador Pictures

Kermit Maynard about to be hit while trying to save Ann Sheridan in a scene from *Red Blood of Courage* (1935) filmed at the settling ponds near Big Bear Lake.
Photo courtesy of Alex Thompson

CAST OF CODE OF THE MOUNTED:
Kermit Maynard .... Sgt. Jim Wilson
Lillian Miles .... Jean
Directed by .... Sam Newfield
Produced by ... Ambassador Pictures

Lillian Miles looks up at her hero, Kermit Maynard (riding a white horse), in a scene from *Code of the Mounted* (1935) filmed in the San Bernardino Mountains.

1-Col. Scene Mat, No. 3A-3

SNOW BLOCKS TRAILS; TIMBER WOLVES LOOT FILM PLAYERS' FOOD

A pack of timber wolves, that made off with a good share of the rations for the cast of "Wilderness Mail" while on location deep in the snow country, nearly caused a serious shortage of food.

It was just at a time when the roads leading to the "location" were blocked with snow, and for a time it looked as though the company would have to exist on beans.

While Kermit Maynard, the star of "Wilderness Mail," was on an other location with Director Forrest Sheldon, Paul Hurst, and Dick Curtis, who both have a dislike for beans as a steady diet, took matters into their own hands and mushed to a nearby lake and, after chopping a hole in the ice, dropped in improvised fishing lines. Soon they were pulling out several big fish that weighed as much as 18 pounds.

The cast of "Wilderness Mail" cheered their arrival, and that night feasted on planked fish steak, delicious and cooked as only old woodsmen can prepare it.

The next day the roads were opened and a fresh load of supplies were rushed to the location camp. But Dick and Paul continued their fishing, the cast afterwards enjoying several other fish dinners.

CAST OF WILDERNESS MAIL:
Kermit Maynard .... Rance and Keith Raine
Doris Brook .... Lila Landau
Fred Kohler .... Lobo McBain
Directed by .... Forrest Sheldon
Produced by .... Ambassador Pictures

Hollywood hype for the film
Wilderness Mail (1935)

Kermit Maynard holding a gun on (left to right) Syd Saylor, Fred Kohler and Dick Curtis in a scene from *Wilderness Mail* (1935) filmed at Big Bear Lake in February 1935.

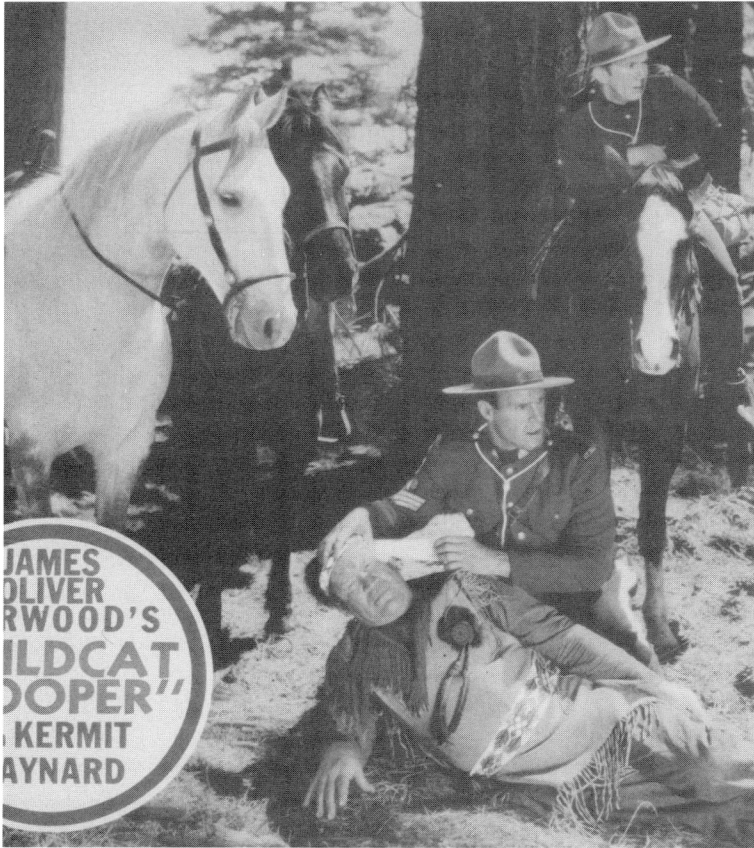

Kermit Maynard ministers to a wounded Jim Thorpe in a scene from *Wildcat Trooper* (1936) filmed at Big Bear Lake.

CAST OF WILDCAT TROOPER:
Kermit Maynard .... Sgt. Gale Farrell
Lois Wilde .... Ruth Reynolds
Jim Thorpe .... Wounded Indian
Directed by .... Elmer Clifton
Produced by ... Ambassador Pictures

Kermit Maynard stops Hobart Bosworth while Eddie Phillips holds Lois Wilde in a scene from *Wildcat Trooper* (1936).

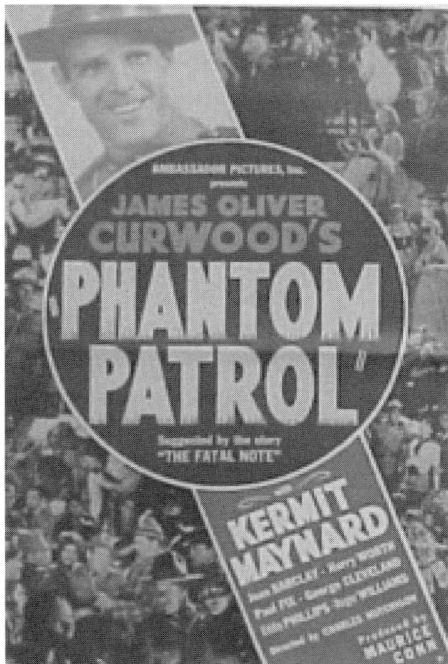

Pressbook for
Phantom Patrol (1936)

Kermit Maynard holds Joan Barclay
while Julian Rivero (in colorful gaucho
outfit) is taken into custody in a
scene from *Phantom Patrol* (1936)
filmed at Big Bear Lake.

EIGHT GIRLS IN A BOAT
(1934)

CAST:
Dorothy Wilson .... Christa Storm
Douglass Montgomery .... David Perrin
Barbara Barondess .... Pickles
Directed by .... Richard Wallace
Produced by ..... Paramount Pictures

Three of the contest winners on the cover of the sheet music "A Day Without You" written for the film *Eight Girls in a Boat* (1934) filmed at Lake Arrowhead (Adele Pearce in the center).

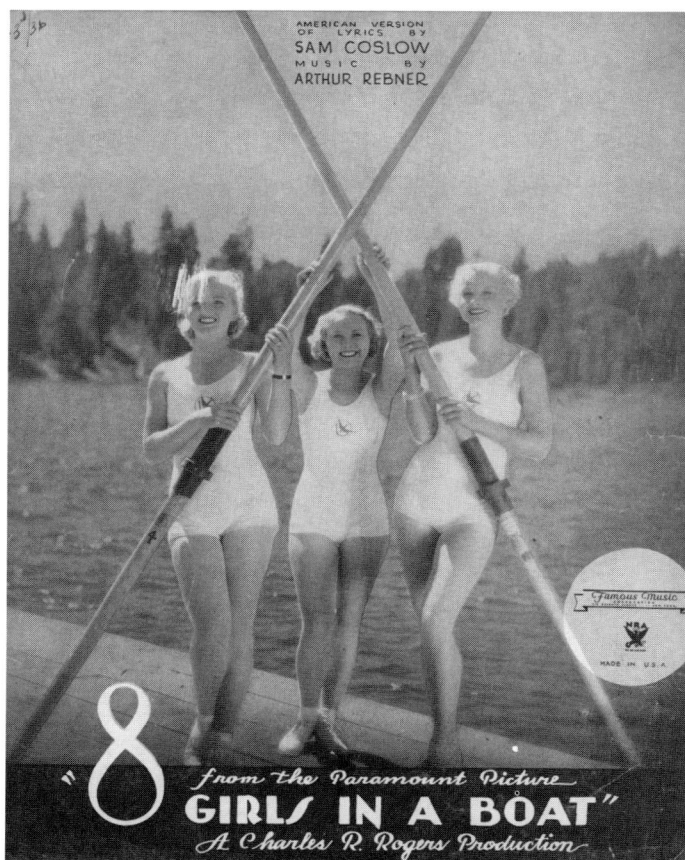

In the second of two films by the same name, (the first is a German version made in 1932), *Eight Girls in a Boat* is a romantic drama with a couple of musical numbers thrown in. Christa Storm (Dorothy Wilson) finds herself pregnant while she is attending an exclusive school for girls in Switzerland. She keeps it a secret from all except for her lover, David Perrin (Douglass Montgomery), who is studying medicine at a nearby university. Christa, who has been sheltered all of her life and been sent to boarding schools, is afraid to confide in her father whom she rarely sees. David wants to do the right thing, ie. marriage, but his father will have none of it and refuses his permission to marry. Of course, all ends well in this Depression era feel-good story. In order to promote the film early, Paramount conducted a series of beauty contests in eight locations all over the country. The winners were promised a screen test and a small role in an upcoming production which turned out to be *Eight Girls in a Boat*. The eight winners ended up learning how to crew a scull which was used in the film on Lake Arrowhead. Of the eight beauties, only Adele Pearce ever made another movie and that was just one.

Canadian-born Douglass Montgomery grew up near Hollywood. He joined M-G-M and made his first film in 1930. Because of his dashing and handsome good looks, M-G-M slated him for stardom. Unfortunately for Montgomery, other than a memorable role in *The Mystery of Edwin Drood* (made at Universal Studios in 1935), his star never ascended in filmdom. He drifted from movie lot to movie lot during the remainder of the Thirties and then left Hollywood just before WWII. Curiously, M-G-M must have considered him for a role in the epic GWTW, because he made several screen tests with various female stars who were being considered for the part of Scarlett O'Hara, two of whom were Joan Bennett and Jean Arthur. After the war he made a couple of films in Europe before retiring from the screen in 1948.

Twenty-five year old Dorothy Wilson was a stunning beauty who came to Hollywood at the height of the Depression. She made twenty films in the span of five years, none of them remarkable. In 1935, she starred with Will Rogers in his last film, *In Old Kentucky*, which was released three months after his tragic air crash in Alaska. She retired from acting in 1937 and died in 1998 at the age of eighty-eight.

Stage actress and silent screen veteran, Barbara Barondess was twenty-six years old when she made *8 Girls in a Boat*. She appeared in almost thirty films from 1925 to 1940, before leaving Hollywood. One of the first to join the newly formed Screen Actors Guild (SAG), she bitterly complained about the way actresses were being treated in the early Thirties. She remembered that she had to jump into the cold waters of Lake Arrowhead twenty times one day, for just one take in *8 Girls in a Boat*. She was married to a silent film comedian, Douglas MacLean, and became active in drama classes later in life. She died in 2000 at the age of ninety-three.

Cast and crew on location at Lake Arrowhead for the film *Eight Girls in a Boat* (1934) Photo courtesy of The Academy of Motion Picture Arts and Sciences

SPLENDOR (1935)

```
CAST:
Miriam Hopkins ...... Phyllis Manning
Joel McCrea ...... Brighton Lorrimore
David Niven ........ Clancey Lorrimore
Directed by ................. Elliott Nugent
Produced by ........ Goldwyn Pictures
```

The rich and powerful Lorrimore family faces financial ruin unless they can marry off their only son, Brighton (Joel McCrea) to wealthy socialite Edith Gilbert (Ruth Weston). To their dismay, Brighton returns from a holiday trip with a new bride, southern-belle Phyllis (Miriam Hopkins) who is penniless. The family plots to separate the two, but in the true Hollywood spirit, boy gets girl in the end. Oddly enough, Lake Arrowhead is the holiday setting for our two lovers as they cavort among the pines and bracken fern in still photos from the film, but the scenes must have been cut in later versions as they don't appear on the abbreviated variation that is shown on video. For once, it would be nice to see the director's cut with the entire film intact.

This was Joel McCrea's second film with Miriam Hopkins made in the San Bernardino Mountains (the first was *The Richest Girl in the World*-1934). The thirty year old actor was one of the handsomest leading men in Hollywood and, although he wanted to work in Westerns, was usually cast in romantic comedies, in which he excelled. In his later years in films, he did achieve his lifetime dream and became one of the most beloved of cowboy stars. He met his future wife, actress Francis Dee, on the RKO Studio set in 1933 where they were working on a movie

Miriam Hopkins and Joel McCrea among the bracken fern in the film *Splendor* (1935)
Photo courtesy of
The Academy of Motion Picture
Arts and Sciences

together. In one of the longest enduring Hollywood marriages of stars, McCrea and Dee were married fifty-seven years until his death in 1990.

The southern-belle accent came naturally to thirty-two year old Miriam Hopkins as she had been born in Georgia. Hopkins was at the top of her popularity in the mid-Thirties, but producers were beginning to shun her by 1938, when she made no movies. Because she was born in Georgia, she set her mind on playing the part of Scarlett O'Hara, but it was obvious that David O. Selznick was looking for a much younger woman, finally choosing twenty-five year old Vivien Leigh to play the part. Hopkins continued making films sporadically through the Forties, Fifties and Sixties with occasional appearances on television. She retired in 1968 and died four years later at the age of seventy.

In what was to be his first significant role, twenty-five year old David Niven plays the part of the snooty younger brother to McCrea. London-born Niven came to the United States in the early Thirties to try his hand at acting. *Splendor* thrust him into the limelight and he received critical acclaim for his role. He made twenty movies in five years, but after filming *Raffles* (1940) in which he played the lead, Niven left Hollywood to join the Army in England. He never spoke of his war time experiences, but General Dwight D. Eisenhower awarded him the Legionnaire of the Order of Merit (the highest American order that can be earned by a non-citizen of the United States). After the war, Niven returned to films and worked steadily up until his death in 1983. In 1959, he won both the Golden Globe and the Oscar for Best Actor playing opposite Deborah Kerr in *Separate Tables* (1958).

Another British actor present on the set of *Splendor* was forty-one year old Arthur Treacher, who defined the perfect English butler in so many movies of the era, like P.G. Wodhouse's *Jeeves* series. Treacher made nearly eighty films in his career, but in later years would be known for lending his name to various commercial enterprises, such as the popular, Arthur Treacher's Fish & Chips.

Miriam Hopkins and Joel McCrea on location at Lake Arrowhead for the film *Splendor* (1935)
Photo courtesy of
The Academy of Motion Picture
Arts and Sciences

MAGNIFICENT OBSESSION (1935)

CAST:

Irene Dunne .... Helen Hudson
Robert Taylor .... Bob Merrick
Betty Furness .... Joyce Hudson
Directed by .... John M. Stahl
Produced by .... Universal Pictures

Universal Studios bought the rights to the moralistic 1929 novel, *Magnificent Obsession,* by clergyman Lloyd C. Douglas and made it into one of the best melodramas of the era. Playboy Bob Merrick (Robert Taylor) recklessly runs through life. When he causes the death of a noted physician, he callously shrugs it off until he meets the widow, Helen Hudson (Irene Dunne). His advances toward her reinforce his inconsiderate ways and redemption doesn't occur until he causes her blindness. Over a period of years he drops out of the social life and dedicates his life to not only being a doctor, but a specialist bent on curing the woman he has harmed in so many ways. In order to make audiences buy the love affair between thirty-seven year old Dunne and the twenty-three year old Taylor, they aged him gracefully over a period of time, graying his widows-peak hairline. The movie was remade by Universal in 1954 and starred Jane Wyman opposite young Rock Hudson and was also filmed at Lake Arrowhead. The 1935 version is probably closer to the original novel as Douglas helped write the script.

Magnificent Obsession was Robert Taylor's breakout role in movies. Audiences and fellow workers loved him immediately, but critics panned him unjustly because he was "too pretty." He was born with the unlikely name of Spangler Arlington Brugh and wanted to be a musician. While studying in college, he was spotted by an M-G-M scout and signed by the studio. His striking good looks and deep voice ensured him a lifetime of

Irene Dunne and Cora Sue Collins in a scene from *Magnificent Obsession* (1935)

starring roles and matinee idol status. When WWII broke out, he enlisted in the U.S. Navy. The Navy was smart enough to use his movie talents rather than have him subjected to combat. He directed and narrated seventeen training films during that time. Over his thirty plus years in Hollywood, Taylor had screen credits in nearly one hundred films and television plays. A heavy smoker, he died prematurely at the age of fifty-seven in 1969 of lung cancer.

Kentucky-born Irene Dunne was trained as an opera singer, but once rejected by the Metropolitan Opera Company, she tried her luck with musicals eventually landing on Broadway. Her starring role in a touring production of Ziegfeld's *Showboat* led to a contract with RKO. Always a star, she made close to sixty film and television appearances over the next twenty-five years. One of the least remembered actresses of her time, Dunne was nominated by the Academy five

Contemporary lobby card circa 1935

Robert Taylor carries Irene Dunne in a scene from *Magnificent Obsession* (1935). Photo courtesy of The Academy of Motion Picture Arts and Sciences

times as best actress, but never won the Oscar, losing out to Marie Dressler, Vivien Leigh, and Jane Wyman. Ironically, she also lost out two years in a row to Luise Rainer. Rainer won the Best Actress Award for her starring role in *The Great Ziegfeld* in 1936, the story of the man Dunne always credited with discovering her and the following year for Pearl S. Buck's *The Good Earth* (1937). For her part in *Magnificent Obsession*, Dunne received a salary of $150,000 in the midst of the depression, a sum that would be the eqivalent to some of the exaggerated salaries paid to some stars today.

Also included in the cast was Charles Butterworth, who played the unlikely fiancé to young Betty Furness, who played the part of the stepdaughter. Furness later made television history as the best remembered commercial spokesperson for opening and closing Westinghouse refrigerators.

Robert Taylor (standing left) in a scene from *Magnificent Obsession* (1935)

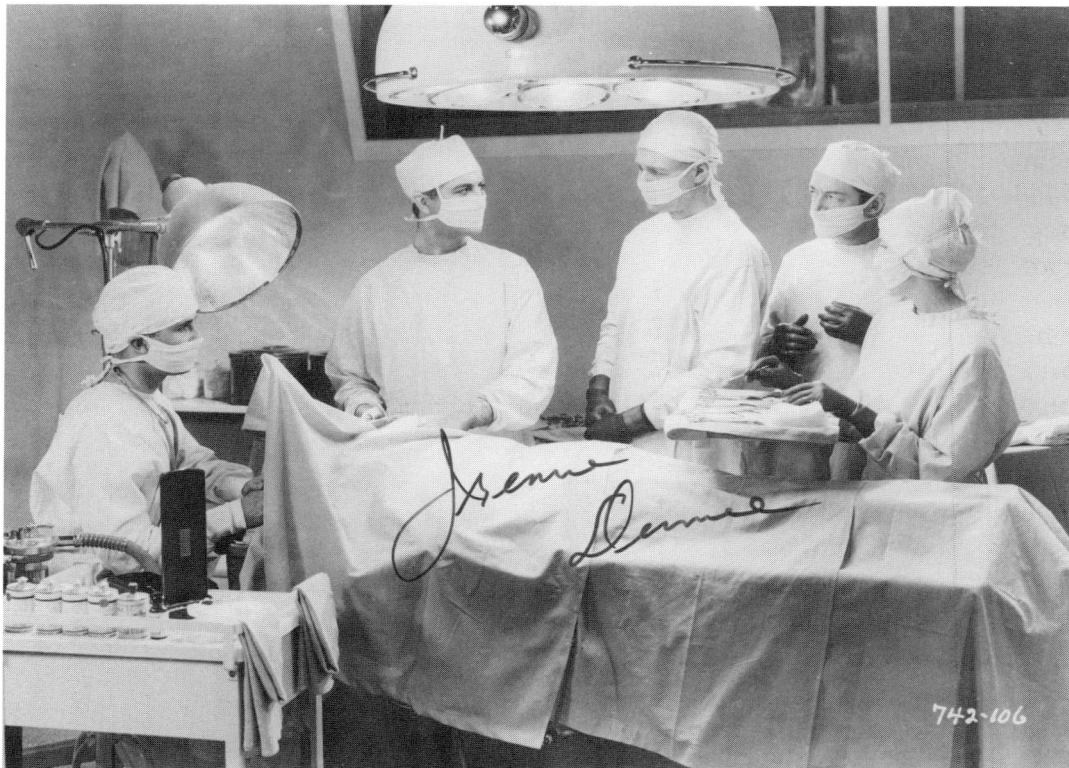

IN PERSON (1935)

Back in 1935, when a director told an actress to jump, she jumped. So it was when director William Seiter told Ginger Rogers to take a dive into Cedar Lake. He requested Rogers to dive in, swim thirty or so feet away from the camera and then resurface. Rogers protested after she tested the water and found it freezing, even in August. "Right," he replied, "But—you will swim underwater for thirty feet and I'll have the camera right on you. When you come up for air, George (George Brent) will see you for the first time without your phony makeup on. And then get out of the water and run to your cabin." Always the trooper, Rogers obediently did the scene, freezing all the way back to her cabin. Making matters worse, the Hays Office, the official censor in Hollywood, protested about Rogers' two piece bathing suit, claiming it showed too much flesh. Little did the censor know, but if the camera could have seen underwater, Rogers' suit, which was a size too big to begin with, got larger as it got wet and was sliding off her body.

The script for *In Person* was based on a novel by Samuel Hopkins Adams, about an agoraphobic actress who seeks refuge in a mountain retreat with her psychologist. RKO wanted to showcase Ginger Rogers' singing voice so they turned it into a comedy with songs by Oscar Levant. Rogers sings three original songs, unfortunately none of them memorable. Rogers accepted the role that had been turned down by many

```
CAST:
Ginger Rogers .............Carol Corliss
George Brent ................. Emory Muir
Alan Mowbray .............. Jay Holmes
Directed by ........... William A. Seiter
Produced by .............. RKO Pictures
```

Ginger Rogers
circa 1935

George Brent
circa (1935)

others, notably Katherine Hepburn, because the character had to look ridiculous in glasses and false teeth.

By the time Ginger Rogers made *In Person*, she was already a big star at RKO with more than forty pictures made in the span of six years. Born Virginia Katherine McMath, twenty-four year old Rogers had won a dance contest at the age of fourteen, which led to a vaudeville act and ultimately to a screen test. From her first film in 1929 until she retired in 1965, Rogers amassed over one hundred movie and television credits. Her portrayal of a girl from the wrong side of the tracks in *Kitty Foyle* (1940) won her an Oscar for Best Actress. After her movie career, Rogers continued on Broadway and in musical comedies. She died at the age of eighty-four in 1995.

Thirty-one year old George Brent came to America under a cloud in the early 1920s. As George Nolan (his real name), Irish-born Brent had been active with the IRA during the rebellions shortly after WWI in his native country. He began acting and was signed by RKO Studios in 1930, where he stayed for the next twenty years playing opposite some of the biggest named actresses of the day. The six foot one inch actor was usually the suave, sophisticated elitist in his films. Brent's career spanned twenty plus years until he retired from films in the late 1950s. Curiously, he came back twenty years later and made one more picture (*Born Again*-1978) shortly before his death in 1979 at the age of seventy-five. A very popular actor during the height of his career, he was married to Australian actress Constance Worth during the 1930s and to Ann Sheridan during the 1940s.

English-born actor Alan Mowbray began acting in films during the early 1930s after a successful Broadway career. Never a leading man, Mowbray perfected the upper-class, snobbish windbag persona that followed him throughout his long screen life. In his three decades of acting before the camera, Mowbray had more than one hundred and fifty movie and television credits. Mowbray was also one of the founding members of the Screen Actors Guild of America.

Alan Mowbray
circa 1940s

Ginger Rogers, Joan Breslau and George
Brent in a scene from *In Person* (1935)
Photo courtesy of
The Academy of Motion Picture
Arts and Sciences

FIGHTING SHADOWS (1935)

```
CAST:
Tim McCoy ...................... Tim O'Hara
Geneva Mitchell ...... Martha Harrison
Ward Bond .................. Brad Harrison
Si Jenks ...................... Hank Bascom
Directed by .................. David Selman
Produced by ....... Columbia Pictures
```

Royal Canadian Mountie Tim O'Hara (Tim McCoy) is sent to Indian River (Big Bear Lake) to investigate a suspicious fur-trading racket. On his way there, he encounters a burning cabin and the body of a trapper along with a note warning others to beware or they might face the same fate. Through a misunderstanding, Brad Harrison (Ward Bond) accuses O'Hara of killing one of the thieves and hiding behind his uniform. Harrison's sister, Martha (Geneva Mitchell), is mainly window dressing in this fisticuff melodrama that finds McCoy battling everyone except Mitchell. There are no mushy kissing sequences in this predominantly male movie as Col. Tim McCoy was always uncomfortable doing a love scene.

At five feet eleven inches tall, with piercing blue eyes and a ramrod straight stance, Tim McCoy was considered one of the best of the 1930s cowboy heroes. Born in Michigan, McCoy went west to Wyoming where he honed the real skills of a cowboy, roping and riding. When WWI broke out, McCoy entered the Army and mustered out with the rank of Lt. Colonel, a title he used throughout his career. In 1923, he acted as liaison and consultant to director James Cruze, who was filming *The Covered Wagon* on location in Wyoming (he actually procured many of the Indians used in the picture because he was able to communicate with them). This eventually led him to Hollywood and an acting career of his own. From 1925 until the beginning of WWII, McCoy starred in close to ninety Western features. Again with the outbreak of war in 1941, McCoy returned to the armed forces where he was awarded several decorations for his service with the Army Air Corps in Europe. His intention was to retire from films after the war, but in 1952 with the

Tim McCoy, Geneva Mitchell and Ward Bond in a scene from *Fighting Shadows* (1935)

popularity of television becoming evident, McCoy hosted his own weekly series, *The Tim McCoy Show*. He made a few more cameo appearances over the following years, most notably as a U.S. Calvary Colonel in Mike Todd's *Around the World in Eighty Days* (1956).

Not many men could stand toe to toe with six foot four inch John Wayne, but his one-time football roommate from the University of Southern California, Ward Bond, was one of them. Together they entered the movies on a lark and both went on to become screen legends, Wayne as superstar and Bond as one of the best character actors in Hollywood. During Bond's earlier days in film, he was more likely to be cast as the heavy due to his gruff and burly looks. Interestingly, he is remembered more for his popular television series, *Wagon Train*, than for the two hundred and fifty films he made. Sadly, he died of a massive heart attack at the age of fifty-seven at the peak of his success in 1960.

Twenty-seven year old Geneva Mitchell was a dancer in the Ziegfeld Follies prior to coming to Hollywood in 1929. Over the next six years, she was cast in close to sixty films, serving as a utility player bouncing from one studio to the next, wherever work was to be found among the major studios or the independents. In 1936, she left the film industry only to emerge five years later in a cameo role and then six years later in a small bit part. She died in 1949 at the age of forty-one.

One of the most colorful characters in Hollywood was veteran vaudevillian, Si Jenks. Jenks did not begin to act in films until he was well into his mid-fifties. He specialized in appearing as the old, toothless codger in hundreds of movies over the next two decades. In 1939, he appeared in three of the most famous films of that year, *Gone With the Wind, Drums Along the Mohawk*, and *Stagecoach*. A great lover of the San Bernardino Mountains, Si Jenks was a frequent visitor to the Big Bear Lake area where he had made *Fighting Shadows* back in 1935.

Tim McCoy (in RCMP uniform) and Ward Bond (in checkered shirt) battle the bad guys in a scene from *Fighting Shadows* (1935).

THE TEST (1935)

In this tale from "poverty row" producer Reliable Pictures, Rinnie (Rin-Tin-Tin, Jr.) is asked to guard the furs of his master, fur trapper Brule Conway (Grant Withers). When Rinnie is lured away by a female dog (Nanette), Conway's winter catch of furs is stolen by Pepite La Joie (Monte Blue) and his henchmen led by Black Wolf (Art Ortego). Rinnie is told to track down Pepite and recover the furs including a valuable blue fox pelt that was supposed to be a present to the daughter of the trading company's factor. Beth McVey (Grace Ford), the factor's daughter, believes Rinnie is up to the task, whereas Conway has his doubts about the dog since the dog had abandoned his post to begin with. After a series of adventures, Rinnie masterfully captures the evil doers single-handedly and wins Nanette while Conway wins the hand of Beth.

Reliable sent the cast and crew to Big Bear Lake in the winter of 1934-35 to film this northwest tale from the pen of James Oliver Curwood. Unfortunately, Rinnie is not his father and looks too scrawny to be effective. However, the scenery around wintertime Big Bear is magnificent and well photographed.

Thirty-one year old Grant Withers had worked as an oil company salesman and as a reporter before turning to acting in 1926. At six foot three inches, the handsome and strapping Withers soon became a leading man of silent films and easily made the transition to talkies because of his deep voice. In the 1930s, he appeared in tens of "B" movies before his star waned and he became a character actor who specialized in bad guy roles. He joined the loose group around John Ford and can be seen in many of Ford's classic westerns. In 1931, Withers created a scandal by marrying an underage young starlet by the name of Loretta Young. After eight months of putting up with the hard drinking Withers, Young, with the backing

Grant Withers
circa 1930s

and urging of her studio, had the marriage annulled. Never at a loss for work, Withers made over two hundred film and television appearances before committing suicide in 1959 at the age of fifty-five.

One actress that didn't find a lot of work during the depression was Grace Ford. She made only four films in the span of three years and then left the industry. The twenty-two year old blonde was pretty, but her voice and acting left a lot to be desired.

One of the great silent stars, Monte Blue, who was part Cherokee Indian, grew up in an orphanage in Indiana. During the early 1910s, he became a handyman at movie studios before being pressed into stunt work and bit parts. Blue's first major film was D. W. Griffith's *Birth of a Nation* in 1915. Later he worked for C. B. DeMille and became a leading man at Warner Brothers Studios. He retired from films just before the Wall Street Crash in 1929, but was forced to go back into the movies when he learned that he had lost his fortune. With his swarthy looks, Blue was usually cast in ethnic roles during the 1930s. He too never lacked for work as Warner Brothers kept him busy out of respect for his earlier work. In his four decades of film work, Blue is credited with more than two hundred and fifty movie appearances, his last being that of Geronimo in *Apache* (1954).

Art Ortego, who played the part of an Indian in many silent, as well as, talking pictures, was actually Hispanic, like his former wife, Mona Darkfeather. They starred in several earlier films made in the San Bernardino Mountains in the 1910s. Ortego's career in films spanned four decades and included more than one hundred and seventy films.

Grace Ford
circa 1937

Monte Blue
circa 1930s

ROCKY MOUNTAIN MYSTERY
(1935)

CAST:
Randolph Scott .... Larry Sutton
Ann Sheridan .... Rita Ballard
Mrs. Leslie Carter .... Mrs. Borg
Directed by .... Charles Barton
Produced by ..... Paramount Pictures

Randolph Scott
circa (1940s)

In the depression era Thirties, Paramount Studios wanted to get the most out of its stars. In 1935, it teamed veteran Western actor Randolph Scott with Ann Sheridan, one of Paramount's ingenues, to make a quickie "oater" in the mountains. They sent their cast and crew up to Big Bear Valley where they shot a majority of *Rocky Mountain Mystery* on Gold Mountain near the site of "Lucky" Baldwin's abandoned mine. Instead of gold, the plot revolves around radium, a rare element that was in the news during the 1930s, but one which most people knew little about.

Larry Sutton (Randolph Scott) is sent to the Ballard mine to take over as chief engineer and investigate the murder of the former engineer, Adolph Borg. Sutton and Deputy Tex Murdock (Charles "Chic" Sale) find themselves with bodies all over the place as mysteriously, people keep dying. [At some point, the audience must have asked themselves if the dangerous radium had something to do with it, but the screenwriter missed a real opportunity in not exploring this issue.] The upshot is the Borgs are trying to oust the Ballards from their claim, including one of the nieces, Rita Ballard (Ann Sheridan), with whom Sutton has fallen in love. The evil head of the Borg clan is Mrs. Borg (Mrs. Leslie Carter) who receives her comeuppance in the end.

Thirty-six year old Randolph Scott had been making movies since 1928, when he appeared as an extra in several silent films before being selected to coach Gary Cooper in a Virginia dialect for *The Virginian* (1929), a film he also had a bit part in. Spotted by Paramount scouts, he signed with the studio that year and this led to his being offered leads in their Westerns. He was equally comfortable acting in romantic comedies, but will always be remembered best for the numerous Westerns where he portrayed the stoic-faced good guy. A shrewd business-man, Scott invested in real estate and retired from the screen in 1962 with over one hundred and twenty film and television credits.

Billed as Clara Lou Sheridan, by the end of 1935 Sheridan was tired of the grind Paramount had put her through (she had been cast in nineteen pictures in two years) and she signed with Warner Brothers. With the change of studios also came a name change to Ann. Over the next few years she appeared in dozens of films, usually as a gangster's moll who tries to reform him. She worked with the best of the "gangsters": James Cagney, George Raft, and Humphrey Bogart. In 1942, Sheridan was known as the "Oomph Girl" and was one of the most popular pin-up girls in the country, rivaling Betty Grable for top honors among GIs. That year she got the chance to act with Ronald Reagan in *King's Row*, one of her best performances. Although she didn't get nominated for an Oscar, she did win a Golden Apple award as the most cooperative actress. Sheridan continued to act in movies and television throughout the Fifties and Sixties, before dying of cancer in 1967 at the age of fifty-two.

One of the most interesting bit players in this drama is Mrs. Leslie Carter who plays Mrs. Borg. Born Caroline Louise Dudley, Carter went by the name of the socially prominent man who had divorced her in 1889 and taken her child away in a scandalous courtroom affair. She hated the man so much that she vowed to spread his name all over the world by becoming an actress. Much to Mr. Leslie Carter's dismay, the green-eyed socialite with flaming red hair teamed up with impresario David Belasco and became one of the most famous actresses of the late 1890s and early 1900s. Known for her "emotional" school of acting and mannered histrionics, she became the "American Sarah Bernhardt" on the stage. She went through at least three fortunes and bankruptcies and traveled like

Ann Sheridan circa 1935

Mrs. Leslie Carter Post Card (1900s) with error incorrectly listing her as "Miss"

an empress with her own private railway car and a personal retinue of seven. At the age of fifty-three, she reenacted two of her most famous stage roles for the silent screen, Madame Du Barry and Maryland Calvert, two women who had been wronged by the men they loved. Neither film was a success and she went back to the stage and vaudeville, but never to the acclaim she had received earlier. Mrs. Carter died two years after making *Rocky Mountain Mystery* at the age of seventy-five. In 1940, Warner Brothers Studios produced her life story, *The Lady with Red Hair*, starring Miriam Hopkins as Carter and Claude Rains as Belasco.

Charles "Chic" Sale and Randolph Scott
supposedly inside the "Lucky" Baldwin
gold mine in a scene from *Rocky Mountain
Mystery* (1935)
Photo courtesy of
The Academy of Motion Picture
Arts and Sciences

BIOGRAPHY OF
A BACHELOR GIRL (1935)

In the early 1930s, M-G-M Studios purchased the rights to a brilliant play by S.N. Behrman called *Biography of a Bachelor Girl*. Troubles immediately arose from the movie watchdog agency, the Hays Office. They objected to any and all references about sex, but the play was all about sex. The film was made in the late summer of 1934 in Lake Arrowhead, but with a subdued script and as some critics said, the wrong actors. In a classic exchange of letters that began a witch hunt, the Hays Office learns from a Catholic movie censoring federation of the line: "Of course you were always interesting, even fornicationally." The Hays Office searched the film, but couldn't find the offensive line in the movie. Finally, after many viewings it was caught and the real line was: "You used to be quite a nice boy—even fun occasionally."

Bohemian artist Marion Forsythe (Ann Harding) is thought to have led a sordid past and is asked to reveal all in her memoirs by editor Richard Kurt (Robert Montgomery). When all of her possessions start to be removed from her apartment by process servers, Marion reluctantly agrees to reveal all in a book for $2,000 in advance money. Marion's former lover, Leander "Bunny" Nolan (Edward Everett Horton), learns of the book from his then fiancé Slade Kinnicott (Una Merkle), and decides to put a stop to it because he plans to become a senator. While painting a portrait of the aspiring senator, Leander offers Marion a bribe not to publish her autobiography. Richard learns of the betrayal and instantly dislikes Leander. Richard spirits

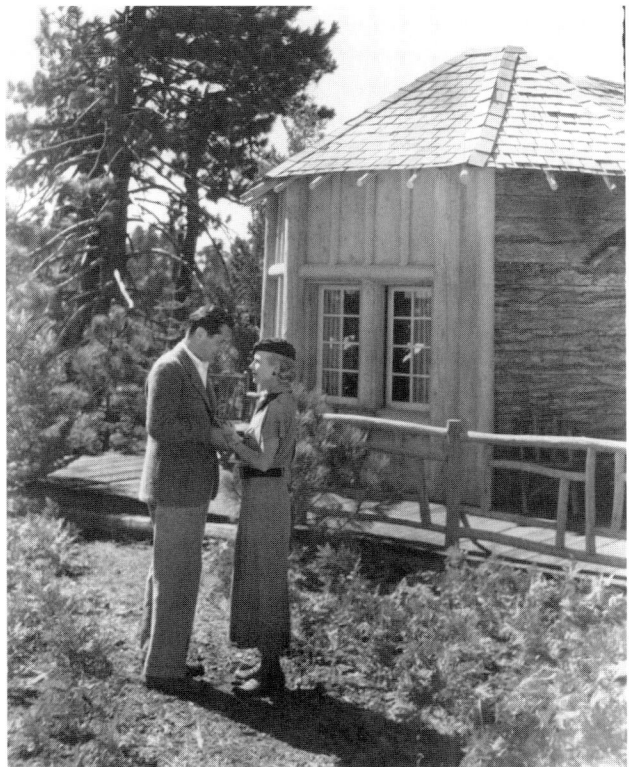

Robert Montgomery and Ann Hardin in a scene at Lake Arrowhead in the film *Biography of a Bachelor Girl* (1935)
Photo courtesy of
The Academy of Motion Picture
Arts and Sciences

Ann Hardin in a scene from the film
Biography of a Bachelor Girl (1935)

Edward Everett Horton

Marion away from all the distractions of city life to his cabin in Maine where they can write in peace. Unfortunately, they create a scandal by their propinquity and are soon joined in Maine by the rest of the cast in this romantic farce.

Handsome and tall, Robert Montgomery was the epitome of the 1930s leading man. Extremely popular with audiences, Montgomery was in the stable of M-G-M players for many years. His WWII years were spent in the U. S. Navy, where he distinguished himself and attained the rank of Commander. After the war he came back to acting and starred in the innovative film noir classic by Raymond Chandler, *Lady in the Lake*, a story of a murder at Lake Arrowhead. In later years, he enjoyed directing and became a staple of television by hosting the very popular *Robert Montgomery Presents* show which ran from 1950 to 1957.

It was suggested that Ann Harding was too genteel to play the part of Marion, a part better suited to Norma Shearer, but M-G-M cast her in the lead anyway. The reviews were less than enthusiastic. One went so far as to say: "it is too talky talkie." Thirty-three year old Ann Harding had been a successful Broadway actress before taking on Hollywood. In her first film, Pathé Studios *Paris Bound* (1929), she appeared opposite Frederic March. Over the next decade she perfected the role of the gentle refined heroine in a series of tearjerkers. When her popularity waned, she slipped into character roles ending in 1956 with her last appearance in *The Man in the Gray Flannel Suit,* once again playing opposite Frederic March.

It just seems like Edward Everett Horton was in every comedy made during the 1930s. The grinning, lanky Horton was a stage actor before coming to Hollywood in 1922. When sound arrived, his cracking voice was actually laughable, but he made it his signature from then on. The lovable comedic character actor had over one hundred and fifty screen and television credits in his fifty years in Hollywood.

This was pioneer cinematographer James Wong Howe's second film at Lake Arrowhead. The black and white scenes are spectacular, but not enough to make the rest of the film palatable to audiences of the day. Innovative and original, Howe was one of the most prolific cameramen of his era. Chinese-born Howe was nominated by the Academy nine times as Best Cinematographer and won the Oscar twice.

Cinematographer James Wong Howe and director Edward Griffith discussing a scene in the film *Biography of a Bachelor Girl.* (Note the image of Ann Harding on the camera screen.)
Photo courtesy of
The Academy of Motion Picture
Arts and Sciences

PETER IBBETSON (1935)

CAST:
Gary Cooper .... Peter Ibbetson
Ann Harding .... Mary Towers
Ida Lupino .... Agnes
Directed by .... Henry Hathaway
Produced by ..... Paramount Pictures

In this tale of lifetime soul mates, director Henry Hathaway has crafted a surrealistic melodrama that played well with depression era audiences abroad. Based on an 1891 novel by English author George Du Maurier (grandfather of writer Daphne Du Maurier), *Peter Ibbetson* was first made into a stage play in 1917 starring John and Lionel Barrymore. In 1921, Famous Players/Lasky bought the rights and called it *Forever,* starring Wallace Reid. Then in 1931, the story was made into an opera and premiered at the Metropolitan Opera House. Paramount Studios, the successor of Famous Players/Lasky, then bought the rights to the opera, with the intention of making it a musical to showcase Jennette McDonald. When they found that she was unavailable, they reverted back to a drama.

From childhood, Peter Ibbetson (Gary Cooper) is in love with Mary (Ann Harding), who later marries and becomes the Duchess of Towers. When they meet once more as adults, architect Peter is commissioned to build new

Ann Harding and Gary Cooper in a scene from the film *Peter Ibbetson* (1935)

stables for the Duke. When the Duke learns of their love for one another, he confronts Peter and is inadvertently killed. Peter is thrown in prison and dreams of being free with Mary at his side.

The initial trailers for the film prominently displayed Cooper and Harding climbing on the rocks in and around Big Bear Lake. Although the film didn't do well at local box offices, it was well received in Europe. The movie was nominated for Best Musical Score by the Academy, but it lost out to Max Steiner's score in *The Informer* (1935).

Thirty-four year old Gary Cooper was at the top of the fan charts by the mid 1930s. The tall, lanky "Coop," as he was called, was just a year away from his first Academy Award nomination for his part in Frank Capra's comedy, *Mr. Deeds Goes to Town*. He lost out that year to Paul Muni, but would be selected once more in 1941 for his portrayal of *Sergeant York*. This time he won and would go on to receive three more nominations and one more Oscar for *High Noon* in 1950. In 1939, according to the U.S. Treasury Department, Gary Cooper was the nation's top wage earner but because he was so well liked no one envied the $482,819 he was paid.

In the same year that she appeared in *Biography of a Bachelor Girl* (1935), thirty-four year old Ann Harding was playing the part she had perfected for the screen, the genteel heroine who suffers long and hard. Harding continued to be cast in the same type roles and finally quit in 1937 when she married musical conductor Werner Janssen. When she returned to films five years later, she was once again cast as the long-suffering woman, but this time as a character actress. She continued with a few films throughout the 1940s and 1950s and then switched to television where she amassed almost as many credits as with her films. Harding is one of the least remembered of the major actresses of the Golden Age of Films. She died in 1981 at the age of eighty.

In a minor role, twenty-one year old English-born Ida Lupino plays Agnes, the cockney seductress who meets Peter in a museum. At the time, Paramount wanted to showcase the young ingenue as the "English Jean Harlow" with thin arched eyebrows, bleached hair and a Kewpie-doll mouth. Lupino broke out of this mold later and played the roles she is best remembered for, the hard, tough woman who knew what she wanted. In real life she made the same choice

This contemporary playbill shows a dramatic scene from the film *Peter Ibbetson (1935)*.

Ida Lupino
circa 1935

and got behind the cameras as a director for both films and in television.

Playing the part of young Peter, ten year old Dickie Moore was a veteran child actor with close to fifty film credits by the time he made *Peter Ibbetson*. He went on to make another forty plus movies before retiring at the age of twenty-seven in 1952. He is best remembered for giving Shirley Temple her first onscreen kiss in *Miss Annie Rooney* (1942). Playing opposite Moore was nine year old Virginia Weidler in only her third picture. She too made forty more films before she retired in 1943 at the age of seventeen.

Ann Harding and Gary Cooper
on location at Big Bear Lake in the film
Peter Ibbetson (1935)
Photo courtesy of
The Academy of Motion Picture
Arts and Sciences

SKULL AND CROWN (1935)

Reliable Pictures returned to Big Bear Lake once more in 1935 to film another Rin-Tin-Tin, Jr. film. Rinty* is asked to do the impossible—track down the killer of the sister of his master. Ranger Bob Franklin (Regis Toomey) is on the trail of the notorious bandit, El Zorro, wanted for various crimes. When his sister, Barbara (Lois January), is shot and killed by the Mexican outlaw [Zorro fans would not like this version], Bob and Rinty trail the killer and his gang to their lair. The lair is actually the Norton Ranch where the leader of the gang, King (Jack Mower), is holding John Norton and his daughter Ann (Molly O'Day) hostage. At the ranch Bob is captured, but Rinty breaks through a glass window and saves the day by eating through the ropes and attacking Zorro, who turns out to be King in disguise.

Thirty-seven year old Regis Toomey began as a singer and Broadway actor before a throat ailment cut short his singing career. He entered the movie industry in 1929 and after a few leading roles, producers were more likely to cast the affable actor as the sidekick to their main star. He appeared in hundreds of character parts and was usually the Irish cop or sergeant who was killed early in the film. A good friend of Dick Powell, he once again played sidekick in many Powell-created TV series during the 1950s and 1960s. He died in 1991 at the age of ninety-three.

A popular leading man in the 1920s, forty-eight year old Jack Mulhall's star had faded by 1935 when he played one of the bad guys in *Skull and Crown*. He was especially good as the villain and appeared in

CAST:	
Regis Toomey	Bob Franklin
Molly O'Day	Ann Norton
Lois January	Barbara Franklin
Directed by	Elmer Clifton
Produced by	Reliable Pictures

Regis Toomey
circa 1935

*Reliable couldn't make up their mind whether to call him Rinnie or Rinty.

Molly O'Day
circa 1930s

Regis Toomey on dog sled
on location at Big Bear Lake in the film
Skull and Crown (1935)
Photo courtesy of
The Academy of Motion Picture
Arts and Sciences

dozens of "B" serials during this time and throughout the 1940s. A consummate working actor, Mulhall took his craft seriously and was a board member of the Screen Actors Guild. He had over three hundred and fifty credits in films and television and died at the age of ninety-two in 1979.

Oddly enough, twenty-four year old Molly O'Day was at the end of her career when she made *Skull and Crown* in 1935. Her career began with Hal Roach in his quickie, two reel *Our Gang* comedies, and escalated to starring opposite Richard Barthelmess in *The Patent Leather Kid* (1927) when she beat out eleven hundred other Hollywood hopefuls for the role. In 1928, she was named a WAMPAS Baby Star at the age of seventeen. Although she only made nineteen major films, fans remember the bright-eyed Irish lass to this day.

Twenty-two year old Lois January had made sixteen pictures in two years with various studios in the early 1930s. *Skull and Crown* was her first Western and because of her riding abilities, she was the leading lady in several more in the following years. She effectively retired in 1937, made a few cameo appearances in several movies, including *The Wizard of Oz* (1939) and then stayed active singing in cabaret clubs and on Broadway for the rest of her life, with occasional bit parts in television.

Although he was really too old to tussle with the younger actors, Jack Mower was able to put up a convincing act with both Regis Toomey and Rinty. Mower began acting in the silent era at the age of twenty-six in 1916. Although tall, he never was a leading man. A very capable character actor, Mower was able to amass more than three hundred and sixty film credits in the four decades that he was in the industry.

NEVADA (1935)

When Westerns were adaptations of novels, they rose above the crowd of trash that was massed produced by the "poverty row" studios. So it was with Zane Grey's 1926 novel *Nevada*, filmed in Big Bear Valley by Paramount Pictures. One of the young extras was Tom Core, a long-time resident and historian in Big Bear, who remembers being asked to ride up a hill and shoot a rifle with blanks. Unfortunately, the film is almost lost. The author was able to locate a copy at the UCLA Film Archives in Hollywood, but due to shrinkage it is almost unwatchable because it jumps so badly. Nevertheless, the storyline makes the movie a better than average Western, even today. This is the second of three times the story was filmed; the first starred Gary Cooper in 1927 and the third, in 1944, starred Robert Mitchum.

Jim "Nevada" Lacey (Buster Crabbe) is an itinerant cowhand that loves to skirt the law. When he joins Ben Ide's cattle drive, the ranchers are leery of him and his past. This is especially true for Clem Dillon (Monte Blue), who is sweet on Ide's daughter, Hettie (Kathleen Burke), who in turn has an eye for the new young stranger, Nevada. With talk of William McKinley becoming President, one by one the ranchers find that they are losing their men to murder. Of course, Nevada is suspected and is sent packing. When Nevada follows one of the gang to their hideout, he learns of a plan to steal all the cattle and rustle them down to old Mexico. In the end, Clem turns out to be the traitor and Nevada wins the heart of Hettie.

Like John Wayne before him, twenty-eight year old Larry "Buster" Crabbe began in films as a stunt actor while still attending University of Southern California. After winning a Gold Medal for swimming in the 1932 World Olympics, Crabbe signed a contract with Para-

```
CAST:
Buster Crabbe ........ "Nevada" Lacey
Kathleen Burke .................. Hettie Ide
Monte Blue ...................... Clem Dillon
Directed by ............... Charles Barton
Produced by ..... Paramount Pictures
```

Poster for *Nevada* (1935)

Buster Crabbe and Kathleen Burke in a scene from *Nevada* (1935)

mount who wanted to capitalize on his good looks and athletic abilities. During the early 1930s he appeared in several Zane Grey Westerns, including *To the Last Man* (1933), also filmed at Big Bear Lake, before being offered the role that he is best remembered for — *Flash Gordon* in 1936. Later he would become another science fiction hero, Buck Rogers. In the 1940s, Crabbe once more turned to Westerns and made a series of unremarkable "B" films. In later years, Crabbe associated himself with a swimming pool construction company, but kept his hand in the film industry by doing cameo roles every so often. Crabbe died in 1983 at the age of seventy-six.

Twenty-two year old Kathleen Burke, who had just made another Zane Grey film at Big Bear (*Rocky Mountain Mystery*-1935), started her film career by winning a contest to play Lota, the Panther Woman in Paramount's *Island of Lost Souls* (1933). This film also had an uncredited role by Buster Crabbe as one of the "beasts." Burke made seven pictures in 1935 and then she drifted from studio to studio, picking up bit parts. She retired in 1938 at the age of twenty-five after making twenty plus films.

Making a return trip to Big Bear Lake, Monte Blue once again played the villain. Actually, this was Blue's third trip in 1935. Earlier in the year, he had appeared with Kermit Maynard as his sidekick in the James Oliver Curwood Royal Canadian Mounted Police tale, *Trails of the Wild*. Forty-five year old Blue, who had been a popular silent star, was a full-time character actor by this time. From 1915 until his death in 1963, Blue appeared in almost three hundred film and television shows.

Buster Crabbe in
Nevada (1935)
Photo courtesy of
The Academy of Motion Picture
Arts and Sciences

Buster Crabbe and unidentified
actors in a scene from
Nevada (1935)
(Note Clark's Grade in the
background.)

SILENT CODE (1935)

CAST:
Kane Richmond .... Cpl. Jerry Hale
Blanche Mehaffey .... Helen Brent
Directed by .... Stuart Paton
Produced by ... International Pictures

Blanche Mehaffey
circa 1935
Photo courtesy of Les Adams

Newly assigned Royal Canadian Mounted Police Corporal Jerry Hale (Kane Richmond) finds a dying man who turns out to be the brother-in-law of the factor (head man) of the trading post, Peter Barkley (Barney Furey). Helen Brent (Blanche Mehaffey), the daughter of the murdered man, works for the factor, but doesn't trust him as he cheats the miners shamelessly. Hale is then framed for the murder when he produces the old miner's map of where the treasure is hidden. When the police inspector follows the map, but finds no gold, things look bleak for Hale. Thrown into the plot is the murdered man's dog, Rex, who knows who the real killers are and where the treasure is cached.

International Pictures, another one of the "poverty row" producers, chose the San Bernardino Mountains for this tale of twisted loyalties. The area looks suspiciously like Crestline and Valley of Enchantment near Camp Seely, but no production notes confirm the location.

Twenty-nine year old Kane Richmond began his career in the movie industry as a film booker for the States Rights organization, before Universal Studios asked him to act in front of the cameras. He started out in Universal's two-reelers *The Leather Pushers*, a series about the boxing profession in the late 1920s. During the Thirties he played bit parts in "A" pictures and the heroes in "B" movies. He became a leading man in serials at Republic Pictures in the late 1930s and early Forties. Richmond left the industry in 1948 to pursue a career in the fashion industry, but made occasional cameo appearances on screen into the Sixties. Richmond died in 1973 at the age of sixty-seven with close to one hundred film and television credits.

Blanche Mehaffey, a former WAMPAS Baby Star (1924), appeared in a dozen productions before making the transition to talkies.

Mehaffey broke into show business as a dancer with the Ziegfeld Follies in the early 1920s and moved into the moving picture industry in 1923 as a bit player. By the late Twenties, she had been married and divorced and began a career as a "B" movie queen that continued throughout the 1930s. She retired in 1938 after forty movies and made one comeback movie in 1946 before finally calling it quits. Mehaffey died in 1968 at the age of sixty-one.

Kane Richmond (in uniform) struggles with the bad guys in a scene from *Silent Code* (1935).

TRIGGER TOM (1935)

CAST:

Tom Tyler .... Tom Hunter
Al St. John .... Stub Macey
Bernadene Hayes .... Dorothy
Jergenson
Directed by .... Harry S. Webb
Produced by .... Reliable Pictures

Tom Tyler
circa 1935

The 1930s could almost be called the age of Westerns. Because of the depression, it was imperative that movies be made quickly and cheaply. Westerns fit the bill more so than other genres and for a single dime they were the mainstay of Saturday matinees. Between 1934 and 1936, Reliable Pictures made forty-five films, the majority of them low-budget "oaters." Many of them were made on location in the San Bernardino Mountains, as was *Trigger Tom* which showcased the talents of popular Western hero Tom Tyler.

In one of the most scenic parts of Big Bear, Tom Hunter (Tom Tyler) and his sidekick Stub (Al St. John) attempt to buy a herd of cattle from Rancher Jergenson (John Elliot) and his daughter Dorothy (Bernadene Hayes). His efforts are thwarted by outlaws, led by Scarface Taylor (Bud Osborne) who try to dynamite the pass. After a fight on the top of the rocky pass, Tom rescues Dorothy and secures the herd for delivery. In one of the strangest shootouts in movie history, two of the old codgers hide behind huge kites made from blankets and fire at one another until one of them is shot.

Born Vincent Markowski of Lithuanian descent, Tyler came to the movies as a stunt man, but because he was tall, strikingly handsome and had a magnificent physique (he was a weight-lifting champion), he quickly became a silent Western hero in the mid 1920s. His transition to talkies was considered smooth as he had a strong voice tinged with just a slight accent. During the Thirties, Tyler worked for nearly all of the "poverty row" producers and consequently, never earned large sums for his work. By the end of the decade, Tyler was reduced to taking character roles. In the 1940s, his career revived with his portrayal of caped crusader, Captain Marvel. Unfortunately, his health failed in the next few years and he was reduced once more to bit parts. In his thirty years of films, Tyler is credited with almost two hundred appearances. He died of heart failure in 1954 at the age of fifty.

Blonde Bernadene Hayes was one of the hundreds of hopeful starlets that called Hollywood their home. This was probably her only starring role. From 1934 until her retirement in 1954, Hayes made nearly sixty films, none of them memorable.

Once again, Bud Osborne played the villain Scarface Taylor. Although fifty-two years old, Osborne put up a good fight on the mountain pass. He was known as one of the best four-horse teamsters Hollywood had. In his five decade career, Osborne appeared in more than five hundred pictures, many of them made on location in the San Bernardino Mountains.

Tom Tyler and Bud Osborne (right) battle it out on top of the cliffs above Big Bear Lake in a scene from *Trigger Tom* (1935).

THE TRAIL OF THE LONESOME PINE (1936)

Sylvia Sidney and Henry Fonda on location
at Cedar Lake for the film
The Trail of the Lonesome Pine (1936)
Photo courtesy of
The Academy of Motion Picture
Arts and Sciences

In the summer of 1935, Paramount Pictures brought a crew to Bartlett's Lake (now Cedar Lake) to construct a set for the John W. Fox novel, *The Trail of the Lonesome Pine*. Tom Core, a local Big Bear resident and historian, remembers working on the set where he helped build the water wheel and house on Cedar Lake which was predominant in the film. This was Paramount's fifth remake of the beloved story (some say "the best tearjerker of all time") and they must have finally gotten it right because it has never been made again. The elaborate set was necessary because Paramount was about to shoot the first outdoor movie ever made in Technicolor.

Jack Hale (Fred MacMurray) is a young railroad surveyor who has been hired to find the best possible route for a new line through the Blue Ridge Mountains. Inadvertently, he starts up a long simmering feud between the Tolliver clan and the Falin clan with tragic results to young Buddie Tolliver, played by George McFarland who would be better remembered as "Spanky" in the *Our Gang* comedies. Complicating matters even more, Jack falls in love with one of the hillbilly daughters, June (Sylvia Sidney) who is betrothed to her cousin, Dave (Henry Fonda).

The film was directed by Henry Hathaway, who was born with the unlikely name of Marquis Henri Leonard de Fiennes, to a theatrical family. His grandfather had been commissioned by the King of Belgians to acquire the Sandwich Islands (Hawaiian Islands), hence the inherited title.

Hathaway began his film career as a child actor in Westerns directed by Allan Dwan. His career was interrupted when WWI broke out and he enlisted in the Army. After the war Hathaway became an assistant director, with credits for *Ben Hur* (1925) and *Mantrap* (1926). In the Thirties, he became a full director and made several trips into the San Bernardino Mountains to film: *To the Last Man* (1933), *Now and Forever* (1934), and *Peter Ibbetson* (1935). His love of the mountains was obvious as he made four more trips, to film: *Spawn of the North* (1938), *Brigham Young* (1940), *The Shepherd of the Hills* (1941) and finally, *North to Alaska* (1960). The last two movies were made with one of his favorite actors, John Wayne. Amazingly, Hathaway, who directed some of the finest movies produced in Hollywood, was only nominated for an Oscar once. He won the Best Director award in 1936 for *The Lives of a Bengal Lancer* (1935). Hathaway died in 1985 just short of his eighty-seventh birthday.

Twenty-seven year old Fred MacMurray started his film career at the end of the silent era as an extra. His big break came when he was cast opposite Katharine Hepburn in *Alice Adams* (1935). One of the most endeared actors in Hollywood, he was equally delightful playing comedy (as the crazy professor who invents "flubber" in *The Absent-Minded Professor*-1961), or the calculating lover of Barbara Stanwyck in *Double Indemnity* (1944). With a career that spanned close to seven decades, it is surprising to note that MacMurray never garnered even an Oscar nomination. He will best be remembered for his long running TV series, *My Three Sons* (1960-1972). He died at the age of eighty-three in 1991.

Petite and pretty, twenty-six year old Sylvia Sidney had some of the most expressive eyes in

Fred MacMurray and Tuffy on location at Cedar Lake for the film
The Trail of the Lonesome Pine (1936)
Photo courtesy of Jerry Orvedahl

Hollywood. Bronx-born Sidney's career began on Broadway where she was a rising star. Her first film was a silent that high-lighted Broadway actresses of the day, *Broadway Nights* (1927). In 1931, she was asked to replace Clara Bow and play oppo-site Gary Cooper in the crime-drama *City Streets*. The film was an instant hit and secured Sidney's place among the leading actresses of the day. Over the next seventy years, Sidney worked in films and televi-sion with a final appearance as the gravelly voiced "Grandma Florence" in the wacky Tim Burton comedy, *Mars Attacks!* (1996). Sidney was nominated for both an Oscar and an Emmy, and won a Golden Globe award in 1986. She died of throat cancer in 1999, a month before her eighty-ninth birthday.

The ever youthful looking, Ne-braska-born Henry Fonda had third billing in this film, his fourth since he began his career on the screen. A consummate stage actor, Fonda returned time and again to the legitimate stage which was his first love. His sympathetic portrayal of the underdog was his lifelong signature and led to his first Oscar nomination for Best Actor in *The Grapes of Wrath* (1940). Ironically, he lost to his long time friend, Jimmy Stewart, in *The Philadelphia Story* (1940). Fonda returned to the San Bernardino Mountains in 1938 to film *Spawn of the North* and again to star in *Wild Geese Calling* (1941).

Beulah Bondi tends Henry Fonda in this re-issued lobby card for the film *The Trail of the Lonesome Pine* (1936).

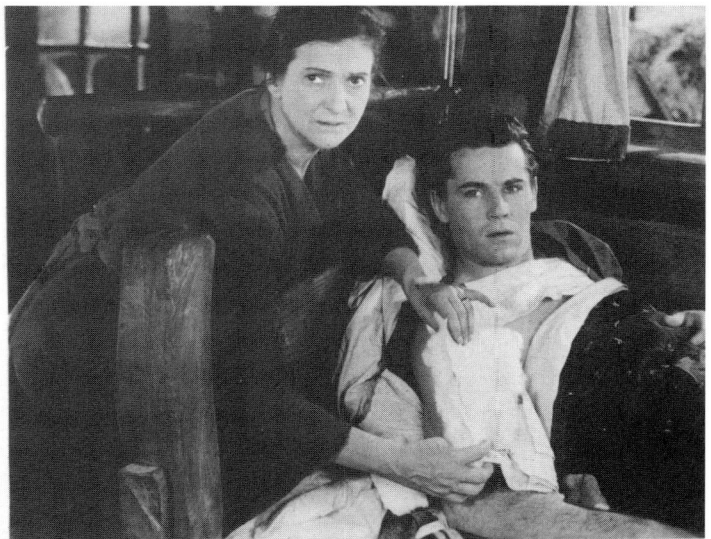

FRED MacMURRAY
SYLVIA SIDNEY
HENRY FONDA

with FRED STONE · NIGEL BRUCE
ROBERT BARRAT · BEULAH BONDI
SPANKY McFARLAND · FUZZY KNIGHT
Based on John Fox, Jr.'s Famous Novel · Directed by Henry Hathaway
A Walter Wanger Production
A PARAMOUNT RE-RELEASE

THE TRAIL OF THE LONESOME PINE

CARYL OF THE MOUNTAINS (1936)

Reliable Pictures sent a crew to the Big Bear area after the snows had fallen in 1936, to film the James Oliver Curwood saga, *Caryl of the Mountains*. Once more Rinty (Rin-Tin-Tin, Jr.) must save the day after his owner, trapper Jean Foray (Josef Swickard), is murdered. During the killing, Rinty is wounded trying to save his master. Foray's niece, Caryl (Lois Wilde), arrives at the cabin under a cloud of suspicion. Her employer has reported the theft of some bonds that she is believed to have taken. Sgt. Brad Sheridan (Francis X. Bushman, Jr.) is asked to investigate the murder and renews an old flame with Caryl until he finds out she is wanted for embezzlement. Caryl reveals she only took the bonds to protect them from being stolen by her boss, Pres. Enos Colvin (Robert Walker). In the end, only Rinty knows where the bonds are hidden and corners the man who killed his master, none other than Colvin.

Thirty-three year old Ralph E. Bushman was the son of Francis X. Bushman (known as the first King of Hollywood) and began using his father's name when he found it had better recognition. At six foot two inches, Bushman was the epitome of the strapping, handsome young hero, but he was not his father and his acting was considered second-rate at best. Bushman made more than thirty films and made the transition to talkies when he starred in *Caryl of the Mountains*. After that he played a few character roles and finally retired in 1946.

One of the many young starlets in Hollywood was twenty-seven year old Lois Wilde who appeared in

CAST:
Lois Wilde .... Caryl Foray
Francis X. Bushman, Jr.   ....Brad Sheridan
Directed by .... Bernard B. Ray
Produced by .... Reliable Pictures

1930s post card of
Francis X. Bushman, Jr.

Lois Wilde circa 1936
Photo courtesy of Paramount Pictures
and Frank Ralbovsky

twelve pictures in two years and then disappeared from the scene for fifteen years. In 1952, she was in an uncredited role in a "B" movie called *Steel Town* which was filmed in Fontana at the Kaiser Steel Mill. Again she disappeared for another fifteen years, until she once more pops up in a terrible Sci-Fi movie called *Sharad of Atlantis*, made for television. She died in 1995 at the age of eighty-six.

Once again, Reliable Pictures used old silent stars, Robert Walker and George Chesebro, as the villains and Rinty's enemies. The pair of villains had crossed paths with Rinty in the movie *Skull and Crown* (1935), which was also filmed in Big Bear. Another ex-silent star and probably the best actor in the entire production was seventy year old, white-haired Josef Swickard who had been born in Coblenz, Germany. From 1912 until his death in 1940, Swickard appeared in over one hundred and sixty film productions.

1930s photo of Reliable Pictures studio at the corner of Beachwood and Sunset Blvd. in Hollywood

STRAIGHT FROM THE SHOULDER (1936)

In the early part of the summer of 1936, Paramount Pictures sent a crew and cast up to Bartlett's Lake (now Cedar Lake) to film *Straight From the Shoulder,* from a short story by Lucian Cary in *The Saturday Evening Post*. This time, Paramount did use the existing set they had constructed for *The Trail of the Lonesome Pine* (1936) and the water wheel is quite prominent.

Gail Pyne (Katherine Locke), granddaughter of Jedediah Pyne (Andy Clyde), decides to leave the lakeside cabin she grew up in and take a job in the big city. She begins work with a commercial artist and widower, Curt Hayden (Ralph Bellamy), only to find that their lives are in danger when they witness a gangland killing. Utilizing his artistic talents, Curt is able to draw the killers, but when he goes to testify against them at the trial, he is shot. Gail convinces Curt and his son to hide out at the old cabin next to the lake until he recuperates from his wound. Curt's son Johnny (David Holt) is unhappy with the budding relationship growing between his father and Gail, but is buoyed up by the fact that her grandfather is building a child-size rifle for him to shoot. When the killer's gang finds out where Curt has been hiding, they capture the son and grandfather and lay in wait to kill Curt. When the pair arrive, the killers fire but unbeknownst to them, Johnny has plugged the barrel of the killer's gun and the rifle backfires. Gail then uses the child-

CAST:	
Ralph Bellamy	Curt Hayden
Katherine Locke	Gail Pyne
Andy Clyde	Jedediah Pyne
Directed by	Stuart Heisler
Produced by	Paramount Pictures

Katherine Locke and Ralph Bellamy on location at Big Bear Lake for the movie *Straight from the Shoulder* (1936) Photo courtesy of The Academy of Motion Picture Arts and Sciences

size rifle to disarm the second killer and thus gains the respect of young Johnny.

Thirty-two year old Ralph Bellamy knew he wanted to be an actor since the days he lobbied to become the president of his high school drama club. After a few years on Broadway, Bellamy came west and in 1931 began in movies with bit parts. The deep-voiced actor was soon starring in films, but by the late thirties, he was always the guy who lost the girl to the likes of Cary Grant. In the Forties, Bellamy once more saw his stock rise when he starred in a series of *Ellery Queen* mysteries. Because of an uncanny likeness, he is best remembered for his portrayal of President Franklin D. Roosevelt in the stage play and later the movie *Sunrise at Campobello*. *Life Magazine* even portrayed him on the cover, in February, 1958, striking a pose with a dog that looked exactly like the one FDR owned and loved, Fala.

Ralph Bellamy on the cover of
Life Magazine as he appeared in the play
Sunrise at Campobello

Russian-born Katherine Locke was a Broadway actress who enjoyed dabbling in films. Raised on the east coast and trained in classical piano, Locke rebelled and headed west to join a group of vibrant actors known as the "potboilers." *Straight from the Shoulder* was her debut film and critics loved the twenty-six year old brunette, but her heart longed for the Great White Way. In 1937, she was the toast of Broadway when she co-starred with John Garfield in the comedy, *Having Wonderful Time*. (A year later, RKO Studios bought the film rights and starred Ginger Rogers and Douglas Fairbanks, Jr. in the movie version, which ironically was also filmed at Cedar Lake.) In twenty years of screen acting Locke only appeared eight times, but never again as the star. She died at the age of eighty-five in 1995.

Another one of the great character actors was forty-four year old Scottish-born Andy Clyde. The wiry Scot with the walrus mustache began with Mack Sennett as a comedian and was famous for his double-take. His film credits include being Hopalong Cassidy's sidekick and spanned four decades with more than three hundred film and television appearances.

Born in 1886, Lucian Cary, who wrote the story, was one of the shooting world's greatest writers. His J. M. Pyne character was utilized in many of his short stories which brought tales of target shooting, hunting and adventure to the reader.

1930s post card of movie set at Cedar Lake
(mislabled incorrectly as Big Bear Lake)
Photo courtesy of the Russ Keller Collection
Photoscan by Roger Hatheway

GIRL OF THE OZARKS (1936)

CAST:
Virginia Weidler .... Edie Moseley
Henrietta Crosman .... Granny Moseley
Leif Erickson .... Tom Bolton
Elizabeth Russell .... Gail Rogers
Directed by .... William Shea
Produced by ..... Paramount Pictures

In the heart of the depression, no other part of the country was poorer than the people of the Ozarks, and the Moseley family was the poorest in the county. Practically wearing rags, little Edie Moseley (Virginia Weidler) tries to make the best of things in a one room schoolhouse to the taunts of the other children. When she becomes incorrigible, the town elders take things into their own hands and threaten to place her in a county home. Tom Bolton (Leif Erickson), the town's editor, agrees to be her guardian because her mother is too sick to get out of bed and her grandmother, Granny Moseley (Henrietta Crosman), is as incorrigible as little Edie. Gail Rogers (Elizabeth Russell), the daughter of the town's leading citizen, arrives from Philadelphia where she has spent the last two years becoming citified. Tom loves Gail, but she sees no future with him as he won't leave the small town. Later Gail realizes that life with Tom in a small town is still better than life in the city without him. When they marry, their first act is to adopt little Edie who has lost everyone in her family.

Surprisingly, Paramount didn't use the elaborate set they built for *The Trail of the Lonesome Pine* (1936), but shot existing buildings in and around Big Bear Lake. They also recognized the drawing power of Henrietta Crosman, one of the premier actresses of her day and gave her second billing over Leif Erickson and Elizabeth Russell.

Seventy-five year old Henrietta Crosman was a leading actress on Broadway, where she played the parts of Grand Dames as well as Shakespeare. She began her film career in 1914 in a movie adapted from a stage play to show

Elizabeth Russell and Leif Erickson look on approvingly at Virginia Weidler in a scene from *Girl of the Ozarks* (1936).

off her talents. Over the next two decades she made occasional film appearances but always returned to her first love, the legitimate stage. She made one more film after *Girl of the Ozarks* and then retired. She died in 1944 at the age of eighty-three.

Leif Erickson (pronounced "life") was born William Anderson in 1911. Before graduating from high school, Erickson decided to take a job singing and playing the trombone with an orchestra that was touring the country. Paramount offered the tall, good-looking, brawny Erickson a contract in 1935 and his first bit part was as a corpse in a Zane Grey Western. His next two pictures were also Zane Grey Westerns, where he had speaking parts, also shot in Big Bear, *Nevada* (1935) and *Drift Fence* (1936). In *Girl of the Ozarks*, Erickson shows off his deep rich voice with a couple of songs, but critics felt his acting was just so-so. He quickly slipped into character roles and secondary parts. His career was placed on hold when WWII broke out and he enlisted in the Navy. After the war, Hollywood was in transition and parts were scarce to all but the best of actors. He continued acting in secondary roles for the rest of his screen career with close to two hundred and fifty credits during his five decades before the cameras. Erickson is best known for his many television appearances, including the lead role as Big John Cannon in *The High Chaparral* series that ran from 1967 to 1971. At the height of his career, Erickson married one of his leading ladies, actress Frances Farmer who became a *cause celebre* for the mentally ill.

Ten year old Virginia Weidler was already a child star and veteran actress (she had the part

Virginia Weidler entertains the school board with a song and dance during a scene from *Girl of the Ozarks* (1936).

of Mimsey in *Peter Ibbetson*-1935) with nine screen credits when she made *Girl of the Ozarks* in 1936. Weidler's mother was a famous German opera singer who wanted a screen career for her daughter. Her first appearance was to be opposite John Barrymore in *Moby Dick* (1930), but because she refused to remove her dress during a bathing scene (she was all of three), the part went to another child actress. When her career stalled at Paramount Studios in 1938, Weidler signed on at M-G-M. Just as her career was starting to take off, M-G-M signed another child actress, Shirley Temple. It wasn't too long before the two found themselves vying for the same parts. She retired from the screen in 1943 at the age of sixteen and died at the age of forty-one from a heart attack.

Henrietta Crosman (holding a rifle), Virginia Weidler and Leif Erickson as they appeared on a lobby card from the 1930s

FRESHMAN LOVE (1936)

When Billings College continually loses in rowing regattas, Coach Hammond (Frank McHugh), whose job is on the line, decides to fire the entire crew and recruit some real oarsmen. Joan Simpkins (Patricia Ellis), whose father is the college president, agrees to help recruit the best crew for the college by using her feminine wiles on two of the brightest prospects in the nation. At Lake Mistooke (Lake Arrowhead), Joan runs over practicing oarsman Tony Foster (Walter Johnson) with her boat, but convinces him that Billings is the college to go to. At a charity ball, she lands the second prospect, playboy collegian Bob Wilson (Warren Hull), for Billings. Sparks fly when the two oarsmen find that they are vying for the same girl, but in the end they both row for old Billings and win the big Tri-State Regatta to the tune of *Dixie*.

Also called *Rhythm on the River*, (which refers to the music used to get the rowers moving faster), this Warner Brothers' musical comedy featured some great jazz and swing music. Unfortunately, the students look too old to be in college, even twenty-two year old Lloyd Bridges in his first movie role. Nevertheless, the scenic views of Lake Arrowhead and the Village beach alongside McKenzie Ski School make this film a delight to watch.

Nineteen year old Patricia Ellis was the stepdaughter of Broadway director and theatrical producer, Alexander Leftwich. The bright, perky blonde became a contract player for Warner Brothers in 1932 and for the next six years she was credited with forty-four pictures before she married and retired from films in 1939. She died of cancer in 1970 at the age of fifty-four.

As a most unlikely freshman,

CAST:	
Patricia Ellis	Joan Simpkins
Warren Hull	Bob Wilson
Frank McHugh	Tom Hammond
Walter Johnson	Tony Foster
Directed by	William C. McGann
Produced by	Warner Brothers

Patricia Ellis
circa 1936

Warren Hull
circa 1936

thirty-three year old Warren Hull was making his third movie for Warner Brothers where he was also a contract player. Hull had a magnificent deep voice that helped him host many television shows later in his career. His screen credits also included two popular comic book characters, Mandrake in *Mandrake the Magician* (1939) and the lead in *The Green Hornet Strikes Again* (1940).

Equally unlikely as a freshman, Walter Johnson was thirty years old at the time he made *Freshman Love*. His film career spanned only three years when he made ten films for six different studios. He died in 1946 at the age of forty.

Comic relief is supplied by veteran actor Frank McHugh and Mary Treen as sweethearts who can't marry until the coach wins the big race. Character actor McHugh began in films with Howard Hawks' *The Dawn Patrol* (1930), sometimes called the "Greatest Air Epic Ever Made." Over the next thirty-seven years he amassed close to one hundred and fifty screen and television credits. Twenty-nine year old Treen was also a screen veteran and over the next five decades entertained audiences with her plastic face and comic antics.

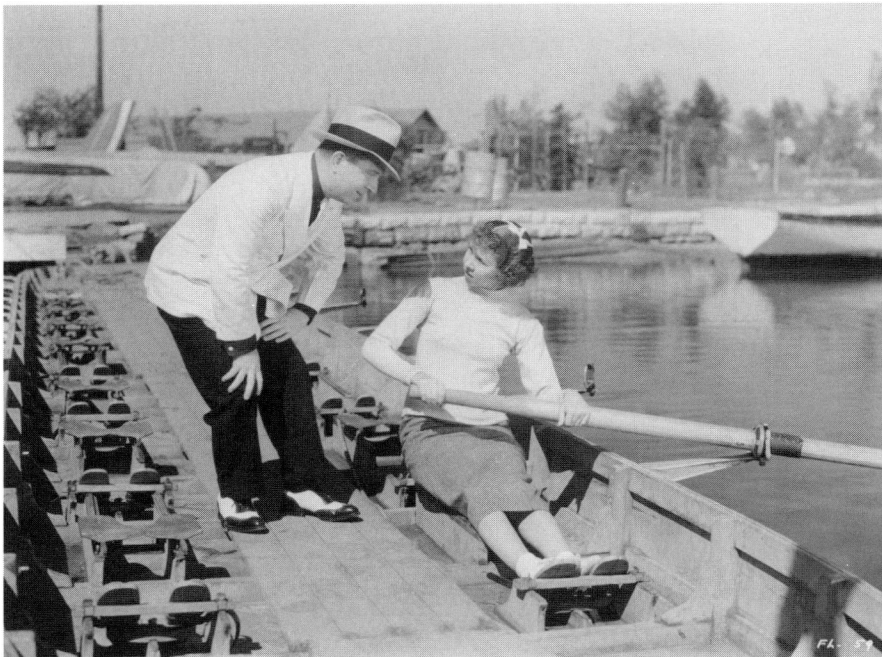

Frank McHugh and Mary Treen in a scene from *Freshman Love* (1936)

DRIFT FENCE (1936)

Paramount's location scouts loved the San Bernardino Mountains, especially in the 1930s. Staying at the Pine Knot cabins in Big Bear Lake, the entire cast and crew of *Drift Fence* were entertained by Tuffy, a mixed breed border collie, owned by Gerhart Orvedahl. Tuffy had been in an earlier Big Bear film, *Nevada* (1935), where his intelligence and talents stood out and so he was asked once more to perform in this Zane Grey Western. Tuffy's most important role was in another film that same year, *The Trail of the Lonesome Pine* (1936), which was shot on location at Cedar Lake with Fred MacMurray (see p.185).

Cowboy Jim Travis (Tom Keene) is persuaded to switch places with a man with a similar name, Traft (Benny Baker), who has inherited a ranch. A provision in the will states that the heir must learn the cattle business, which the real inheritor has no intention of doing. Travis skillfully erects a "drift fence" for cattle containment which impresses the Traft wranglers. The fence is an obstacle to the rustlers headed up by Clay Jackson (Stanley Andrews), who enlists the strong-arm tactics of Travis' next door neighbor, cattleman Slinger Dunn (Buster Crabbe). Slinger is also known as the fastest gun around. Complicating matters, Jackson is sweet on Slinger's sister, Molly (Katherine DeMille). Travis, who is really a Texas Ranger in disguise, eventually convinces Slinger that Jackson is a wanted criminal and not looking out for the Dunn family's best interests. When Slinger and Travis join forces, justice prevails and Jim wins the girl.

Tom Keene is one of the least remembered Western actors. This is possibly due to his numerous name changes. From 1928 to 1930 he was known by his birth name, George Duryea. During the 1930s he was cowboy Tom Keene and then he made another switch in 1944

Tom Keene
circa 1930s

to Richard Powers. In later years he reverted to just Dick Powers. His chance meeting with Ed Wood, Jr. in the waning years of his career led to his inclusion in what has been called "the worst film ever made," *Plan Nine from Outer Space*, written, produced and directed by Ed Wood. A former Broadway actor, Keene had been brought to Hollywood by Cecil B. DeMille in 1928 to play the lead in some of DeMille's films. When he made *Drift Fence* in 1936, Keene was probably at the top of his career having appeared in twenty-eight films to date. After appearing in two so-so Paramount Westerns in 1936, he found himself making pictures for the "poverty row" producers, but at least he was still the star. In all, Keene/Powers/ Duryea is credited with close to one hundred screen appearances in his thirty years of filming.

Canadian-born Katherine DeMille was the adopted daughter of Cecil B. DeMille. She began

Tom Keene, Katherine DeMille and Buster Crabbe in a scene from *Drift Fence* (1936)

appearing in her father's films in the early Thirties and was usually cast as the "other woman." In the late Thirties she broke with Paramount but with a name like DeMille she still had star power, even if it was in a dud like *Charlie Chan at the Olympics* (1937). In 1937, she married actor Anthony Quinn with whom she had two (some say three) children, one of whom drowned in the swimming pool of W. C. Fields, the comedian. DeMille never achieved true stardom and finished her career in supporting roles. She retired in 1949 and made one cameo appearance in 1956. DeMille died in 1995 at the age of eighty-three.

With a magnificent physique, handsome Buster Crabbe, who had just played the good guy in *Nevada* (1935), reverted to the villain in *Drift Fence*. Crabbe graduated from the University of Southern California in 1931 and had been acting in bit parts up until then. After he won an Olympic Gold Medal as a swimmer in the 1932 Olympics at Los Angeles, he was offered a contract with Paramount Pictures. Instead of entering law school where he had been accepted, he chose an acting career. In 1936, Crabbe filmed what would become the quintessential super hero, *Flash Gordon,* at Universal Studios. The film, based on a comic book series, assured Crabbe's future in movies. Crabbe continued to act in movies the rest of his life and had more than one hundred and twenty film and television credits in his fifty years on the screen. He died at the age of seventy-six in 1983.

**Buster Crabbe
circa 1936**

THE LAST OF THE MOHICANS (1936)

In the fifth movie produced from the story by James Fenimore Cooper, Reliance Productions brought a cast and crew back to Big Bear and Cedar Lake in the summer of 1936 to film this tale of the French and Indian War. By this version, Natty Bumppo aka Hawkeye, has been elevated to the lead character and the story's ending has been completely altered. Alice (Binnie Barnes) and Cora (Heather Angel) Munro trek through the wilderness seeking their father, English Col. Munro, at Ft. Henry with the aid of Hawkeye (Randolph Scott) and Major Duncan Heywood (Henry Wilcoxon). At one point, Magua the Huron (Bruce Cabot) captures Cora and Major Heywood, but Hawkeye escapes with Alice. In a duel to the death, Magua wrestles with Uncas (Phillip Reed) atop a cliff and forces him over the edge. Magua's lust for Cora then drives her over the cliff also and she falls mortally wounded beside the dying Uncas. Chingachgook (Robert Barrat), father of Uncas, then kills Magua in revenge for his son's death.

Thirty-eight year old Randolph Scott was a soft-spoken Virginian who had been trained as an engineer. His good looks and interest in acting brought him to Hollywood. Scott's chance meeting with Howard Hughes, who took a liking to him, resulted in a screen test and subsequent contract. At Paramount Studios he became a leading man in a series of parlor romances, but his real love was Westerns. Not wanting to play favorites during WWII, he appeared as a naval officer, a marine and as an airman in patriotic films. After the war, Scott made no pretense of preferring to appear in nothing other than Westerns. He made

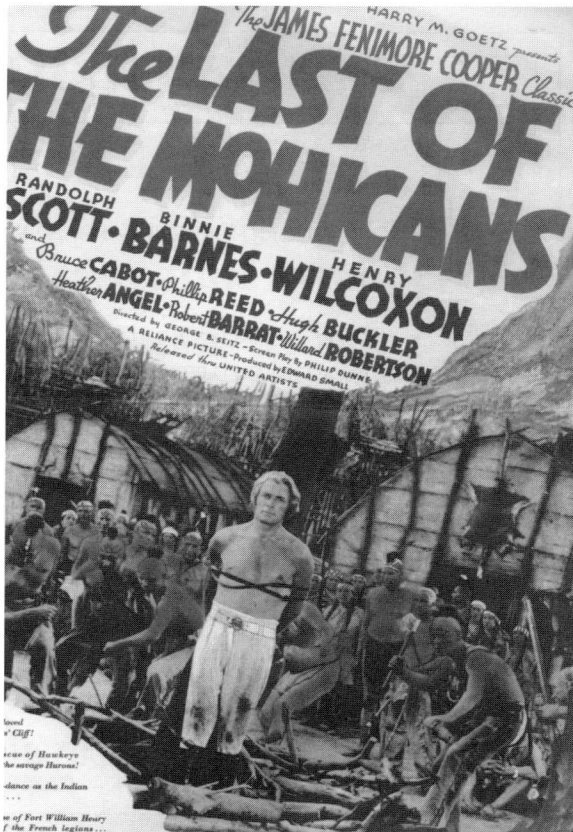

Playbill for *The Last of the Mohicans* circa 1936

nearly forty more "oaters" before his retirement in 1962.

London-born Binnie Barnes had started show business as a cabaret singer and dance hostess. In 1931, Noel Coward wrote a song especially for her to sing in a review. Her first screen appearances were in two reel comedies with Stanley Lupino, Ida's father. She became a star of British films and came to Hollywood in 1934 and starred in a series of dramas, usually as the "other woman." Fed up with films, Barnes left the screen in 1941 for radio. She was occasionally drawn back into movies that interested her over the next three decades. Her final film was a comedy made for television in 1974.

Born in the British West Indies, Henry Wilcoxon had a commanding theatrical presence on film which brought him to England where he became a star. He is best remembered for his roles as the pompous English gentleman. His long association with Cecil B. DeMille led to some of his best roles and later to production duties on films like *The Greatest Show on Earth* (1952) and *The Ten Commandments* (1956). In a career that spanned fifty years, Wilcoxon had more than seventy-five screen and television credits.

Another English import was flaxen-haired twenty-seven year old Heather Angel (her real name). After starring in British films beginning in 1931, she migrated to Hollywood during the mid-Thirties. By the late Thirties, she was being cast in second-rate thrillers as the heroine. When parts dried up for her during the intervening years, she did voice overs for films. Her last appearance was in a television mini-series in 1979. Angel died in 1986 at the age of seventy-seven.

Alternating between good guy/bad guy, thirty-two year old Bruce Cabot had just saved Fay Wray from the clutches of *King Kong* in 1933 and then been asked to menace Heather Angel to her death in *Mohicans*. It is little wonder that Cabot changed his name,

Binnie Barnes
circa 1936

Heather Angel
circa 1936

for he was born Etienne Pelissier Jacques de Bujac, and was brought up by a father in the diplomatic service. In 1932, he corralled David O. Selznick at a cocktail party and hassled him into a screen test. Over the next few years, Cabot starred in a variety of films. When the roles began to dry up in the Forties for the handsome, but sometimes abrasive, actor his long association with drinking buddy, John Wayne, allowed him to extend his career via Wayne vehicles, like *Hatari!* (1962), *The Green Berets* (1968), and *Big Jake* (1971). With more than one hundred screen appearances, Cabot died in 1972 at the age of sixty-eight.

**Phillip Reed struggles with Bruce Cabot (right) as
Heather Angel looks on in a scene from
The Last of the Mohicans (1936).
Photo courtesy of
The Academy of Motion Picture
Arts and Sciences**

SUTTER'S GOLD (1936)

Probably one of the most interesting films made in the San Bernardino Mountains has to be *Sutter's Gold*. Universal Pictures purchased the rights to the 1926 novel, *L'Or,* written by Swiss author Blaise Cendras. Universal's woes began immediately with the story treatment. In 1934, Russian film maker/ director, Sergei M. Eisenstein (he directed the silent Russian classic, *Battleship Potemkin*-1925), was invited to Hollywood to write some scripts. Evidently his script for *L'Or* was turned down by Universal, as was William Faulkner's treatment, for neither received credit for their efforts. Eventually, Bruno Frank, along with three others, was given the film writing credit. Universal chose independent director James Cruze on the strength of his silent screen successes and his film *I Cover the Waterfront* (1933). Unfortunately, they ignored his recent failings. *Sutter's Gold* premiered in Sacramento on March 1, 1936, at the Alhambra Theater. Universal's final expenditure was over $2,000,000 to produce the film and it was a dismal box office failure, costing Cruze his reputation. Only a small portion of the film was made at Barton Flats, a forested area south of Big Bear Lake.

The story concerns the hardships of Swiss-born Johan Sutter, who fled his native land under a cloud of suspicion and eventually landed in California where he attempted to create his own "New Switzerland." Swiss-born Blaise Cendras was himself an exile from his own country and much of his book may be autobiographical, if not the factual history of Johan Sutter.

Rotund Edward Arnold once said, "that as he gained weight, the better the roles he got . . . so he never stopped eating." Born on the Lower East Side of New York City and orphaned at the age of eleven, the forty-six year old actor had been bitten by the acting bug at an early age. His film career started in 1916 with bit parts at Essanay Film Studios in Chicago. He made the

---

CAST:
Edward Arnold .... John Sutter
Lee Tracy .... Pete Perkin
Binnie Barnes .... Countess Elizabeth Bartoffski
Directed by .... James Cruze
Produced by .... Universal Pictures

Premier opening for *Sutter's Gold* circa 1936
Photo courtesy of the *Sacramento Bee*

Edward Arnold at Barton Flats in a scene
from *Sutter's Gold* (1936)

Lee Tracy
circa 1935

transition to talkies because of his deep, and by then theatrical, voice playing the parts of "heavies." In 1935, he was asked by the producers at Universal to pack on even more weight to his already ample girth for the starring role in *Diamond Jim*, the story of the flamboyant gambler "Diamond" Jim Brady. His leading lady was Binnie Barnes who played the part of his paramour, Lillian Russell, and who starred with him again in the ill-fated *Sutter's Gold* the following year. Strangely enough, because of his strong characterization of Sutter in *Sutter's Gold*, Arnold never suffered for parts. His four decades in films netted him more than one hundred film and television credits. Politically active, Arnold worked hard to protect his fellow actors, even taking a controversial stand against the House Un-American Activities Committee. Arnold died in 1956 at the age of sixty-six.

Lee Tracy plays Sutter's partner and just about steals every scene that he is in. Classified as one of the truly great character actors, Tracy almost was black balled from Hollywood because of an incident he pulled while on the set of *Viva Villa!* (1934) on location in Mexico. Tracy got drunk one afternoon and urinated on a passing military parade. The episode enraged Mexican politicos and was about to become an international crisis until M-G-M agreed to do something about it. Not only did they fire Tracy from the set, but they agreed to delete him from scenes already shot. Tracy later redeemed himself, but his reputation was tarnished and many thought he never really lived up to his true potential. He did receive an Oscar nomination for his supporting role in *The Best Man* (1964), as well as a nomination for a Golden Globe. Unfortunately, he lost out on both.

Two of the many uncredited extras in the film were Jim Thorpe and Oscar Apfel. Forty-eight year old Native American Thorpe was one of the greatest living athletes at the time, but struggled with alcoholism. Fifty-eight year old Apfel had been a silent actor, then director, and finally character actor in his three decade career.

DANIEL BOONE (1936)

In the spring and summer of 1936, RKO Studios built an elaborate set near Big Bear to represent early Booneville, Kentucky, and asked local citizens to become involved with their production of *Daniel Boone*. Two of the extras were Fred and Loretta Baker, who owned Andrews Lodge on the lake next to Stillwells Lodge. Like other townsfolk in Big Bear, they had been extras in *Trail of the Lonesome Pine* (1936) and *Girl of the Ozarks* (1936).

Daniel Boone (George O'Brien) is hired to lead a group of settlers, including the family of Virginia Randolph (Heather Angel), into the promised land called "Kain-tu-kee." Standing in their way are hostile Indians led by a white renegade named Simon Girty (John Carradine). Through raids and turmoil, the farmers build their settlement, only to find that it is on land claimed by others and that their prized land is also claimed by the state of Virginia. When the smoke clears and Daniel is freed from the burning stake, a thriving community is built called Booneville.

Thirty-six year old barrel-chested O'Brien was a college athlete and during WWI he enlisted in the Navy and became a boxing champ of the fleet. After the war he drifted west and became an extra and stunt man in Hollywood, where he met director John Ford. Ford liked the tall strapping youth and picked the virtually unknown O'Brien to star in one of his first Westerns, *Iron Horse* (1924). He became a leading man during the Twenties, culminating in his best performance as the seduced husband in the critically acclaimed film *Sunrise* (1927). O'Brien interrupted his acting once more in WWII and returned

CAST:	
George O'Brien	Daniel Boone
Heather Angel	Virginia Randolph
John Carradine	Simon Girty
Directed by	David Howard
Produced by	RKO Radio Pictures

George O'Brien confronts John Carradine (skunk hat) in a scene on the lobby card for *Daniel Boone* (1936).

George O'Brien and Heather Angel on location at Big Bear for the film *Daniel Boone* (1936)
Photo courtesy of Tom Core

to Hollywood a much decorated hero. His patriotism again was shown during the Korean War and during Vietnam when he returned to duty. When O'Brien finally retired with the rank of Captain, he had just been recommended for Admiral. O'Brien's last role in films was as a calvary major in another John Ford classic, *Cheyenne Autumn* (1964).

Petite, English-born Heather Angel (her real birth name) came to Hollywood just before the depression. In 1931, she landed the leads in *Night in Montmarte* and the well-recieved *The Hound of the Baskervilles*. By the Forties, Angel's star had faded and she became a character actress with a few sporadic roles over the next three decades. She died in 1986 at the age of seventy-seven.

One of the great villains of his day, John Carradine had a deep resonant theatrical voice that allowed him to appear larger than life. Whether he was shooting *Jesse James* (1939) in the back or strangling his models in *Bluebeard* (1944), Carradine, extracted the loathing of audiences. In one of the longest careers in Hollywood, Carradine appeared in nearly four hundred film and television episodes in his six decades before the cameras. Sadly, in later years he found his talents only were wanted by "B" producers and he made a slew of exploitation films that left audiences laughing instead of crying. He died at the age of eighty-two in 1986.

Some of the cast and extras on location at Big Bear for the film *Daniel Boone* (1936)
Photo courtesy of Tom Core

Some of the local ladies who played
extras for the film *Daniel Boone* (1936)
Photo courtesy of Tom Core

John Carradine (left) grapples with George
O'Brien on location at Big Bear for the film
Daniel Boone (1936).
Photo courtesy of
The Academy of Motion Picture
Arts and Sciences

PRIVATE NUMBER (1936)

CAST:
Robert Taylor .... Richard Winfield
Loretta Young .... Ellen Neal
Basil Rathbone .... Wroxton
Directed by .... Roy Del Ruth
Produced by .... 20th Century Fox

Lobby card for
***Private Number* (1936)**

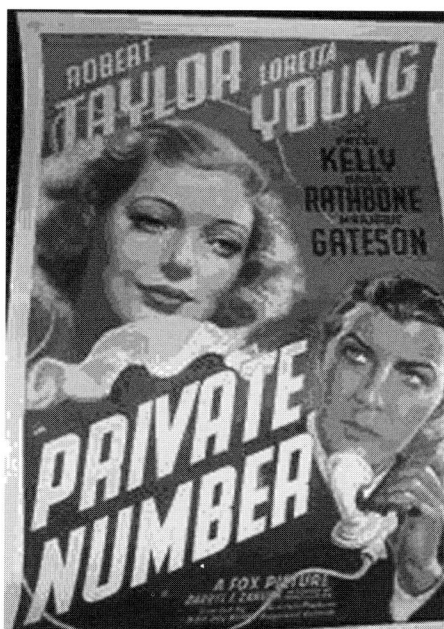

In a classic boy meets girl/boy loses girl/boy gets girl, *Private Number* was a breezy melodrama about a pompous butler attempting to break up the romance between the son of the house, Richard Winfield (Robert Taylor) and one of the servants, Ellen Neal (Loretta Young). Wroxton, the butler (Basil Rathbone), takes a liking to Ellen and hires her as a lady-in-waiting to Mrs. Winfield. After Ellen charms Richard into marriage, Wroxton delights in tormenting the two by dropping hints to the family that she is not worthy of marrying into the family. In one sequence, the original Blue Jay ferry could be seen crossing Lake Arrowhead as Richard and Ellen motored across to a dance at the village.

In a case of being too pretty, Robert Taylor was seen as more of a matinee idol than a serious actor. Just the opposite was the case as he proved in *Magnificent Obsession* (1935), a film that brought him national celebrity status. Taylor came to the role of scion naturally. He was born Spangler Arlington Brugh and his father was a doctor in Nebraska. He studied the cello and in college picked up acting where he was spotted by an M-G-M scout. Even after he was signed to a seven-year contract, M-G-M wasn't sure what to do with him. They changed his name to Robert Taylor and lent him out to several studios. It was at these other studios that he finally made his mark as an actor. When M-G-M finally woke up to the fact that they had a star, they began to give him meatier roles. His better films during the 1930s and 40s include: *Camille* (1937), *Three Comrades* (1938) and *Waterloo Bridge* (1940). During WWII, he served in the Navy and returned to find a changed Hollywood with his type of roles gone. In the 1950s, he began a series of costumed dramas that allowed him to star once more. He also began his television career and hosted several programs. A longtime smoker,

Taylor died of lung cancer in 1969 at the age of fifty-eight.

Before his days as Sherlock Holmes, Basil Rathbone was the ubiquitous villain in many 1930s films, like *David Copperfield* (1935), *A Tale of Two Cities* (1935) and *The Adventures of Robin Hood* (1938). South African-born Rathbone was one of Hollywood's most consummate actors that was never satisfied until the part was just right. His enunciation was so precise that some said you could cut it with a sword, a weapon that he used with better proficiency than his good friend, Errol Flynn. Hopelessly typecast as Sherlock Holmes in some fourteen screenings and hundreds of radio broadcasts, Rathbone left Hollywood during the 1940s and returned to his first love, the stage. He reluctantly returned to Hollywood later to film a few forgettable quickies, in order to finance his lecture tours and Shakespearean recordings. With more than one hundred screen and television credits, he died in 1967 at the age of seventy-five.

Twenty-three year old Loretta Young had been around the acting world since she was three years old. Born Gretchen Young, she was the youngest of three sisters. Both of her older sisters, Sally Blaine and Polly Ann Young, were actresses, but they never attained the success that Loretta garnered in the mid-1930s. Her elopement with co-star Grant Withers in 1930 at the age of seventeen almost caused her to lose her career. She was usually typecast as the sweet innocent and justly so since she grew up in convent schools. Her affair with co-star Clark Gable in *Call of the Wild* (1935), a film that was shot on location at Lake Tahoe, resulted in a child that was never acknowledged until years later. Young won an Oscar in 1947 for her role as the Swedish housekeeper opposite Joseph Cotten in *The Farmer's Daughter* (1947). In later years, she turned to television and hosted The *Loretta Young Show* from 1953 to 1961, where she

Robert Taylor and Loretta Young on location at Lake Arrowhead in a scene from *Private Number* (1936)

earned three Emmy awards. Young died in 2000 at the age of eighty-seven in Palm Springs.

Robert Taylor and Loretta Young decide to motor over to Lake Arrowhead Village in a scene from *Private Number* (1936). Photo courtesy of The Academy of Motion Picture Arts and Sciences

Basil Rathbone interviews Loretta Young in a scene from *Private Number* (1936).

STOLEN HOLIDAY (1936)

Twice in 1936 Lake Arrowhead doubled for the alpine country of Switzerland. The first time, Warner Brothers used the lake for scenes from *Stolen Holiday*, then later that year Universal Pictures made *Three Smart Girls*. *Stolen Holiday* was loosely based on the famous bond scandal in Paris that involved a Russian emigré, Serge Stavisky. The caveat at the beginning of the movie states that this is a work of fiction . . . etc. Nevertheless, the producers followed the real story of Stavisky who either committed suicide or was murdered in 1934.

Nicole Picot (Kay Francis) is a model in a dress shop when she meets a penniless Russian emigré, Stefan Orloff (Claude Rains). With his polished manner and pretense at wealth, he helps her to obtain a prestigious dress salon and she, in turn, helps him enter Paris society. When the bond scandal irrupts, Picot marries Orloff to legitimize him in the eyes of the law and society. In order to assist Orloff, Picot has to spurn the English diplomat she has fallen in love with, Anthony Wayne (Ian Hunter). In the end, there is no question that Orloff, who has caused tremendous damage to the financial health of France, is assassinated by tacit order of the French Government.

Thirty-seven year old Kay Francis was one of the most sophisticated and glamorous stars in Hollywood during the Thirties. Born Katherine Edwina Gibbs in Oklahoma, the statuesque (five foot nine inches) and dark-haired Francis became a stage actress on Broadway during the 1920s. She got her first part in the Marx Brothers film, *Cocoanuts* in 1929. Warner Brothers signed her to a long term contract in 1932 with the intention of making her their leading star. She appeared in dozens of films opposite the top actors in the industry, but the films never were of any

<table>
<tr><td colspan="2">CAST:</td></tr>
<tr><td>Kay Francis ....</td><td>Nicole Picot</td></tr>
<tr><td>Claude Rains ....</td><td>Stefan Orloff</td></tr>
<tr><td>Ian Hunter ....</td><td>Anthony Wayne</td></tr>
<tr><td>Directed by ....</td><td>Michael Curtiz</td></tr>
<tr><td>Produced by ....</td><td>Warner Brothers</td></tr>
</table>

Kay Francis
circa 1936

Kay Francis and Ian Hunter on location at
Lake Arrowhead in a scene from
Stolen Holiday (1936)

consequence. When it became evident that the best roles at Warner's were going to Bette Davis, Francis left and her career spiraled downward into character roles in "B" movies. The often married actress died in 1968 at the age of sixty-nine and left her one million dollar estate to train Seeing Eye dogs.

Suave and sophisticated, forty-seven year old Claude Rains was born in London and started his career on stage at the age of eleven. Rains, who was short and not particularly handsome, was cast in leading roles where the protagonist is not necessarily good looking but sympathetic. His breakthrough role came in 1933 with his portrayal of H. G. Wells' *The Invisible Man*. Although he never won an Oscar, he was nominated four times as Best Supporting Actor, for his roles in classics like *Casablanca* (1942) and *Notorious* (1946). Rains returned to Lake Arrowhead in 1942 to film *Now, Voyager* with Bette Davis and Paul Henreid at the North Shore Tavern (UCLA Conference Center). He died at the age of seventy-eight in 1968.

South African-born Ian Hunter came to Hollywood via the London stage and screen. Tall and handsome, the well-mannered Hunter was generally cast as the upper-class elitist. At thirty-six, he never quite made the "A" list of actors and spent the better part of his career as a character actor. In forty plus years, Hunter made nearly one hundred screen appearances. He returned to Lake Arrowhead in the 1940s to film *Dulcy*, a light comedy starring Ann Sothern. In later years, he made his home and living as an actor in London where he died in 1975.

One of the legends of Hollywood was director Michael Curtiz. Beginning in the earliest days of films in his native Hungary, Mano Kertesz Kaminer (Curtiz) became an actor first and then a director. He directed nearly sixty films in Europe before coming to Hollywood in the mid-Twenties. Curtiz was known for his explosive nature and problems with the English language. He once yelled at an errant assistant: "The next time I want an idiot to do this, I'll do it myself!" In his thirty-five years in Hollywood, Curtiz directed some of the finest movies ever made, including *The Charge of the Light Brigade* (1936), *The Adventures of Robin Hood* (which also included Rains and Hunter in 1938), *Mildred Pierce* (1945) and *White Christmas* (1954). He was nominated four times as Best Director by the Academy, but only won once for his superb direction of *Casablanca* (1942).

Claude Rains and Kay Francis in a scene
from *Stolen Holiday* (1936)

THREE SMART GIRLS (1936)

**Deanna Durbin
circa 1936**

In the opening sequence of the musical *Three Smart Girls*, director Henry Koster made sure the audience paid attention by having "Universal's newest discovery," Deanna Durbin, belt out an operatic scale prior to launching into her debut song while sailing on a Swiss lake (Lake Arrowhead) in the Alps. Actually, Durbin was originally discovered and signed by M-G-M, but when they found that they had two similar stars in Durbin and Judy Garland, they decided to send Garland packing, but a mix-up occurred and Durbin was the one who was out. The cinematographer, Joseph Valentine, took full advantage of the summer boating on Lake Arrowhead with beautiful shots through the trees and close-ups at the water's edge. The sequence of the three sisters running from the boat dock to the house was filmed at the Chateau des Fleurs, a house built on the north shore of Lake Arrowhead by the inventor of the "fairy wafer" (Nabisco's saltine cracker today).

When Penny Craig (Deanna Durbin) and her sisters find that their wealthy father, Judson (Charles Winninger), is to remarry, they try to sabotage the wedding by finding someone else to marry the potential bride, Donna (Binnie Barnes). They enlist the help of Lord Michael Stuart (Ray Milland) and Count Arisztid (Mischa Auer) in their efforts.

In her second film (her first was a musical short at M-G-M with Judy Garland), Canadian-born Deanna Durbin exhibited her operatically trained voice and became a household name immediately. The fourteen-year old was, in fact, the reason Universal did not go bankrupt in the depression era Thirties. Her string of hit movies not only kept them solvent, but made her one of the highest paid stars of the day. A very private person, she was never comfortable with all the adulation shown to her. In 1948, after two failed marriages, she turned her back on Hollywood, married writer/director Charles David and retired to a small village in France where she still lives. She has not granted an interview since that time.

Already a star and veteran actress with more than thirty film credits, thirty-three year old Binnie Barnes received top billing in this feature and justly deserved it. When the director asked her to sing off key, she did a remarkably good job of it, allowing fourteen year old Durbin to find fault with her singing as part of the plot. A former chorus girl and dance-hall hostess, English-born Barnes came to Hollywood in 1934 after impressing audiences with her performance as one of the wives of Henry the Eighth in the British production of *The Private Life of Henry VIII* (1933). She was usually cast as the "other woman," a role she played to perfection. She too left Hollywood in the late Forties for Europe where she made films with her husband, producer Mike Frankovich. She died at the age of ninety-five in 1998.

Fifty-two year old Charles Winninger was one of Hollywood's great character actors, usually playing the part of the harried husband. Winninger was an actor who divided his time between silent films and Broadway. He originated the part of Cap'n Andy in the original Broadway production of *Show Boat* in 1927, and later in the film of the same name in 1936. Other than his role as Cap'n Andy, Winninger will best be remembered as the father of Charlie Farrell, long time owner of the Palm Springs Racquet Club, in the 1956 sitcom, *The Charles Farrell Show*. Winninger retired to Palm Springs where he died in 1969 at the age of eighty-five.

Also included in the international cast of *Three Smart Girls*, was Russian-born Mischa Auer and Welsh-born Ray Milland.

Nan Grey, Barbara Read, and Deanna Durbin (top to bottom) in a publicity still for *Three Smart Girls* (1936)

Milland was also a veteran English actor with more than thirty film credits when he made *Three Smart Girls*. He came to Hollywood in 1931, but did not attain star status until well into the 1940s when his role as an alcoholic, in *Lost Weekend* (1945), shocked the world. In 1946, he received the Best Actor award from the National Board of Review, the Cannes Film Festival, the Golden Globes, and the Academy of Motion Picture Arts and Sciences. Milland played both comedy and drama equally well. In his fifty years of show business, Milland garnered close to two hundred movie and television credits. He died in 1986 at the age of eighty-one.

Deanna Durbin on location at Lake Arrow-head for the film *Three Smart Girls* (1936)
Photo courtesy of
The Academy of Motion Picture
Arts and Sciences

THE LADY FIGHTS BACK
(1937)

Owen Merrill (Kent Taylor) is an engineer sent by a power company to survey the Muskalga River (Lake Arrowhead) for a dam that will ruin the salmon fishing. The manager of the local fishing club, Heather McHale (Irene Hervey), begins a campaign to stop him even though she likes him personally. McHale is also pursued by one of the fishing club members, Doug McKenzie (William Lundigan) who hangs around but loses the girl in the end. After a series of accidents, court orders and a near-death experience, Heather realizes that it was Owen who saved the salmon river by installing a new Norwegian invention, the fish ladder, and agrees to marry him.

Thirty-year old Kent Taylor had been signed by Paramount in 1932 and appeared in nearly fifty pictures before making *The Lady Fights Back*. The handsome six foot tall Taylor became a leading man during the late Thirties in mostly "B" movies. The leading roles dried up for him during the 1940s until he switched to television. In 1951-1952, Kent starred in the popular TV series *Boston Blackie* as the mustached super sleuth. He continued his career in movies in character roles in later years and retired in 1974. Kent died in 1987 at the age of eighty.

Vivacious Irene Hervey was an M-G-M contract actress during the early Thirties and mainly played supporting roles. By 1937, she was freelancing at other studios and picked up some good credits such as playing opposite Jimmy Stewart in *Destry Rides Again* (1939). Married to leading actor and singer Allan Jones, she took time off during the Forties to raise a family which included her son, popular singer Jack Jones. She continued her career through the Fifties and Sixties in minor roles and television,

CAST:	
Irene Hervey	Heather McHale
Kent Taylor	Owen Merrill
William Lundigan	Doug McKenzie
Directed by	Milton Carruth
Produced by	Universal Pictures

Kent Taylor (right) and unidentified actor in a scene from *The Lady Fights Back* (1937)

Irene Hervey and Joe Sawyer in a scene
from *The Lady Fights Back* (1937)

Willie Best
circa 1937

where she acted in supporting roles to Anne Francis in the 1965 TV series *Honey West*. Hervey died in 1998 at the age of eighty-nine.

Twenty-three year old William Lundigan was auditioned because of his strong radio voice that intrigued the head of Universal Studios. In only his second role in movies, the handsome athletic Lundigan muddled along in *The Lady Fights Back*. Unfortunately, Lundigan never achieved super stardom that many thought he might on the silver screen. Once again because of his voice, he landed a choice hosting job on two CBS television series, *Climax* and *Shower of Stars*, where he delivered on-air commercials for the main sponsor, Chrysler Motors. He returned a couple of times to films in supporting roles and retired in 1968. Lundigan died of heart and lung congestion in 1975 at the age of sixty-one.

In a terrible stereotyping of the lazy Negro, sleepy-eyed Willie Best played McTavish, the salmon club's cook, cleaner and handyman. Realizing that he either went along with the caste system in Hollywood or else, Mississippi-born Best made the most of his parts by dragging them out. He usually played the role of a slow, shuffling and superstitious illiterate black male. In the end, Best may have had the last laugh as he found steady work during the height of the Depression and had close to one hundred and twenty screen credits before he died prematurely of cancer in 1962 at the age of forty-eight.

THUNDER TRAIL (1937)

Once more the rocks and cliffs above Big Bear Lake are utilized for their magnificent scenery in a Zane Grey Western thriller, *Arizona Ames* (aka *Thunder Trail*). During a wagon raid, two young brothers, Dick and Bob Ames, are the only survivors of the outlaw gang attack led by Lee Tate (Charles Bickford). Dick is abandoned for dead, but his younger brother is adopted and raised by the family's killer, Tate. Dick is rescued by Rafael Lopez (J. Carrol Naish) and reared as a cowboy. Years later, Dick Ames, who goes by the sobriquet of "Arizona Ames" (Gilbert Roland), recognizes his father's murderer, Tate, in the guise of a legitimate businessman and miner. When Arizona defends the mining claims of Jim Morgan and his daughter, Amy (Marsha Hunt), against Tate, Tate's adopted son Bob (James Craig) becomes embroiled in a fight with his long lost brother. When the brothers finally recognize each other, they join forces to undo their nemesis, Tate. It is inevitable that the two antagonists, Tate and Arizona, have to battle it out on top of the tallest rocks around and true to Zane Grey and Hollywood, goodness prevails.

Considered one of the handsomest men in Hollywood, thirty-two year old Mexican-born Gilbert Roland had thought about following in the footsteps of his father, a professional bullfighter, until the Mexican Revolution forced them to leave Mexico in 1917. He began his career in films as a stand-in for Ramon Novarro in 1925 and was befriended by Rudolph Valentino. In 1927, he starred opposite Norma Talmadge in *Camille*, a big box office hit of the year. Roland's torrid, and sometimes lurid, love affair with Talmadge led to her divorce. In 1941, he married popular star Constance Bennett, one of his former leading ladies in the Thirties. Over the next few years,

CAST:
Gilbert Roland .... Arizona Ames
Charles Bickford .... Lee Tate
Marsha Hunt .... Amy Morgan
J. Carrol Naish .... Rafael Lopez
Directed by .... Charles Barton
Produced by .... Paramount Pictures

Gilbert Roland and Marsha Hunt in an ad for *Thunder Trail* (1937)

he alternated between character roles and leading men. He was the first and only Mexican-born actor to have ever played O. Henry's *Cisco Kid*. Roland made close to one hundred and fifty screen and television appearances in his five decades of films. He died in 1994 at the age of eighty-nine.

Forty-six year old Charles Bickford was known for his tempestuous nature. (At the age of nine, he was accused of attempted murder when he shot at a motorman who had run over his dog.) Bickford began his film life in 1929 in a very auspice manner, he punched out the director, who just happened to be—Cecil B. DeMille. Obviously, it didn't do his career much damage as he was picked to play opposite Greta Garbo in *Anna Christie* (1930) the following year. After a lion mauled him in 1935, the redheaded thespian became a very powerful character actor known for his gruff voice and take-no-prisoners attitude. His legendary fights with studio head Louis B. Mayer, led to his being blacklisted from the studios for several years. Bickford returned to the San Bernardino Mountains in 1957 to play opposite Tony Curtis in *Mister Cory*. He was nominated three times as Best Supporting Actor by the Academy, but never won. He became a staple on the television series, *The Virginian* in 1966, but died the next year of blood poisoning.

J. Carrol Naish
circa 1937

Because of his swarthy complexion, dark eyes and was a good dialectician, J. Carrol Naish played every type of role but that of his own Irish heritage. At the age of sixteen he joined the Navy and literally saw the world, picking up the local flavor and dialects along the way. When he found himself stranded in California in the Twenties, he joined an acting troupe that toured for several years. His film career began with bit parts in the 1930s, but producers were quick to pick up that he could play just about any role they chose for him. Never a leading man, he was considered to be one of the best character actors in Hollywood. He won the Golden Globe Award for Best Supporting Actor in 1946 for his portrayal of the indigent

Mexican father in *A Medal for Benny* (1945) and was also nominated for an Oscar (his second nomination—the first was in 1944 for *Sahara*). He lost out to James Dunn who played the father in the film, *A Tree Grows in Brooklyn* (1945). Naish loved the San Bernardino Mountains and purchased a home in the Lake Arrowhead area during the 1930s. He died in 1973 with more than two hundred film and television credits.

Twenty year old Marsha Hunt had been a Powers model when she was signed by Paramount Pictures in 1935. Paramount immediately cast the slender, pretty girl, with the expressive eyes, in a series of nondescript films that did little for her career. Over the years, she became a character actress and, some say, was "blacklisted" for her "left-wing" causes. A longtime resident of the San Fernando Valley, she has been Honorary Mayor of Sherman Oaks, California, since 1980.

Marsha Hunt
circa 1940s

Gilbert Roland on location at Big Bear in a scene from *Thunder Trail* (1937) Photo courtesy of The Academy of Motion Picture Arts and Sciences

THE AWFUL TRUTH (1937)

In 1936, Columbia Pictures paid cash-strapped RKO $80,000 for the rights to a group of old scripts, among which was *The Awful Truth*, a former Arthur Richmond play from the Twenties. The fact that it had been filmed twice before did not deter Columbia from naming one of its best directors to the film. Writer/director Leo McCarey took one look at the existing script and tore it up. Working with screenwriter Vina Delmar, McCarey crafted one of the great screwball comedies to come out of the Thirties.

Bored socialites, Jerry (Cary Grant) and Lucy Warriner (Irene Dunne) become suspicious of each other's dalliances and decide to divorce. The only bone of contention is the custody of Mr. Smith (Asta of the *Thin Man* series of films), their dog. After the divorce, each plans to re-marry: Lucy to Oklahoma oilman Daniel Leeson (Ralph Bellamy); Jerry to wealthy heiress Barbara Vance (Molly Lamont). When it becomes obvious that each one is trying to sabotage the other's wedding plans, they reconcile at a mountain cabin (Lake Arrowhead) after some madcap antics, including the scuttling of their car along the side of a mountain road.

The Awful Truth is considered to be the movie that made Cary Grant the international

Magazine ad with Cary Grant and Irene Dunne in scenes from *The Awful Truth* (1937) Alexander D'Arcy far right

Why did his wife have to hide Jerry Warriner in the bedroom when her best friend visited her? This and other novel romantic questions are answered uproariously in this brilliant version of a Broadway hit.

"Theodora" goes wilder than ever untangling new angles in this tantalizing love triangle. . . . . See how a society bride's sensational drawing-room dance shocked Park Avenue—and stopped a divorce!

superstar that he became. It was nominated for six Oscars, but noticeably lacking was a nomination for Grant. At the end of the Academy Award ceremonies, only McCarey walked away with the coveted award. At first, Grant had objected to being loaned out to Harry Cohn's Columbia Pictures and asked to be removed from the picture. He even offered several thousand dollars and a free picture to Cohn, but the studio boss held Grant to his contract. In a strange bit of déjB vu, Grant actually married a dime store heiress, Barbara Hutton, at the home of his agent, Frank Vincent, at Lake Arrowhead five years later.

Cary Grant and Irene Dunne in a scene from *The Awful Truth* (1937)

Kentucky-born Irene Dunne, who did her best to lose any childhood accent, got a chance to revert back to her southern roots as she parodied a phony accent in a song she sings for Cary's fiancée (she sounds a bit like an effected Katharine Hepburn). The thirty-nine year old actress was trained as an operatic singer and musician and appeared on Broadway. During her career, Dunne was nominated as Best Actress five times, including her role in *The Awful Truth*, but never won. After a career that lasted more than twenty-five years, she retired in 1955 and died in 1990 at the age of ninety-two.

Veteran director Leo McCarey was considered by the overly professional cast to be a washed-up drunk and mediocre has-been. Ralph Bellamy recalled years later a time when McCarey walked onto the set, after an obvious night out drinking, with a crumpled-up piece of paper that was to be the script for the day. The cast's pleas to have him removed as director fell on deaf ears, as Harry Cohn was so pleased with the results that he was once heard to have been laughing uproariously at some of the rushes he watched. McCarey, who had honed his comedic skills with Hal Roach and the *Our Gang* series and was the genius behind the pairing of Stan Laurel and Oliver Hardy, had the last laugh as he walked away with the Oscar for Best Director for the film the following year. His loose style of

Asta
circa 1937

directing later became the norm in the frantic bustle of Hollywood film making. He was nominated six times for an Oscar and won again in 1946 for his direction of Bing Crosby in *Going My Way* (1945). As writer/director, McCarey had more than one hundred and fifty screen credits before he died at the age of seventy-one in 1968.

Asta, a wire-haired terrier, was actually Skippy to his owners. With the tremendous success of the *Thin Man* series of films during the 1930s, Skippy became Asta. Grant and Asta teamed up once more in another Thirties comedy, *Bringing Up Baby* (1938), in which they were teamed with the real Katharine Hepburn.

Cary Grant and Irene Dunne in a scene from
The Awful Truth (1937) filmed at Lake Arrowhead

Photo courtesy of The Academy of Motion
Picture Arts and Sciences

PARK AVENUE LOGGER
(1937)

Wealthy timber magnate Mike Curran, who came up the hard way, feels his son Grant (George O'Brien) is too intellectual and a real sissy. In actual fact, Grant is a professional wrestler, the "Masked Marvel," but is afraid to tell his father. Subsequently, Curran sends his son to Oregon to learn the lumber business from the ground up. At a logging contest Grant meets Peggy O'Shea (Beatrice Roberts), the daughter of the owner of a rival logging outfit. Like any greenhorn, Grant is picked upon by the biggest bullies in the logging camp, but uses his wrestling experience to overcome adversity. After a series of mysterious accidents that derail trains from both logging concerns and threaten their valuable government contracts, Grant learns that the real culprits are none other than the foreman of the O'Shea company, Paul Sanger (Ward Bond) and the foreman of his father's company, Ben Morton (Willard Robertson). Filmed in Crestline and Oregon, *Park Avenue Logger* was released as both *Tall Timber* and *Millionaire Playboy* at various times in 1937.

Thirty-seven year old silent star George O'Brien was nearing the end of his leading man days when he made this film for RKO Pictures (he made twenty films with them in four years). The son of a policeman who became police chief of San Francisco, Navy veteran O'Brien reenlisted in the Navy when WWII broke out and upon his return found that the studios were no longer interested in him. His long association with John Ford led to a few minor parts in later years and he retired in 1964 at the age of sixty-four. O'Brien died in 1985 at the age of eighty-five.

Beatrice Roberts broke into films as an extra in 1933. She is best remembered

CAST:	
George O'Brien	Grant Curran
Beatrice Roberts	Peggy O'Shea
Ward Bond	Paul Sanger
Willard Robertson	Ben Morton
Directed by	David Howard
Produced by	RKO Pictures

George O'Brien in a publicity still for
Park Avenue Logger (1937)
Photo courtesy of
The Academy of Motion Picture
Arts and Sciences

George O'Brien and Beatrice Roberts in a scene from *Park Avenue Logger* (1937) filmed in Crestline.
Photo courtesy of Les Adams

Ward Bond
circa 1950s

for her portrayal the following year as the evil Queen Azura in *Flash Gordon's Trip to Mars* (1938) with Buster Crabbe. In the span of sixteen years, Roberts played in more than forty films as a bit player and in uncredited roles. She retired in 1949, but made a comeback film in 1966 when she reappeared again as Azura, Queen of Mars, in the television movie, *Deadly Ray from Mars* (1966).

Fifty-one year old Willard Robertson was a practicing attorney who gave up the profession to become an actor. In his career that spanned almost twenty years, Robertson usually portrayed men of authority such as judges, military officers, policemen and even lawyers. He worked in films until he died in 1948 at the age of sixty-two, with close to one hundred and fifty film credits.

Perennial good guy/bad guy, Ward Bond was a contemporary of his fellow USC collegian, John Wayne. Known for his lack of tact, his screen persona usually mirrored his own feelings. As the president of the ultra right-wing Motion Picture Alliance for the Preservation of American Ideals during the 1950s, he was an ardent proponent of the Hollywood witch hunts during that period and the blacklisting of left-wing leaning actors. He is best remembered for all the supporting roles he played in the epics of John Ford that starred John Wayne. He died in 1960 at the age of fifty-seven from a massive heart attack.

HIGH, WIDE AND HANDSOME (1937)

In a most unlikely plot for a musical (the building of a pipeline in Pennsylvania), Jerome Kern and Oscar Hammerstein II produced an expensive and disappointing film called *High, Wide and Handsome* (1937) for Paramount Studios. A costly village was constructed in the Chino Valley and nearby hills as the setting for early Titusville, Pennsylvania. The production also needed some forest scenes and for these they traveled to Big Bear. The film never knows which way to go — to be a true drama or stick to the lightness of a musical. Consequently, it does neither and Kern and Hammerstein's efforts reflect the overall mood by producing six totally forgettable songs, including *High, Wide and Handsome*.

Irene Dunne, who had a decent voice, played the lead as the rebellious and itinerant daughter (Sally Watterson) of a snake oil salesman (Raymond Walburn) who is stranded in a small Pennsylvania town. When their wagon is destroyed in a fire, the Wattersons are taken in by the Cortlandts and their son, Peter (Randolph Scott). Peter's attempt at building a pipeline to sell oil in nearby Philadelphia is thwarted temporarily by railroad tycoon Walt Brennan (Alan Hale), but in the end the pipeline goes through and Peter wins the girl. Unfortunately, the box office reflected what critics had said and the film did poorly. About the only good thing to say about the movie is that least we didn't have to hear Randolph Scott sing!

Dunne, who made three films in the San Bernardino Mountains in a span of two years, was musically trained and a Broadway star when she came to Hollywood in 1930. Her career in the Thirties vacillated back

Lobby card for
High, Wide and Handsome (1937)

and forth between comedies, dramas and musicals, and she was nominated five times for a Best Actress Oscar. She never won, but her performance in the classic tearjerker, *I Remember Mama* (1948) is still thought to be her best. In 1957, President Dwight Eisenhower appointed the still very popular star, as a special U.S. delegate to the United Nations. Her later years were devoted to charities and she died in 1990 at the age of ninety-one.

The lead role of Peter Cortlandt was an easy choice for Paramount to make, as they had one of the most popular stars of the 1930s under contract in the form of tall and handsome Randolph Scott. At the time, Scott was living with his friend and fellow thespian, Cary Grant, in Malibu. The two bachelors were dating a bevy of beauties at the time and kept the gossip columns filled with their antics. This was the only film Scott made in 1937 as the production was long and dragged-out. By this time, Scott had established himself in the Western genre and probably objected to being ill-placed in a musical. His performance was lacking, but it did little damage to his career as he went on to film nearly seventy more films over the next two decades, the majority of which were Westerns.

Twenty-three year old Dorothy Lamour (the 1931 Miss New Orleans) was a big band singer and dancer before coming to Hollywood. Her performance the year before in *The Jungle Princess* (1936) and subsequent south sea adventure films earned her the moniker "the sarong girl." In *High, Wide and Handsome,* the dark-haired beauty steals the scenes she was in whether she is singing or acting. Lamour is best remembered as the love interest in all the successful "Road to . . . " comedies that co-starred Bing Crosby and Bob Hope. Her finest performances came in 1940 when she was cast opposite Tyrone Power in the crime drama, *Johnny Apollo* (1940) and opposite Henry Fonda in *Chad Hanna* (1940). In later years she did radio, television and an occasional movie, the last being a forgettable Steven King story, *Creepshow 2* (1987). Lamour died in 1996 at the age of eighty-one.

Rounding out the cast was the great character actor, Russian-born Akim Tamiroff. Even

Dorothy Lamour
circa 1937

though he had a very heavy accent, he could play a wide variety of ethnic characters from a French banker to a middle-east potentate and be believable. Tamiroff returned to Lake Arrowhead the following year and co-starred with Lamour and Henry Fonda in the award winning film, *Spawn of the North* (1938). Tamiroff appeared in close to one hundred and thirty films in his four decades of film making. Tamiroff died in 1972 at the age of seventy-one.

Scene from
High, Wide and Handsome (1937)

Publicity still of Randolph Scott and Ben Blue (right) for
High, Wide and Handsome (1937)

HEIDI (1937)

At the apex of her career as a child star, Fox Studios sent nine year old Shirley Temple back up to Lake Arrowhead to film the enchanting children's tale, *Heidi*. Johanna Spyri's story of a poor orphaned Swiss waif had pulled on the heartstrings of adoring children and adults since it was first written before the turn of the century. Fox could not have asked for a better vehicle for its diminutive star. It was an instant success and merchandising bonanza for the studio which churned out Heidi dolls, Heidi coloring books and Heidi clothing. Although most of the film was shot in a studio, there are several scenes that were made in an area off Highway 18 which is now known as Switzer Park. Temple and her family were housed at the Arrowhead Springs Hotel which was partially owned by several movie producers, including Darryl F. Zanuck, head of Twentith Century Fox.

One of Temple's friends, Marcia Mae Jones, who played the little crippled girl, Klara, recalled years later that the security surrounding Shirley was tremendous, even when they went to Lake Arrowhead Village to play miniature golf they were surrounded by body guards.

Fifty-one year old Jean Hersholt, who played Shirley's grandfather, was born in Denmark and had been acting in silent films from 1906 in his native country. He came to the states during the 1910s and played extras in the early days of Hollywood. By the Twenties, Hersholt was a leading man and starred in some of the classics of the period, such as Erich von Stroheim's *Greed* (1925). When the talkies arrived, Hersholt slipped into character roles. He is still

Jean Hersholt as he appeared in
Heidi (1937)

remembered for his sympathetic portrayal of the kindly Dr. Christian in a series of films in the late Thirties and early Forties. Hersholt, known for his great compassion and charity, never was nominated by the Academy but it paid him an even greater honor by naming its Humanitarian Award after him.

Shirley Temple had appeared twice before in films made in the San Bernardino Mountains, *To The Last Man* in 1933 and *Now and Forever* in 1934. She returned three years later to make another children's fantasy, *The Blue Bird* (1940). A frequent guest to the mountains, Temple was once Grand Marshall for a parade in the mountains during the Fifties. She retired from the screen in the early 1960s and devoted the rest of her life to public service. She has been a delegate to the United Nations and our Ambassador to both the Republics of Ghana and Czechoslovakia.

One of the best character actors in Hollywood, Sidney Blackmer began his film career in the cliff-hanging *Perils of Pauline* (1914). Preferring Broadway to Hollywood, over the years Blackmer vacillated back and forth between the two. From handsome leading man in the early Thirties to the actor who played Teddy Roosevelt more often than any other actor, Blackmer remained before audiences close to six decades. He enjoyed working in television and worked up to the year he died in 1973 at the age of seventy-eight.

Pioneer director Allan Dwan returned to the mountains to direct Temple and Hersholt in *Heidi*. Dwan started out as an electrical engineer and was hired for his expertise in lighting. When he was sent to the West Coast by Flying A Studios from Chicago, he found that the director of their San Juan Capistrano unit was off on a

Shirley Temple, Sidney Blackmer and Marcia Mae Jones in a scene from *Heidi* (1937)

drunken bender. He quickly cabled back to the home office advising that the venture should be abandoned, but Chicago returned his wire advising him that he was now the new director. Dwan never looked back and over the next five decades directed more than two hundred movies, wrote more than forty films, produced thirty-four pictures and became one of the true legends of Hollywood.

Shirley Temple, Jean Hersholt, Pauline Moore and Thomas Beck in a scene from *Heidi* (1937) filmed at Switzer Park

TRUE CONFESSION (1937)

In August of 1937, Paramount Studios sent two of its most popular stars (Carole Lombard and Fred MacMurray) to Lake Arrowhead to the delight of the local citizenry. They were there to film *True Confession*, based on the Louis Verneuil play, *Mon Crime*, a screwball comedy about a wife who can't seem to ever tell the truth. Besides the playful antics of Lombard and MacMurray, the locals were also entertained by one of the most recognized faces of the silent era, an aged John Barrymore, who played a drunken rascal.

The murder of a rich but lecherous cad leads to the arrest of Lombard who had worked for him, but left when his advances became too much. MacMurray, as her naive attorney husband, believes she is guilty, but gets her off in a sensational jury trial. The fireworks begin when he finds that his wife has lied about the murder, lied about being pregnant and seems to lie about everything.

Even though it was August, the lake temperature was reportedly only forty-five degrees. Lombard was asked to race into the lake and swim to a float, but pretend to drown thereby causing MacMurray to race to her aid. Lombard found the water so cold that when she ran in she

```
CAST:
Carole Lombard ......... Helen Bartlett
Fred MacMurray .... Kenneth Bartlett
John Barrymore .................. Charley
Directed by ............ Wesley Ruggles
Produced by .... Paramount Pictures
```

Photo story in Life Magazine, December 13, 1937, for the film *True Confession* (1937) Lombard enters lake (left), Lombard finds the water is cold (middle), Lombard being rescued by MacMurray (right)

was, in fact, dangerously close to drowning because she was experiencing hypothermia and MacMurray actually did have to help her make it to the float.

One thing the locals were not aware of was the presence of the King of Hollywood, Clark Gable, who was dating Lombard on the sly because his second wife, Rhea, was reluctant to give him a divorce. On the pretense that he needed a vacation, he rented a cabin in Lake Arrowhead just to be near Lombard during the shoot.

Born Jane Peters in 1908, Lombard was signed to a one picture contract at the age of twelve, based on her stunning looks. Unable to find more acting jobs afterwards, she was not seen again for another four years, when she signed with Fox Studios. A horrendous auto accident in 1926 almost ended her career when the left side of her face was severely injured and scarred. The new art of plastic surgery saved her looks and she became a staple at Mack Sennett Studios, where she honed her comedic talents that would later be her *tour de force*. Lombard could be both funny and sexy at the same time. She was a master of the rapid-fire dialogue* necessary to carry farcical comedies. That, along with her wry double takes, made her an actress that has rarely been equaled in Hollywood.

Lombard eventually became the third Mrs. Gable and the couple were inseparable until WWII broke out and Lombard was asked to participate in a war bond drive. At the end of the

Fred MacMurray and Carole Lombard relaxing on the set of
True Confession **(1937)**
Photo courtesy of
The Academy of Motion Picture
Arts and Sciences

*This had not always been the case. Lombard was cast in C.B. DeMille's first talkie, but was fired for bungling her lines.

tour, her plane crashed near Las Vegas and she died at the age of thirty-three and at the height of her career. One of her best parts could be said to have been her last, in the Ernst Lubitsch classic *To Be or Not to Be* (1942) with Jack Benny and a young Robert Stack. Lombard never viewed her performance as it was released two months after her death.

Twenty-nine year old Fred MacMurray was a popular star during the Thirties known for his light comedies, of which *True Confession* was definitely one according to the critics. His best part, however, came when he contemplated murder in the film noir classic, *Double Indemnity* (1944). The film was nominated for seven Oscars, but conspicuously absent was a Best Actor nomination for MacMurray. In later years, MacMurray found that comedy was once more his forte and sparkled in films like *The Absent-Minded Professor* (1961) and the long running TV series, *My Three Sons*. MacMurray died in 1991 at the age of eighty-three with close to five hundred film and television credits.

One of the great silent stars and matinee idols, John Barrymore was known as the "Great Profile" because of his handsome face. He was part of the famous theatrical Barrymore family which included Lionel and Ethel. Actually, the family name was Blyth, but their father Maurice, also a famous actor, used the stage name of Barrymore. John gravitated to the silver screen early in the 1910s and by the end of the era, was one of the highest paid actors in Hollywood. With his strong voice (some say too theatrical), he easily made the transition into talkies. A consummate roué, Barrymore's conquests, love affairs and marriages were the grist that kept the tabloids running at that time. By 1937, Barrymore's drinking and carousing had taken a terrible

John Barrymore in a scene from
True Confession (1937)
filmed at Lake Arrowhead.
Photo courtesy of
The Academy of Motion Picture
Arts and Sciences

toll on his physique, but his former brilliance was still evident in *True Confession* and a year later in another film made at Lake Arrowhead, *Spawn of the North* (1938). Barrymore's fall from the lofty heights of stardom is considered one of the great tragedies of Hollywood. He died of acute alcoholism in 1942 at the age of sixty.

Fred MacMurray and Carole Lombard
featured on the lobby card of
***True Confession* (1937)**

DOWN IN ARKANSAW
(1938)

In the late 1920s, a group calling themselves the Ozark Boys, successfully toured the vaudeville circuit for several years. It was comprised of Leon Weaver, his younger brother Frank and Frank's wife, June Weaver, who went by the name of Elviry. Leon is credited with popularizing the musical saw which earned him a place in the Ozark Hall of Fame. During the month of August 1938, Republic Pictures signed the three entertainers to star in the hillbilly tale, *Down in Arkansaw*. The movie was such a smash with depression era audiences, which could relate to the down and out mountain folk, that it spawned a series of eleven more films for the trio over the next four years. One of their films, *Grand Ole Opry* (1940), brought to the screen the popular radio program that 1930s audiences had tuned into for years.

When John Parker (Ralph Byrd) is sent to build a dam in Pine Ridge (Lake Arrowhead), he meets resistance in the form of Cicero and Abner Weaver and Elviry (Leon and Frank Weaver, June Weaver). John, who represents the power company, tricks the Weavers into accepting a court summons by putting on a phony talent show. (This was the producer's sneaky way of showcasing the musical talents of the group). John is quickly smitten by the Weaver's daughter, Mary (June Storey), who is engaged to Juble Butler (Guinn "Big Boy" Williams). After a series of misadventures, John manages to eventually show the citizens of Pine Ridge the advantages of moving from their homes by constructing a modern prefab home with all the latest innovations of the day.

Born in Ozark, Missouri, fifty-six year old Leon Weaver was

CAST:	
June Weaver	Elviry Weaver
Frank Weaver	Cicero Weaver
Leon Weaver	Abner Weaver
June Storey	Mary Weaver
Ralph Byrd	John Parker
Directed by	Nick Grinde
Produced by	Republic Pictures

Frank Weaver (on left with arm around June Storey), unidentified actor, Ralph Byrd, Leon Weaver (holding rifle), and another unidentified actor in a scene from *Down in Arkansaw* (1938)

Frank Weaver and Leon Weaver watch
Elviry in a scene from
Friendly Neighbors (1940)

Ralph Byrd (holding mike) in a scene from
Down in Arkansaw (1938) filmed at Lake
Arrowhead. (Guinn "Big Boy" Williams is
facing left and in a t-shirt).

nine years older than his brother Frank. In the Twenties they formed a group to tour in vaudeville and somewhere along the line, Leon married a Chicago-born lady, June Weaver, who went by the stage name of Elviry. Later, she evidently divorced the one brother and married the younger brother, Frank. Although Leon popularized the musical saw, it was Elviry who pioneered the lap-style of playing which produced more vibration and used a violin bow to obtain the dismal whine that we know today. Leon was the first to make his film debut in 1938 for RKO in a murder mystery, playing of course — a hillbilly.

Twenty-nine year old Ralph Byrd began as a bit actor in 1935 and progressed to leading man parts on the "B" circuit. In 1937, Byrd was the first of many actors to portray the famous Chester Gould comic book hero, *Dick Tracy*. The movie was a box office smash and Byrd found himself forever typecast as the pencil-thin mustached crime fighter. In all, he made five sequels not including the television series that ran from 1950 through 1951. Byrd's career ended prematurely in 1952 at the age of forty-three when he was stricken with a heart attack.

Vivacious blonde, Canadian-born June Storey was twenty when she starred for the first time in *Down in Arkansaw*. Her performance was noted by another Republic player, singing cowboy Gene Autry. He cast her opposite him the following year in *Home on the Prairie* (1939). This helped her attain leading lady status for the next two years in ten of Autry's Westerns. By the mid-Forties, she found only supporting roles and retired in 1949 at the age of thirty-one.

Another one of the great character actors was Guinn "Big Boy" Williams, who had started in the silent era and made the transition to talkies. His friend and co-worker, Will Rogers, is credited with giving Williams his nickname of "Big Boy." Born in Texas, Williams was the son of a U.S. Congressman. In his earlier years, Williams had played professional baseball and was a rodeo performer. He is best known for his gravelly voice and hulking appearance. Although good looking, Williams was never a leading man and contented himself with his supporting roles. From 1919 until his death in 1962, Williams performed in over two hundred film roles.

Ralph Byrd and June Storey on the set of *Down in Arkansaw* (1938) filmed at Lake Arrowhead.
Photo courtesy of
The Academy of Motion Picture
Arts and Sciences

TOM SAWYER, DETECTIVE (1938)

CAST:
Billy Cook .... Tom Sawyer
Donald O'Connor .... Huckleberry Finn
Porter Hall .... Silas Phelps
William Haade .... Jake/Jupiter
Directed by .... Louis King
Produced by .... Paramount Pictures

With the caveat that "this story is true . . . not invented, I've just changed the actors, the scenes and some details, which aren't important . . . well, only a couple," Mark Twain opened his novella, *Tom Sawyer, Detective*. In the late summer of 1938, Paramount Pictures dispatched a cast and crew to Lake Arrowhead. Movie Point and the lake were used to represent the shoreline of the Mississippi River. In this sequel to Twain's *Tom Sawyer* and *Huckleberry Finn*, many of the same characters are still around. Tom (Billy Cook) and Huck (Donald O'Connor) are sent downstream to Arkansas for a summer vacation. On the steamboat they meet Jake Dunlap (William Haade) who is hiding two diamonds in his shoe. When he is killed and mistaken for his twin brother Jupiter, the two boys become detectives to prove the innocence of Parson Silas Phelps, their benefactor.

In his first picture, ten year old Billy Cook was at the apex of his career. He never became a big star even though Paramount had big plans for him. He starred twice more with Donald O'Connor in *Sons of the Legion* (1938) and *Beau Geste* (1939). After a short career of ten pictures, Cook retired in 1942 at the age of fourteen.

Born into a vaudevillian family, Donald O'Connor began his screen life in 1937 with two of his brothers in the film *Melody for Two*. The scenes were deleted, but O'Connor's debut persuaded Paramount to sign the thirteen year old actor/dancer to a contract. For the next few years he sang and danced his way through a series of juvenile roles. His big break came in 1950 when he starred in *Francis* (the talking mule). This led to a series of five sequels over the next five years. O'Connor is best remembered for his supporting role in *Singing in the Rain* (1952) and his exuberant dancing skit, "Make 'Em Laugh." After filming the skit, O'Connor admitted years later that he had to take a three day bed rest. Although retired from movies,

Lobby card for
***Tom Sawyer, Detective* (1938)**

O'Connor is currently active in show business. He worked in television from the earliest days and produced some shows for Milton Berle. He won a Golden Globe for his performance in *Singing in the Rain* in 1953 and an Emmy the following year for his television work.

Two other members of the cast were Si Jenks and Etta McDaniel. Sixty-two year old Jenks was one of the most colorful character actors around. He was a frequent visitor to the San Bernardino Mountains and died in 1970 at the age of ninety-four with over one hundred and fifty film credits.

Etta McDaniel was the older sister of Hattie McDaniel who starred the next year in *Gone With The Wind* (1939) and won an Oscar for Best Supporting Actress. Etta never was as famous as her younger sister, but found steady work in Hollywood. She died in 1946 at the age of fifty-six.

Donald O'Connor (left), unidentified actor (center) and Billy Cook (right) playing mumbletypeg on the set of *Tom Sawyer, Detective* (1938). Photo courtesy of The Academy of Motion Picture Arts and Sciences

HAVING WONDERFUL TIME (1938)

CAST:

Ginger Rogers .... Teddy Shaw
Douglas Fairbanks, Jr. .... Chick Kirkland
Lucille Ball .... Miriam
Red Skelton .... Itchy Faulkner
Directed by .... Alfred Santell
Produced by .... RKO Pictures

Douglas Fairbanks, Jr. and Ginger Rogers taking a break on location at Cedar Lake for the movie *Having WonderfulTime* (1938).
Photo Courtesy of Tom Core

If the bosses of RKO Studios had realized what they had in the summer of 1937, it is possible that their studio might still be around. What they had was probably the greatest cast of comedians supporting RKO's two stars, Ginger Rogers and Douglas Fairbanks, Jr.

Utilizing Arthur Kober's popular Yiddish satirical play, director Alfred Santell reworked the story of a bored New York typist who escapes the heat of the city for the relaxation of a Catskill Mountains' summer resort. Her mother's hope is that Teddy (Ginger Rogers) will find love. When Teddy meets Chick Kirkland (Douglas Fairbanks, Jr.), she is anything but enamored with him. Eventually he wins her over and true love prevails. Unfortunately, critics and audiences were not kind to the movie, despite all the talent, and it was considered a flop.

The film was shot at Cedar Lake and parts of Big Bear Lake in the late summer of 1937. The film introduced the new talent of Richard Skelton, later known as "Red" because of his carrot-colored hair. Unbelievably, many of his comedic routines ended up on the cutting room floor and RKO lost his talents to M-G-M a year later. Two of Rogers' roommates are twenty-seven year old Lucille Ball and thirty-year old Eve Arden. Both of these ladies became huge successes with their own television programs at the dawn of the television age. Rounding out the cast was comedy actor Jack Carson, who also hosted his own television program in the 1950s.

Ginger Rogers was no stranger to Cedar Lake as she had tested the waters two years earlier in the movie *In Person* (1935) and almost lost her bathing suit while swimming underwater in one scene. Actually, Rogers had looked forward to working with one of the most popular stars of the 1930s, Douglas Fairbanks, Jr. It wasn't until later, when she found out that he always referred to her as "that chorus girl," that she came to feel her two weeks of filming in the mountains was not such a wonderful time.

Even after Red Skelton went to M-G-M, his talents weren't appreciated and they cast him in supporting roles alongside other established actors. When down-and-out, silent screen comedian Buster Keaton took him under his wing, Skelton's career began to flourish with a series of comedies that showcased Red's rubber-faced antics. It wasn't until the roles began to dry up in the late Forties that Skelton came into his own on television in *The Red Skelton Show*, which aired for twenty years. One of the most beloved of comedians, Skelton later became known for his art work. He died in 1997 of pneumonia at the age of eighty-four.

A former Ziegfeld Girl and Golden Girl, Lucille Ball was always known for her gutsy approach to life and take charge attitude. When her film career seemed to be faltering in the late Forties, CBS Television asked her to create the roll of a scatterbrained wife with her husband Desi Arnez. Over the next three decades, she owned television with her group of hit series: *I Love Lucy, The Lucy-Desi Comedy Hour, The Lucille Ball Show,* and *Here's Lucy.* At one time, it was estimated that an episode of the famous sitcom was airing twenty-four hours a day somewhere on the planet. Ironically, Ball ended up buying the RKO studio lot from the defunct company and changed its name to Desilu Studios. Ball died in 1989 at the age of seventy-seven after undergoing heart surgery.

Never as popular as his superstar father, Douglas Fairbanks, Jr. still managed to carve out a long and distinguished career for himself. Beginning as a child actor in silent films, Fairbanks became a star during the Twenties and Thirties. He also had his own television show, *Douglas Fairbanks, Jr. Presents,* that aired from 1953

Ginger Rogers, Lee Bowman and Lucille Ball in a scene from *Having WonderfulTime* (1938)

through 1957. In 1949, Anglophile Fairbanks was knighted by King George VI, for his service to the Crown and possibly for his duty during WWII as a naval commander, where he won the Silver Star and Legion of Merit. Actor, producer and writer, Fairbanks died in 2000 at the age of eighty with more than a hundred film and television credits.

Douglas Fairbanks, Jr. and Ginger Rogers
on location at Cedar Lake for the movie
Having WonderfulTime (1938)
Photo courtesy of
The Academy of Motion Picture
Arts and Sciences

PRISON FARM (1938)

One of the most popular themes used by film makers during the 1930s was prison reform. Whether this was because of the increase in crime or from social consciousness is not certain, but studios dwelled upon the subject.

Larry Harrison (Lloyd Nolan) is a small time hood and con-artist. When he inadvertently kills an armored car driver and escapes with nine thousand dollars, his girlfriend Jean (Shirley Ross) is unwittingly caught up in his escapade. Both end up at the county prison farm, where obviously, Jean doesn't belong. On the prison farm, Jean is punished for infractions and made to work overtime in slave-labor conditions in the prison laundry by Chief Matron Brand (Marjorie Main). After the death of another inmate in the laundry, Jean is befriended by prison doctor, Dr. Rol Conrad (John Howard). When Larry is shot while trying to bribe a guard (J. Carrol Naish) and escape, his deathbed confession exonerates Jean and she wins a pardon and the hand of the doctor.

Most of the movie was shot on location in and around Crestline and possibly at Camp Seely. The film is notable for several reasons. It is the debut of star-to-be, William Holden, who plays a bare-chested prisoner and it features a group of former silent stars in the waning years of their careers, such as Mae Busch, who was known as the "Versatile Vamp," and Anna Q. Nilsson, who starred in *The Way of the Strong* in 1919.

Born Bea Gaunt in 1913, Shirley Ross began her career as a big band vocalist. In 1933, she began as a bit player with M-G-M and a year later introduced, in Harlem style blackface, the Rogers & Hart tune *The Bad in Every Man* in the movie *Manhattan Melodrama* (1934). The tune eventually acquired new lyrics, became known as *Blue Moon*, one of the

CAST:
Shirley Ross .... Jean Forrest
Lloyd Nolan .... Larry Harrison
Marjorie Main .... Chief Matron Brand
William Holden .... Convict
Directed by .... Louis King
Produced by ..... Paramount Pictures

Lloyd Nolan
circa 1937

sentimental favorites of the era. In 1935, she signed with Paramount Studios and sang opposite Bing Crosby in *Waikiki Wedding* (1937) and helped Bob Hope introduce what would become his signature song, *Thanks for the Memory*, in the *Big Broadcast of 1938*. Her incongruous role in *Prison Farm* was seen as a step backward by most critics. She later said that it was probably her most difficult role, because she had to wash clothes for four straight days during the shoot and her hands suffered horribly. She made a total of thirty films in the span of twelve years and then retired from the silver screen in 1945 at the age of thirty-two.

Thirty-six year old Lloyd Nolan was born into a wealthy shoe family business, but at an early age rebelled at being a part of it. Nolan honed his acting skills at the prestigious Pasadena Playhouse, along with fellow cast member in *Prison Farm*, William Holden. Always considered a second-echelon leading man, Nolan never achieved superstardom that some feel he deserved. His best role came in 1953, when he originated the part of the paranoid Captain Queeg in the Broadway version of Herman Wouk's *The Caine Mutiny*. Unfortunately, he was not even considered for the role in the movie version which went to his good friend, Humphrey Bogart. In later years, Nolan turned to television and made more than thirty appearances, which included his Emmy winning performance as Captain Queeg in *The Caine Mutiny Court-Martial* in 1955 on the *Ford Star Jubilee* television program. Nolan died of lung cancer in 1985 at the age of eighty-three.

Paramount Studios was looking for an entree for the handsome, blond William Franklin Beedle from the day they signed him to a contract. Within a year they had changed his name to William Holden and starred him opposite one of the biggest names at that time, Barbara Stanwyck in *Golden Boy* (1939). Over the next four decades, Holden became one of the most highly respected actors in Hollywood with over one hundred film and television credits. He was nominated for an

William Holden
circa 1940s

Oscar for Best Actor three times and won for his performance as the embittered and cynical POW in *Stalag 17* (1953). He too died of lung cancer in 1981 at the age of seventy-three.

[Note: A copy of *Prison Farm* exists at the UCLA Film Archives.]

Shirley Ross (left) confronts Marjorie Main and unidentified actress in a scene from *Prison Farm* (1938) filmed in Crestline. Photo courtesy of The Academy of Motion Picture Arts and Sciences

OF HUMAN HEARTS (1938)

```
CAST:
Walter Huston ............ Ethan Wilkins
James Stewart .......... Jason Wilkins
Beulah Bondi ............... Mary Wilkins
Directed by ............. Clarence Brown
Produced by ........... M-G-M Pictures
```

Guy Kibbee, Clem Bevans and Walter Huston (left to right) discussing a scene for the film *Of Human Hearts* (1938).

In October 1937, Walter Fig (a volunteer fire lookout) reported from the Butler Peak watchtower that he had sighted a column of smoke in the sky over Lake Arrowhead. Within minutes, a district ranger was on the scene, but what he saw was no fire, it was a reproduction of a steamboat churning its way up Blue Jay Bay belching black smoke. Thus, the mountain residents became aware of yet another movie being made in their midst.

M-G-M Studios chose Movie Point on Lake Arrowhead to build an elaborate set replicating a small Ohio River village for the Honore Morrow story, *Benefits Forgot*. The studio chose one of its top directors, Clarence Brown, to lead the troop of actors which included Walter Huston, James Stewart, Beulah Bondi, and Gene Lockhart. Huston didn't have far to go after a day of shooting as he was a resident of the mountains at the time. Gene Lockhart and his family, including his daughter, June Lockhart, would eventually purchase a home in Lake Arrowhead the following year.

The story revolves around Jason Wilkins' (James Stewart) inability to cope with his stern, circuit-preaching father (Walter Huston) who wants him to follow in his footsteps. However, Jason chooses a career in medicine and through his mother's (Beulah Bondi) sacrifices is able to graduate as a doctor. Jason is immediately caught up in the Civil War and pressed into service, but forgets to write home. When Mrs. Wilkins writes a personal letter to President Lincoln for news of her son, Lincoln sends for him and scolds him for not remembering his family. A shamed Jason rushes home and all is forgiven.

Because mother nature refused to cooperate, there was no snow falling on Lake Arrowhead during the filming. Brown decided to spray the trees white and spread hundreds of yards of white muslin on the set to create the necessary winter scenario. As remembered years later, a local historian, Pauliena LaFuze, related that during the dismantling of the set afterwards, the depression-era residents were offered the muslin, but by the time she got there, the welcomed gift already had been snapped up by others.

Schooled as an engineer, Walter Huston soon found that his love of the stage outweighed his engineering skills. A successful stage actor on Broadway, he made the transition into silent pictures and eventually talkies. Alternating throughout his career between leading man and character actor, Huston was nominated for an Oscar four times, once as Best Actor (*Dodsworth*-1936), and three times as Best Supporting Actor. He finally won in 1949 for his portrayal of the crusty old miner in his son John's classic, *The Treasure of Sierra Madre* (1948). Huston built his home in the Running Springs area during the 1930s depression utilizing itinerant laborers. His home was later converted to a private school. Canadian-born Huston died in 1950 one day after his sixty-sixth birthday.

Twenty-nine year old Jimmy Stewart came to Hollywood via Broadway and Princeton University. Trying to decide what to do with the shy youth, M-G-M, at first, gave him supporting roles in some "A" movies and the lead in a couple of "B" movies. By 1939, he had found his niche as the retiring, "ah shucks" everyday man in roles that 1930s audiences could relate to in films including: *It's a Wonderful World*; *Mr. Smith Goes to Washington*; and *Destry Rides Again*. Stewart joined the U.S. Air Force when WWII broke out and flew missions over enemy territory. He eventually attained the rank of Colonel and received numerous decorations for his service. Stewart was nominated by the Academy as Best Actor four times. He won the coveted award in 1941 for his role as the tabloid reporter in the sophisticated comedy, *The Philadelphia Story* (1940). Stewart is best remembered for his role as the dispirited banker, George Bailey, in *It's a Wonderful Life* (1946), a classic Christmas tale that is still shown regularly.

One of the great character actresses from the 1930s, Beulah Bondi began as a stock com-

James Stewart in a scene from
Of Human Hearts (1938)
Photo courtesy of The Academy of Motion Picture Arts and Sciences

Beulah Bondi
circa 1940s

pany actress and eventually wound up on Broadway. Early on, directors cast her as the older woman, a part she played to perfection. For her role as the self-sacrificing mother in *Of Human Hearts*, Bondi was nominated for an Oscar as Best Supporting Actress, along with Billie Burke for *Merrily We Live* (1938) — another film that was made in Lake Arrowhead. Unfortunately, both actresses lost to Fay Bainter for her part as the meanspirited aunt in *Jezebel* (1938). Bondi was active in films through the Sixties and retired in 1973 with close to eighty movie and television credits. She died of complications from an accident tripping over her cat, in 1981 at the age of ninety-two.

James Stewart (back turned) and Ann Rutherford in a scene from *Of Human Hearts* (1938) on location at Lake Arrowhead
Photo courtesy of The Academy of Motion Picture Arts and Sciences

SPAWN OF THE NORTH
(1938)

Considered by some to be one of the best pictures (from an historical point of view) ever made at Lake Arrowhead, Paramount's *Spawn of the North* garnered an Honorary Oscar for its special effects. Two years in the making, part of the film was shot at Totem Pole Point, a peninsula that juts out into Blue Jay Bay. The big question has always been: Did Paramount place the five totems there or were they already there from another movie? For many years it was thought that they were from a 1930 movie called *River's End*. When this author finally located a print of the film at the UCLA Film Archives and reviewed it, it was obvious that this was not the film as there are no scenes with totems in the movie. This discovery, along with an exhaustive three year search for any other films with totems, has led this author to believe that, in 1936, Paramount Pictures contracted with John Dexter, a local lumberman, to cut down and drag five huge logs down to the peninsula, where they were then erected and carved as totems by Paramount workmen.

The plot of the movie revolves around the spawning of salmon in Alaska; the friendship between two fishermen, Tyler Dawson (George Raft) and Jim Kimmerlee (Henry Fonda) since boyhood; and fish piracy by rogue Russians. In one memorable scene, Jim is courting Dian Turlon (Louise Platt) next to the lake by picking various plants for her to identify by smell. She correctly identifies each after a sniff, even a dogwood, which, of course, has no smell. In another scene, Native American Eskimos perform a ceremonial dance for the annual salmon run. This dance was performed by Madam Sojin, a noted Japanese dancer, who was madeup

Theater bill for
Spawn of the North (1938)

251

George Raft, Dorothy Lamour and Henry Fonda in a Paramount Studios publicity shot for *Spawn of the North* (1938)

Henry Hathaway and Louise Platt relax with Hathaway's dog on the set of *Spawn of the North* (1938).
Photo courtesy of The Academy of Motion Picture Arts and Sciences

to look like an Eskimo.

Rounding out the cast were Dorothy Lamour as the good-hearted girlfriend of Raft; John Barrymore as the verbose editor of the local paper; Akim Tamiroff as the Russian pirate; and a trained seal that could not stay away from water. Director Henry Hathaway also brought along a talisman, his English Sheepdog, Lucky, who was a delight to the cast, but didn't get into the movie.

Remembered for his great tough-guy and character roles, it is hard to imagine that George Raft began in pictures as a song and dance man. Raft was born in "Hell's Kitchen," considered one of the meanest sections of New York City in 1895. This is where he learned to dance and made friends with some of the local gangsters. His gangster connections followed him throughout his career and some say actually helped it, as he never learned to act. Paramount Studios did its best to salvage his reputation in the mid-Thirties by placing him in parts of shady but still sympathetic roles, such as *Spawn of the North*. Raft will always be known as the guy who gave Humphrey Bogart his big break, when he turned down the roles of "Mad Dog" Earle in *High Sierra* (1941) and Sam Spade in the *Maltese Falcon* (1941), the latter because he considered the script no better than a "B" movie. Raft made his own series of "B" pictures during the Forties, such as *Outpost in Morocco* (1949). His career hit the skids in the 1950s, when he attempted to finance his own television program and ran into trouble with the Internal Revenue Service at the same time. Ironically, his last bit part was in the movie *The Man with Bogart's Face* (1980), the year he died at age eighty-five.

Twenty-three year old Louise Platt was a Broadway stage actress before coming to Hollywood in 1938. Highly touted, she was the first actress to be tested for the role of Scarlett O'Hara by David O. Selznick for his film *Gone with the Wind* (1939). Although she did not get the part, she impressed John Ford enough that he cast her in his epic western film *Stagecoach* (1939), in the memorable part of the pregnant wife attempting to reach her husband. She left Hollywood after making only eight films to return to the legitimate stage, where she flourished in roles such as Anne Boleyn in *Anne of a Thousand Days*, opposite Rex Harrison in 1948.

Henry Fonda and Louise Platt get set for a scene in *Spawn of the North* (1938) on location at Totem Pole Point.
Photo courtesy ofThe Academy of Motion Picture Arts and Sciences

Madam Sojin (with knife) in a scene
from *Spawn of the North* (1938) on
location at Totem Pole Point
Photo courtesy of The Academy of
Motion Picture Arts and Sciences

Crew setup for a scene in
Spawn of the North (1938) on location at
Totem Pole Point
Photo courtesy of The Academy of Motion
Picture Arts and Sciences

THE GOLDWYN FOLLIES
(1938)

In the summer of 1937, Samuel Goldwyn Productions (not to be confused with M-G-M, from which he was ousted) arrived with a cast and crew at Lake Arrowhead to film *The Goldwyn Follies,* a lavish musical. The film debuted the talents of popular radio star Edgar Bergen and his alter-ego, Charlie McCarthy. It was also the debut of twenty-one year old operatic singer, Vera Zorina, who Goldwyn had imported from Europe.

Movie producer Oliver Merlin (Adolphe Menjou) hires Hazel Dawes (Andrea Leeds) off the street to critique his movies which have been failing at the box office. She convinces him to hire a short order cook Danny Beecher (Kenny Baker) to be in Merlin's next film because he can sing. Things go wrong when Oliver falls in love with Hazel, who is in love with Danny. Mixed into the plot are The Ritz Brothers, whose zany antics are almost embarrassing.* The film's saving grace is the fact that it is the very first film shot at Lake Arrowhead in Technicolor and has a host of songs from the pen of George Gershwin, including the classic, *Love Walked In.* Unfortunately, this was Gershwin's last film as he died during the filming in July 1937, from a brain tumor.

Known for his slick moustache, dapper forty-eight year old Adolphe Menjou was considered the best-dressed man in Hollywood. A Cornell trained graduate engineer, he began his acting career in 1915 as a silent extra. His big break came when he played opposite Rudolph Valentino in *The Sheik* (1921). Throughout the 1920s he honed his image as the impeccably dressed, upper-class snob. When sound arrived, he easily made the transition and going against the grain of his earlier parts, played the hard-boiled editor in *The Front Page* (1931) opposite

*The Ritz Brothers were Goldwyn's answer to the highly popular Marx Brothers.

CAST:
Adolphe Menjou .... Oliver Merlin
Andrea Leeds .... Hazel Dawes
Kenny Baker .... Danny Beecher
Directed by .... George Marshall
Produced by .... Samuel Goldwyn
Pictures

Adolphe Menjou
circa 1930s

Pat O'Brien. The performance earned Menjou his only Oscar nomination as Best Actor, but he lost out to Lionel Barrymore at the Awards ceremony. A little more than a quarter of a century later, he was nominated for a Golden Laurel as Best Supporting Actor for his portrayal as the hypocritical French officer in *Paths of Glory* (1957). Again he lost out, this time to Red Buttons. Menjou died in 1963 at the age of seventy-three with more than one hundred and fifty film and television credits.

Twenty-four year old Andrea Leeds was born Antoinette Lees in Butte, Montana. Leeds briefly attended UCLA before entering films as a bit player in 1935. Her casting as the aspiring, but neurotic and suicidal actress in RKO's *Stage Door* (1937) led to her only Oscar nomination for Best Supporting Actress. She lost to Alice Brady the following year, but

Vera Zorina (seated in peasant dress) being made up for a scene in *The Goldwyn Follies* (1938). Photo courtesy of The Academy of Motion Picture Arts and Sciences

Goldwyn liked her performance so much that he signed her for the lead in *The Goldwyn Follies.* Leeds made six more undistinguished films in the late 1930s and then retired from the screen after marrying wealthy sportsman Robert S. Howard. She died in Palm Springs at the age of sixty-nine in 1984.

Kenny Baker was a nightclub singer during the 1930s and a regular performer on radio with the *Jack Benny Show*. The twenty-six year old tenor was never an actor, but muddled through the late Thirties into the 1940s in several more singing vehicles before retiring from films in 1947.

Andrea Leeds in a Goldwyn Studios publicity photo

Caricature of the cast of The Goldwyn Follies (1938) drawn by Al Hirschfeld

Left to right: Adolphe Menjou, Kenny Baker, Vera Zorina, Andrea Leeds, Charlie McCarthy, Edgar Bergen

Drawn by Al Hirschfeld

SWISS MISS (1938)

CAST:
Stan Laurel .... Himself
Oliver Hardy .... Himself
Della Lind .... Anna Albert
Walter Woolf King .... Victor Albert
Directed by .... John G. Blystone
Produced by .... Hal Roach Studios

Stan Laurel and Oliver Hardy are up to their ears in cheese in a scene from *Swiss Miss* (1938).

It was a member of the Sons of the Desert, the official fan club of comics Laurel and Hardy, that informed this author of the fact that one of the films the duo made was partially shot on location at Lake Arrowhead. Sometime in fall of 1937, Hal Roach Studios sent the cast and crew up to the mountain resort to film sequences of *Swiss Miss*. This was a big-budgeted, overblown, mixture of highbrow opera and lowbrow comedy that almost flopped. Luckily, Stan and Ollie saved it with some of their best sight gags. Still critics panned it and worse yet, it has not been highly thought of by the Sons of the Desert as one of Laurel and Hardy's best efforts.

With true fuzzy logic, the boys go to Switzerland to sell mousetraps because that is where cheese is made, therefore, there must be mice. At an inn they meet Anna (Della Lind), who is posing as a chambermaid to be close to her famous composer husband, Victor (Walter Woolf King), who wishes to be alone in order to compose his new opera. The boys are forced to work at the inn to pay off a bad debt they have run up. In classic slapstick, Stan and Ollie attempt to push a piano over a rope bridge hung precariously over a gorge and are met halfway by a gorilla. A gorilla in Switzerland? Don't even ask!

English-born Stan Laurel was forty-eight when he made *Swiss Miss*, and had already made more than one hundred and seventy films since he began in the silent era in 1917. A former English music hall entertainer, Laurel had come over to the states with the Fred Karno musical-comedy troupe that included Charlie Chaplin. Deciding to stay, Laurel slipped into vaudeville and finally ended up on the West Coast in small bit parts with the movie studios. Although considered an adequate comedian, it wasn't until his pairing with Oliver Hardy that he and Hardy became truly famous.

Soft-spoken with just a hint of a southern accent, Oliver Hardy was born in Georgia in 1892. Always on the plump side, Hardy was a gifted singer and had entered show business through minstrel shows at the age of eight. Known as Babe Hardy, he began his picture career with Lubin Company in 1913. Hardy made more than three hundred one-reelers before his teaming with Laurel in 1927. Together, they made more than one hundred and forty films in the next two decades. After a contract dispute with Hal Roach, the team split up in 1939, but were reunited when Twenthith Century Fox took an interest in them in the early 1940s. Unfortunately, they lacked the old fire and the films they made were considered second rate. After 1945, no one in Hollywood was interested in the team any longer. In 1950, they attempted a comeback with a miserably scripted French/Italian film called *Atoll K*, which has been deemed a sad epitaph for the boys to have ended on. Hardy died of a stroke in 1957, and Laurel died in 1965 after a heart attack.

Stan Laurel and Oliver Hardy attempt to move a piano over a mountain in a scene from *Swiss Miss* (1938).
Photo courtesy of The Academy of Motion Picture Arts and Sciences

In her first, last and only American film, Austrian-born Grete Natzler, aka Della Lind, debuted as the beautiful musical star that she was. Originally brought to the states by Paramount Studios, it is unclear how she ended up in a Hal Roach comedy. She began as a Viennese musical comedy star and became an actress in films prior to 1930 before moving onto British films. Her career after *Swiss Miss* is a mystery and she may have returned to Europe. She eventually came back to the states as she died in Key West, Florida, in 1999 a few days before her ninety-third birthday.

After a move to Salt Lake City from California, Walter Woolf King began singing in Mormon churches and decided to make music his life. As a baritone, he sang on the vaudeville circuit before landing on Broadway in light comedies and operettas during the 1920s. In 1930, he signed with Warner Brothers, but the first film was a disaster and King ended up suing the studio over bad publicity. He returned to Broadway and vacillated over the next few years between the stage and Hollywood. Never a leading star, King continued his film career into the 1940s, before becoming an actor's agent. When television appeared, King hosted a popular talent show, *Lights, Camera, Action* (1950), and continued as a bit player in both television and movies until he retired in 1978. In the last year before his death, King was often seen around Hollywood with his leading lady of four decades earlier, Della Lind.

Walter Woolf King strolling along a mountain path near Lake Arrowhead in a scene from *Swiss Miss* (1938).
Photo courtesy of The Academy of Motion Picture Arts and Sciences

MERRILY WE LIVE
(1938)

During the heart of the Depression, audiences enjoyed being entertained by the difficulties of the wealthy class. In 1937, Hal Roach Studios bought the rights to the novel, *The Dark Chapter* by E. J. Rath, which had been adapted to the stage in 1926 as a comedy.

Wealthy and eccentric Mrs. Emily Kilbourne (Billie Burke) is determined to rehabilitate tramps that happen to stop by their mansion. After the last hobo makes off with the family silver, writer Wade Rawlins (Brian Aherne) is mistaken for one after his car stalls on a mountain road and rolls down a cliff. When he asks to use the phone, Mrs. Kilbourne hires him as the new chauffeur but daughter Jerry Kilbourne (Constance Bennett) is fed up with the parade of vagrants her mother has imposed upon her family. After a series of misadventures, the family fortune is in danger of being lost until the lowly chauffeur saves the day and wins over the daughter.

If viewing the film today, local historians can be treated to scenes of the original oiled highway (Highway 18) and the red-rock pillars linked together by chain above Waterman Canyon. In one scene of the movie, Aherne stopped to fill up his overheated car utilizing one of the water troughs built by the CCC (California Conservation Corps). Portions of the film were also made at the Arrowhead Springs Hotel.

Thirty-four year old Constance Bennett was one of the superstars of the 1930s. Bennett was the daughter of matinee idol Richard Bennett and was brought up in finishing schools. After an annulled marriage at the age of sixteen, she entered show business and silent films in the 1910s. In the Twenties she became a star, even

```
CAST:
Constance Bennett ................... Jerry
                                  Kilbourne
Brian Aherne .............. Wade Rawlins
Billie Burke .............. Emily Kilbourne
Directed by ......... Norman Z. McLeod
Produced by ....... Hal Roach Studios
```

Lobby card for
Merrily We Live (1938)

Billie Burke as she appeared in 1920. She was described as: medium height, with blonde hair and blue eyes.

Brian Aherne

making some serial Westerns before retiring after her marriage to a wealthy businessman. When her marriage failed in 1929, she reentered the talkies and rebuilt her career. She is best remembered for her sophisticated comedies like *Merrily We Live* and as Marion Kerby, the beautiful ghost in the *Topper* series of films during the Thirties. Bennett earned a military honor for providing shows to servicemen during the Berlin Airlift, while she was married to an Air Force Colonel. She died in 1965 from a cerebral hemorrhage after finishing her last film, *Madam X* with Lana Turner. As the wife of a military officer, she is buried at Arlington National Cemetery.

Forty-nine year old Billie Burke began as a stage actress in London and eventually ended on Broadway. She made her screen debut in 1916 by immediately playing leading roles. By 1921, she had retired from the screen and was married to Florenz Ziegfeld of the famed Ziegfeld Follies. She probably would have remained so, except for the Wall Street Crash that wiped out their fortune. When Ziegfeld died in 1932, she found a second career in Hollywood as the lovable scatterbrained socialite in numerous films. She was nominated for an Oscar for her role in *Merrily We Live* (1938), but lost out to Fay Bainter for her role in *Jezebel*. Although not nominated for it, her most famous role is as the "good witch" in the perennial children's fantasy, *The Wizard of Oz* (1939). Burke's screen career spanned more than fifty years with more than eighty-five film credits. She died at the age of eighty-four in 1970.

English-born Brian Aherne began as a child actor on the stage before entering British silent films in 1924. He made his stage debut on Broadway and then drifted into Hollywood where he usually played the upper-class sophisticate in numerous films during the 1930s. His next film after *Merrily We Live* was in the role of Emperor Maximilian in *Juarez* (1939), which earned him an Oscar nomination for Best Supporting Actor. He lost out to Thomas Mitchell for his part in the John Ford classic *Stagecoach* (1939). Aherne continued in films and on Broadway and retired from films in 1968.

Brian Aherne up a tree and Constance Bennett in the car in a scene from *Merrily We Live* (1938)
Photo courtesy of The Academy of Motion Picture Arts and Sciences

HEART OF THE NORTH (1938)

CAST:
Dick Foran .... Sgt. Alan Baker
Gloria Dickson ..... Joyce MacMillan
Directed by .... Lewis Seiler
Produced by .... Warner Brothers

Dick Foran
circa 1938

In what has to be a real mystery, Warner Brothers sent a cast and crew to Cedar Lake to film a very expensive Royal Canadian Mountie movie called *Heart of the North*, utilizing the new Technicolor process. Neither the stars nor the script rated such a costly treatment (the film cost an astronomical $400,000 to produce) and it is a wonder why it was made other than to highlight Dick Foran's singing talents. The script was so weak that Vincent Sherman, a brilliant scriptwriter, was asked to see if he could mend it. Sherman later claimed that he got credit for the script, but in actual fact, lent little to salvage it. A copy of the film exists at the UCLA Film Archives, where the author viewed it, but time has faded the crisp colors to muddy hues and the chance for this film to ever be restored is probably nil.

When an RCMP corporal is murdered in front of his daughter during a robbery aboard the Arctic Queen, Sgt. Alan Baker (Dick Foran) is sent to put things right. The corporal's daughter, Judy (Janet Chapman), is placed in the care of Joyce MacMillan (Gloria Dickson) after the death of Judy's father. When Alan refuses to arrest Joyce's brother for the crime, Alan is placed in custody himself. Eventually, he finds the gang responsible for the robbery by utilizing a plane in his search efforts.

One of the props constructed for the movie was a steamboat. It was later dismantled and taken to Hollywood to be used as a set. It was seen in at least two other movies that were filmed at Cedar Lake.

Red-haired Dick Foran was a radio and band singer when Warner Brothers decided they needed a singing cowboy to flesh out their repertoire of actors and signed him to a long term contract. He appeared in several "A" pictures in supporting roles before he mounted his horse and starred in a series of forgotten Westerns. After Warner Brothers dropped him, he became a character actor for the next three decades. Foran died in 1979 at the age of sixty-nine with more than two hundred film and television credits.

Twenty-two year old Gloria Dickson was a fresh ingenue signed to a three-year contract with Warner Brothers when she made *Heart of the North.* She briefly starred in a couple of other "B" movies and then was relegated to minor roles. Many feel that Warner never gave her the scripts she needed to fulfill her true potential as a serious actress. After a series of disastrous marriages, the first to makeup artist Perc Westmore and the second to director Ralph Murphy, her career bottomed out in Hollywood in the early Forties. She died in a house fire, caused by her discarded cigarette, in 1945 at the age of twenty-eight.

Gloria Dickson
circa 1940s

Steamboat on Cedar Lake in a scene from
Heart of the North (1938)
Photo courtesy of The Academy of Motion
Picture Arts and Sciences

DANGER FLIGHT (1939)

During the 1930s, youngsters were treated to a weekly comic strip featuring the exploits of *Tailspin Tommy*, an extraordinary aviator who could fly circles around the bad guys. Monogram Pictures bought the rights to the comic strip and produced several films led by real-life aviator John Trent, who portrayed Tailspin Tommy (today the name "Tailspin" seems ludicrous). *Danger Flight*, which was the fourth and last of the series, was filmed at the airport in Big Bear Valley.

In *Danger Flight*, Tommy forms a flying club for young boys. When Whitey (Tommy Baker), the orphaned brother of a gang member, finds Tailspin Tommy's downed plane and rescues Tailspin (John Trent), he is lauded as a hero by Tailspin, his girl-friend Betty Lou (Marjorie Reynolds) and the press. Whitey's evil brother, Duke, then takes advantage of the situation and with the unwitting help of Whitey downs Tailspin's plane with a hefty payroll as the prize. Thinking Whitey has betrayed him, Tailspin escapes and then realizes the young boy had nothing to do with the robbery, when he is aided by Whitey in apprehending the true criminals led by Skeeter Milligan (Milburn Stone).

Handsome and rugged, thirty-three year old John Trent was the epitome of the comic book hero. It is possible that Trent could have been a big star except for one fatal flaw, he couldn't act. In his first film, *Sky Spyder* (1931), he plays a mail pilot which he had been in real life. His next opportunity to fly and act didn't come until eight years later in the first of the *Tailspin* dramas, *Mystery Plane* (1939). Trent had appeared in some minor roles in the intervening years as a character actor. He made only one more film after *Danger Flight* and then faded from the motion

Magazine ad for the successful *Tailspin Tommy* series of films in the late 1930s

picture industry. Nothing more is known of him after 1941 except that he died in 1966 at the age of sixty.

Beautiful twenty-two year old Marjorie Reynolds provided the love interest for Tailspin. She had been starring in a series of "B" Westerns beginning in 1937, before landing the role of Betty Lou Barnes in the *Tailspin* series. Alternating back and forth between blonde and brunette, it was felt that Reynolds was another actress who never lived up to her true potential. Her one big chance came when she starred opposite Bing Crosby in the classic *Holiday Inn* (1942), which introduced the song *White Christmas*. Unfortunately, it did not lead to her being considered an "A" actress and she was again relegated to playing minor character roles for the remainder of her movie career. In 1953, she switched to television and became the wife of William Bendix for the critically acclaimed weekly show, *Life of Riley*. Reynolds appeared in more than sixty films and a like number of television episodes. She died in 1997 just short of her eightieth birthday.

Before he was the loveable "Doc" Adams on the hit western series *Gunsmoke*, Milburn Stone had played the heavy in a slew of "B" Westerns produced in the 1930s. A former song and dance man in vaudeville, Stone began his career in movies in bit parts in 1934. Blessed with a deep throaty voice, Stone made nearly one hundred and fifty films in the span of twenty-three years. This number is small in comparison to his more than six hundred appearances in the blockbuster TV series, *Gunsmoke*, which earned him an Emmy in 1968. Stone died in La Jolla, California, in 1980 at the age of seventy-six.

Marjorie Reynolds
circa 1939

Milburn Stone as he appeared
in the *Gunsmoke* series
circa 1960s

OUTPOST OF THE MOUNTIES (1939)

The premier year of the Golden Age of movies has always been considered to be 1939. More great films were released that year than any year before or since. It was also the year Columbia Pictures decided to send a crew to Lake Arrowhead to film a Charles Starrett "B" movie called *Outpost of the Mounties*. It was notable for only one fact; Columbia utilized the existing totems on Totem Pole Point, a peninsula of land jutting into Blue Jay Bay, as a backdrop for the film.

When Sgt. Neal Crawford (Charles Starrett) leads a contingent of Royal Canadian Mounted Police into a mining settlement, his first job is to break up a fight between the trading post factor (the man in charge) and a young hot-headed miner. In the fracas, the young miner loses his knife and when the factor is killed with the same knife a day later, the miner is accused of murder. Only the miner's sister, Norma (Iris Meredith) and Sgt. Crawford believe him innocent and set out to prove it.

Thirty-six year old Charles Starrett was the scion of a wealthy New England family. His bit part in a football movie made at his college started him on a career in show business. In 1936, he signed with Columbia Pictures (he replaced cowboy star Tim McCoy) and over the next sixteen years made more than one hundred "B" Westerns. During the 1940s, he was consistently in the list of top ten favorite cowboy stars. His most famous role was that of the Durango Kid, which accounted for sixty-four of the "oaters." In 1952, Starrett decided to hang up his spurs and left the industry for good. He died in 1986 at his home in Borrego Springs, California, just days before his eighty-third birthday.

A former Golden Girl, blonde, twenty-four year old Iris Meredith was

Iris Meredith and Charles Starrett as they appeared the following year in Columbia Pictures' *Two-Fisted Rangers* (1940)

considered smart as well as talented. Sadly, she
became typecast as a "B" Western heroine early on,
when she was cast opposite Charles Starrett in no
less than twenty features from 1937 through 1940.
After leaving Columbia, she could only find work
with "poverty row" producers like PRC, a ram-
shackle studio that earned the nickname "Pretty
Rotten Crud." Meredith decided to retire in 1943
and married Columbia Pictures' director, Abby
Berlin. Her long battle with cancer, which disfig-
ured her face, never dampened her spirits and she
was a frequent guest at Western film festivals. She
died in 1980 at the age of sixty-five.

Besides Bob Nolan, who sings his trade-
mark song "Tumbling Tumble Weeds," silent
screen star Edmond Cobb appears as one of the
henchmen. Cobb had been a leading man in the
1920s before becoming one of the most enduring
character actors in Hollywood. His career spanned
over fifty years and more than five hundred appearances in films and television.

A contemporary lobby card for Columbia
Picture's *Outpost of the Mounties* (1939)

FANGS OF THE WILD (1939)

Dennis Moore
circa 1930s
Photo courtesy of Les Adams

Another mystery film made in the San Bernardino Mountains is *Fangs of the Wild* produced by Harry S. Webb for Metropolitan Pictures. The date attributed to production has been variously listed as 1938, 1939 and 1941. The interesting fact is that it shows Lake Gregory filled to capacity, so it probably was made sometime after the lake filled up in the summer of 1938. The film was re-released in 1941 and copies of the film that exist only show the 1941 date.

In another beloved Rin-Tin-Tin, Jr. film, Rinty is accused of stealing foxes from a fox farm owned by Larry Dean (Tom London) and his daughter, Carol (Luana Walters). His owner, Don Howard (Dennis Moore), can't believe Rinty would do such a thing, and goes about proving it was another dog that looks almost like Rinty. He enlists the aid of Mae Barton (Mae Busch) to pose as a fox coat buyer in order to find out who is really stealing the pelts. In the end, Rinty is vindicated when he runs down the real culprits and strolls off into the sunset with a new mate, the lookalike, but female of the species. The fox farms used for this movie are believed to have been the ones located in Skyforest along Sycamore Drive, as no farms were known to have existed in the Crestline area.

Thirty-one year old Dennis Moore began his career as a stock player in Texas and moved into the movies around 1936 as a bit player and stunt man. He starred briefly in a few Westerns and then in the Forties moved over to Universal Studios and Republic Pictures to do a series of low-cost serials. He continued as a serial hero, returning to the San Bernardino Mountains to film *Perils of the Wilderness* in 1956. Moore has the distinction of being cast in the last serial made in Hollywood, Columbia's *Blazing the Overland Trail* (1956). During the 1950s, Moore alternated his time between films and television and briefly was a regular in *The New Adventures of Spin and Marty* (1958), a short-lived Western series that featured Harry Carey, Jr. and Annette Funicello. Moore died at the age of fifty-five in 1964, a year before his last TV movie aired.

Luana Walters was a screen veteran with more than thirty films to her credit when she starred in *Fangs of the Wild*. Considered by many as a real screen beauty, she nevertheless was typecast as the Western heroine opposite so many different leading cowboys (thirteen) that she almost tied the record of Joan Barclay at fifteen. Producers and actors liked to work with her, because she was considered the consummate professional who did it with one take and never muffed her lines. She made few pictures after playing the part of Superman's mother in Spencer Gordon Bennet's 1948 serial, *The Adventures of Superman*. After a career that spanned twenty-six years, Walters retired in 1956. Sadly, she only lived another seven years before she died of chronic alcoholism at the age of fifty.

Australian-born Mae Busch was forty-eight and still looked terrific when she made *Fangs of the Wild*. Busch had been a stunning beauty during the silent era and was known as the "Versatile Vamp." She began with Mack Sennett in 1912 and it was rumored she was forced to leave the studio after Mabel Normand (Sennett's fiancée) caught Busch and Sennett together once too often. During her long career, Busch played opposite some of the biggest names in Hollywood and was a favorite of Laurel and Hardy in their comedy films. She is best remembered as the overbearing wife of Ollie in *Sons of the Desert* (1933). Strangely, after her death and cremation in 1946 at the age of fifty-four, no one claimed her ashes until the 1970s, when the official fan club of Laurel and Hardy, The Sons of the Desert, paid for her funeral and interred her remains in Los Angeles. Busch appeared in more than one hundred and twenty films during her thirty-five year career.

Luana Walters
circa 1940s
Photo coutesy of Les Adams

Mae Busch (right) and Beryl Mercer as they appeared in the 1920s

GONE WITH THE WIND (1939)

CAST:
Clark Gable .... Rhett Butler
Vivien Leigh .... Scarlett O'Hara
Everett Brown .... Big Sam
Directed by .... Victor Fleming
Produced by ... Selznick International Pictures

Entire books have been written about Margaret Mitchell's novel and subsequent movie adaptation, so let it suffice to say that it is still one of the most beloved films of all time and it was partially shot at Big Bear Lake. The scenes referred to are after the defeat of the South and the era of Reconstruction has begun. In one scene, Scarlett O'Hara must drive by a dangerous area called Shanty Town (a kind of hobo city of lean-tos and tents inhabited by freed black slaves and white criminals) on her way back to her lumber mill. The producer, David O. Selznick, chose the Big Bear area because it best represented the tall pines of Georgia.

During the scene, Scarlett drives her horse and buggy over a small bridge when she is approached and accosted by two men asking for a handout, one white and one black. While screaming at the top of her lungs, she attempts to beat them off with her buggy whip to no avail and is about to faint when her father's ex-fore-man, Big Sam (Everett Brown), comes to her rescue. The attack by Shanty Town rogues on Scarlett thus gives the Southern townsfolk reason to form a vigilante group and hence the formative birth of the KKK (Ku Klux Klan).

GWTW has been so over analyzed that each frame has been scrutinized for any errors. There are a few for this particular scene. When Big Sam jumps into the buggy, he doesn't say "giddy-up" or anything like that, instead Big Sam yells: "Horse make tracks!" Curiously, the horse knows instinctively to begin to gallop at a rapid pace. Also, when a long shot of the fleeing pair is shown next, Big Sam is no longer in the carriage and Scarlett is driving alone. Added to that, the yellow bonnet she was wearing when attacked is dislodged during the attack, yet it miraculously reappears again in the long shot as she drives away.

Contemporary lobby ad for
Gone With The Wind (1939)

Scarlett's costume, a grey corduroy dress, was salvaged many years later by Jim Tumblin, a former makeup artist, as it was about to be discarded after being used in two additional pictures. The dress can be seen in the Shaw-Tumblin collection at the Gone With The Wind Museum located in Marietta, Georgia.

Vivien Leigh was not the first choice of David O. Selznick. Every actress in Hollywood at the time wanted a crack at the lead. Clark Gable had been named early on, but the coveted role of Scarlett had not been finalized by the time the film was already in production. Most of the money was on Bette Davis to snare the role, but other actresses had been considered, including Lucille Ball, Lana Turner, Tallulah Bankhead and Edythe Marrenner, who later changed her name to Susan Hayward. Born in British India, Leigh had been a bit player in British films since 1935. Her first American film, *A Yank at Oxford* (1938), co-starring Robert Taylor and Maureen O'Sullivan, introduced her to Hollywood.

Everett Brown and Vivien Leigh on location at Big Bear in a scene from Selznick's *Gone With The Wind* (1939) Photo courtesy of The Academy of Motion Picture Arts and Sciences

Clark Gable and Vivien Leigh in a scene from Selznick's *Gone With The Wind* (1939)

Within a year, she landed the prestigious role that led to the first of her two Oscar Awards. Although she only made a total of twenty pictures, she was considered one of the finest actress of the Twentieth Century. Her second Oscar was for her portrayal of the psychotic Blanche DuBois in the film adaptation of Tennessee Williams' play *A Streetcar Named Desire* (1951). Leigh died of chronic tuberculosis at the age of fifty-three in 1967 at her home in London.

Thirty-six year old Everett Brown began his film career as a Polynesian native extra in a Ralph Ince silent called *South Sea Love* (1927). Other than his meaty role in *GWTW*, over the next few years Brown was cast in bit parts, usually as an African chieftain. In all, he made twenty-six films and died shortly after making his last film, *White Witch Doctor* (1953), at the age of fifty-one.

INDEX OF FILMS MADE
IN THE SAN BERNARDINO MOUNTAINS

INDEX OF FILMS MADE
IN THE SAN BERNARDINO MOUNTAINS